ASIA'S CAULDRON

ASIA'S CAULDRON

The South China Sea and
the End of a Stable Pacific

Robert D. Kaplan

RANDOM HOUSE
NEW YORK

Published in the United States by Random House,
an imprint and division of Random House LLC,
a Penguin Random House Company, New York.

RANDOM HOUSE and the HOUSE colophon are registered
trademarks of Random House LLC.

Chapter VI, "America's Colonial Burden," contains material from
an earlier title by Robert D. Kaplan, *Imperial Grunts*
(New York: Random House, 2005).

LIBRARY OF CONGRESS CATALOGING-IN-PUBLICATION DATA
Kaplan, Robert D., author.
Asia's cauldron : the South China Sea and the end of a stable Pacific /
Robert D. Kaplan.
pages   cm
Includes bibliographical references and index.
ISBN 978-0-8129-9432-2
eBook ISBN 978-0-8129-9433-9
1. Pacific Area—Foreign relations. 2. Pacific Area—Politics and
government. 3. South China Sea Region—Strategic aspects.
4. South China Sea—International status. I. Title.
JZ1980.K37 2014
327.59—dc23   2013036100

Printed in the United States of America on acid-free paper

www.atrandom.com

2 4 6 8 9 7 5 3 1

FIRST EDITION

Book design by Dana Leigh Blanchette
Title-page photograph and border art: © iStockphoto.com

TO STEPHEN S. KAPLAN

Whoever is able to write of the great number and infinity of islands there are from the straits of Kampar to Banda and from the straits of Singapore to the islands of Japan, which are beyond China—and between this island and Banda, there must be an area of more than two or three thousand leagues round—whoever is able let him speak of it. And it is certain that many of the islands are worth speaking about, because many have gold, but it would be never ending and tedious. I will only speak of the few in this great abundance with which Malacca is in communication now, or was in the past, and I will touch on others in general terms, so that my project may be completed, and if my project does not carry sufficient weight, may I be forgiven.

THE SUMA ORIENTAL OF TOMÉ PIRES, AN ACCOUNT OF THE EAST,
FROM THE RED SEA TO CHINA, WRITTEN IN MALACCA
AND INDIA IN 1512–1515

For there is no question but a just fear of an imminent danger, though there be no blow given, is a lawful cause of war.

FRANCIS BACON,
"OF EMPIRE," 1612

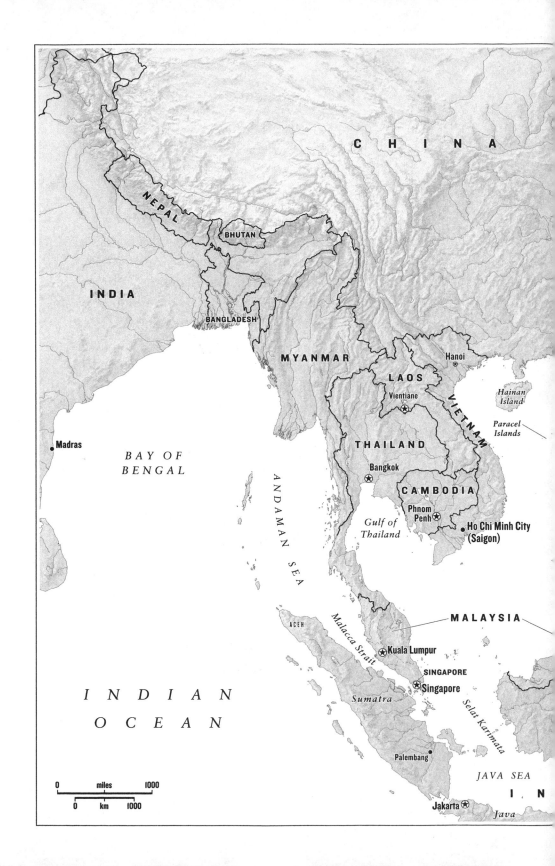

CONTENTS

PROLOGUE

The Ruins of Champa

I walk along jungle trails in the heat-inflicted silence. Blackened, red-brick humps lie strangled in greenery against steep mountains devoured by rain clouds. I am in My Son, in central Vietnam, forty miles inland from the coast of the South China Sea. Flowers and grass grow out of every nonvertical surface of each monument where altars, lamps, and lingas used to be placed, swimming in incense and camphor. Half-destroyed statues that recall India deep in Southeast Asia are embraced by columns in the walls, blotched blue and white with lichen. There are headless gods and time-mottled dancing figures now ferociously explored by insects. The loose bricks are like missing teeth: the monuments so hacked and battered that what remains recall the abstract shapes of modernist sculpture. A lichen-coated linga, the phallic symbol of Shiva's manhood, stands alone and sentinel against the ages.

The size and abundance of Temple Groups B and C hold out the promise of a Vietnamese Angkor Wat, but once I come upon the other temple groups I realize just how little is left of nine centuries of religious life here, stretching from late antiquity to the high Middle Ages. Group A is a mere low pile of rubble, testimony to American helicopter-borne destruction in a war of less relevance to Southeast Asia's future than are these ruins and what they represent.

The fiercest nationalisms are often begot by what, in Freudian terminology, is the narcissism of small differences. What rescues Vietnam from being a mere southern redoubt of Sinic culture is its Khmer and Indian heritage, which allows for a unique confection that is ever so similar and yet ever so different from the civilization of China. Invoking Champa, from the fourth through thirteenth centuries, is to expose the lie of Cold War area studies with which Washington remains enamored, which place Southeast Asia firmly in an East Asia and Pacific realm; while in fact this region is part of an organic continuum that is more properly labeled the Indo-Pacific, whose maritime heart is the South China Sea: for Champa represents a seafaring, piratical race. Squeezed between the Central Highlands and the sea, with numerous rivers and natural harbors at their disposal, with woods, spices, textiles, honey, wax, and metals to trade, the Chams were well placed to benefit from the commerce between the Indian Ocean and the Western Pacific. The French had it right when they designated this region not Southeast Asia, but Indochina.

Witness the medieval Chola Empire of the Hindu Tamils, based in southern India, which sent its fleets throughout this seaboard as far north as China; even as ancient Chinese pottery has been found as far south as Java, and Chinese ships under the medieval Tang and Yuan dynasties ventured as far as Odisha in northeastern India. Long before the North and South Vietnams of the Cold War era, there were northern and southern Vietnams that had existed across this civilizational fault line and across the chasm of the centuries between antiquity and modern times: Dai Viet being a young and insecure kingdom in the north after having been a province of the Chinese Empire for over a thousand years; while to the south lay the Khmer Empire and Champa. Champa, in particular, was the enemy of Dai Viet, prevent-

ing the latter's expansion to the south, until Champa was finally reduced to near ashes by the majority Kinh in the north, with an
underlying sense of guilt felt by northern Vietnam toward southern
Vietnam ever since. Champa, as the historical and cultural represen-
tation of southern Vietnam, was always more closely connected to
the Khmer and Malay worlds than to Sinicized Dai Viet to the north.

In the seventeenth and eighteenth centuries there were, again, effectively two Vietnams: Tonkin in the north ruled by the Le dynasty,
and Cochin China in the south ruled by the Nguyen dynasty. All this,
ultimately, because Vietnam's nearly one-thousand-mile-long coast
lay astride two great civilizations: those of India and China.

Champa entered my consciousness through an illustrated book I had
come upon in a shop in Hanoi years back: *The Art of Champa* by
Jean-François Hubert. Because of its beauty, it was a volume I instantly wanted to own. Champa, writes Hubert, exists "in defiance of
time," its legacy rescued by French archaeologists from the École
Française d'Extrême-Orient in the late nineteenth and early twentieth
centuries, who studied and excavated at My Son and other sites, providing concrete evidence of what is only written about in the Chinese
Dynastic Annals and Embassy Reports. Hubert's text, as elegant as
the accompanying photography, exposed me to this Sanskrit culture,
with its delicious Hindu-Buddhist syncretism (though weighted
heavily in favor of Hinduism). "In the eighth century," says Hubert,
"Champa stretched from the Gate of Annam in the north to the Donnai basin in the south," that is, from just north of the former demili-
tarized zone (DMZ) southward to Saigon. So Hubert's medieval map
suggests a Cold War one. After a Grand Guignol of wars and inva-
sions, the wages of being located on a civilizational fault line, Hindu
Champa finally disappeared under the shadow of the Viets.[1] Vietnam
as we think of it was thus created, even though it is the legacy of this
conquered Hindu world that provides Vietnam with its uniquely non-
Chinese cultural identity.

Hubert's book led me to Da Nang, near the old DMZ, the busiest air base during the Vietnam War. That world is dead, buried under the reality of American-style gated communities, celebrity-brand golf courses, and half-finished five-star resorts and casino complexes that fly the American flag at their entrances stretched along China Beach, south of the city. There are eco-retreats, too. The GIs' jungly hell has become a backpacker's paradise—the country that symbolized war to a generation now has a smile and an intoxicating beat to it.

Situated in downtown Da Nang is the Museum of Cham Sculpture, a 1915 mustard yellow French colonial building where hundreds of statuary recovered by the archaeologists Henri Parmentier and Charles Carpeaux during excavations in 1903 and 1904 at My Son and elsewhere are warehoused in crowded, badly lit, and sweltering conditions, with windows open to the soot and traffic. My obsession with ancient Champa deepened here. Alongside the statuary were coppery black-and-white photographs, taken by these same archaeologists, that represented their subjects better than any color photos could.[2] For the sculptures themselves bear that indeterminate milk-gray hue in some cases, and pale ocher in others, that are more beautiful than any primary color, and are best rendered as a lightened earthen contrast with the darkness all around. Each statue came alive for me, as though it were posing for a photographer in his studio. The Indian world deifies dance, and many of these pieces looked caught in freeze-frame movement.

There was Gajasimha, the mount of Shiva, with an elephant's head and a lion's body, the embodiment of the intelligence of gods and the strength of kings. And Shiva the deity itself, with a gigantic head whose nose was completely broken off, and whose eyes were mightily accepting of all the creations and destructions of the universe. There was a small Vishnu, the Protector, its features so worn away by time that there was only the hint of an eye, which, nevertheless, was frightening in its gaze. Brahma, the god of creation, had three heads rather than the usual four, representing the different directions of the universe, and, with its four arms, holding the various volumes of the Vedas. Yaksa, the nature spirit; Balarama, Vishnu's avatar; Kala, a god of death: the entire Hindu pantheon is here in Da Nang—a place where these Indian gods ruled for close to a thousand years. The most vivid bas-reliefs from a temple at My Son, moved here by the French, recall the German-Jewish intellectual Walter Benjamin's famous vision of history as a vast heap of wreckage of incidents and events that keeps piling higher and higher into infinity, with progress signifying merely more wreckage waiting to happen.

I was not done. The History Museum in Saigon, where there was a room full of Champa sculpture, required a visit. Here amid the dioramas and other exhibits of Song, Yuan, and Ming depredations—in other words, the struggle against China as the thematic core of Vietnamese history—I found Cham remains from as far back as the second century and as far forward as the seventeenth: more evidence of how, despite its overwhelming cultural similarities with China, Vietnam was nevertheless distinct. And it was, to a significant extent, Indian influence that made it so. Without the Indian Subcontinent, in other words, there could not have been a Vietnam in any cultural or aesthetic sense. I turn my head to café au lait dancing stone goddesses with four arms—with full breasts and narrow-yet-fleshy waists: they match exactly the sculptures I once saw in the caves of Ellora east of Mumbai. Lakshmi, a tenth-century statue, an invitation to wealth and sensuality; Shiva, fifteenth century, an iconic stylization that overtakes realism, so that artistic abstraction reigns. Though this Shiva is half carved, such a force of character emerges out of the stone!

I compare the Cham sculptures with the twelfth-century Khmer ones in an adjoining room, themselves confections of Buddhist-Brahminist styles. The beige brown Khmer faces come alive with their mystical acceptance of fate—nothing I have ever seen is so suggestive of being at peace—the shallow brows, the flattish noses, the wide and full lips, the eyes open, even as they seem closed. Khmer, like Champa, is another variant of the confluence of Indian and Chinese civilizations. And yet sometimes so close to one civilization one finds a piece that manifests the other civilization in its entirety: for example, a tenth-century Devi, the female form of the Supreme Lord, from Huong Que in central Vietnam, with the sharpest Aryan features, cast in stunning chocolate orange. This statue is purely of India. It is the only one I saw suited for color rather than black-and-white rendering.

How odd that I begin a geopolitical study of the South China Sea with the delectable, mythic legacy of India. But that is the point. Champa is the lesson I must keep in mind in the course of this report about China's growing influence. My description of the art of Champa is lavish by necessity: for I must never lose sight of the vividness of India's presence in this part of the world at a time when China's gaze seems so overpowering. Yes, as I write, China's advancing presence continues to be *the story* in the South China Sea region, testimony to Beijing's demographic and economic heft. If I do not confront China's rise—if I do not confront the signal trends of recent decades—then there can be no relevance to my observations. Because the future is unknowable, all one can do is write about the present. But the fact that the future is unknowable also means it is open to all manner of possibilities—such as, perhaps, the dramatic weakening or even collapse of the Communist Party (and China, too) from internal economic and social stresses. Thus, Champa offers a lesson in humility: an awareness that because the present is ephemeral, even at its best my analysis can only constitute a period piece. Though I will refer only rarely to Champa again, I hope that my brief albeit intense allusion to it will rescue what follows from mere topicality. Champa represents the long view: for by going back in time we look forward over the horizon. The shadow of China presently looms large, but if at some point very soon China dramatically falters the South China Sea may once again live up to its French colonial description of *Indochina,* where China competes on an equal—rather than a dominant—footing with India and other powers and civilizations.

Moreover, while my study points to a military rivalry between the United States and China, the future—in military as well as economic terms—may be distinctly multipolar, with a country like Vietnam—or Malaysia, Australia, or Singapore—playing off a host of powers against each other. The United States fought against the prospect of a Vietnam unified by the communist North. But once that unification became fact, the new and enlarged Vietnamese state became a much greater threat to communist China than to the United States. Such can be the ironies of history. Champa, because it tells of the centrality of one power at a time when another is now still ascendant, is a symbol of surprises and possibilities yet unseen to the conventional analyst.

The American GIs' Saigon of loud bars and strip joints is gone: entombed in memory under gleaming, backlit facades of *Gucci, Lacoste, Versace*. But these wondrously enigmatic statues in the dusty godown of a museum live on.

ASIA'S CAULDRON

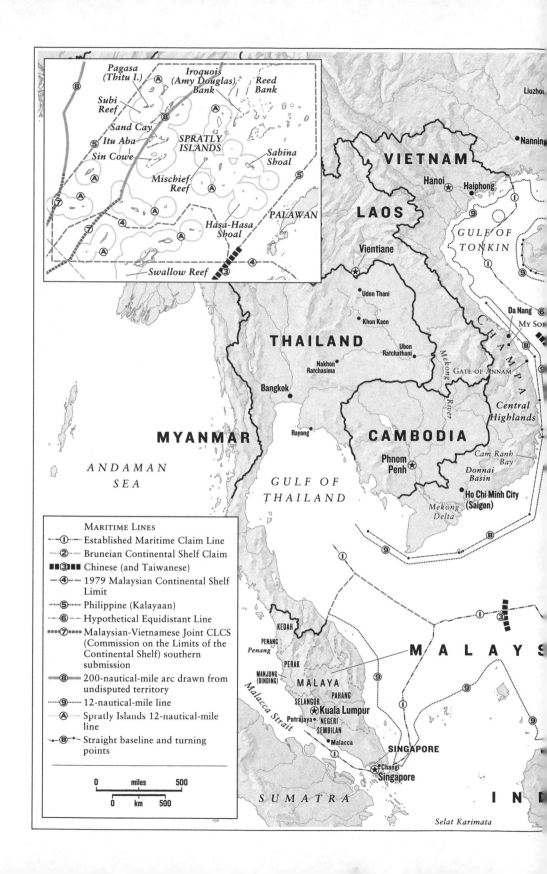

INSET MAP (top left):

Liuzhou

Pagasa
(Thitu I.)

Iroquois
(Amy Douglas)
Bank

Reed
Bank

Subi
Reef

Sand Cay

Itu Aba

Sin Cowe

SPRATLY
ISLANDS

Mischief
Reef

Sabina
Shoal

PALAWAN

Hasa-Hasa
Shoal

Swallow Reef

MAIN MAP:

Nanning

VIETNAM

Hanoi

Haiphong

LAOS

GULF OF
TONKIN

Vientiane

Udon Thani

Khon Kaen

THAILAND

Ubon
Ratchathani

Nakhon
Ratchasima

Mekong
River

Da Nang

My Son

C H A M P A

GATE OF ANNAM

Bangkok

Rayong

CAMBODIA

Phnom
Penh

Central
Highlands

Cam Ranh
Bay

Donnai
Basin

MYANMAR

ANDAMAN
SEA

GULF OF
THAILAND

Ho Chi Minh City
(Saigon)

Mekong
Delta

LEGEND:

MARITIME LINES

-①- Established Maritime Claim Line

-②- Bruneian Continental Shelf Claim

■■③■■ Chinese (and Taiwanese)

-④- 1979 Malaysian Continental Shelf Limit

-⑤- Philippine (Kalayaan)

-⑥- Hypothetical Equidistant Line

■■⑦■■ Malaysian-Vietnamese Joint CLCS (Commission on the Limits of the Continental Shelf) southern submission

-⑧- 200-nautical-mile arc drawn from undisputed territory

⑨ 12-nautical-mile line

Ⓐ Spratly Islands 12-nautical-mile line

-Ⓑ- Straight baseline and turning points

0 — miles — 500

0 — km — 500

KEDAH

PENANG
Penang

PERAK

MANJUNG
(DINDING)

MALAYA

PAHANG

SELANGOR

Kuala Lumpur

Putrajaya

NEGERI
SEMBILAN

Malacca

Malacca Strait

MALAYS

SINGAPORE

Changi
Singapore

SUMATRA

Selat Karimata

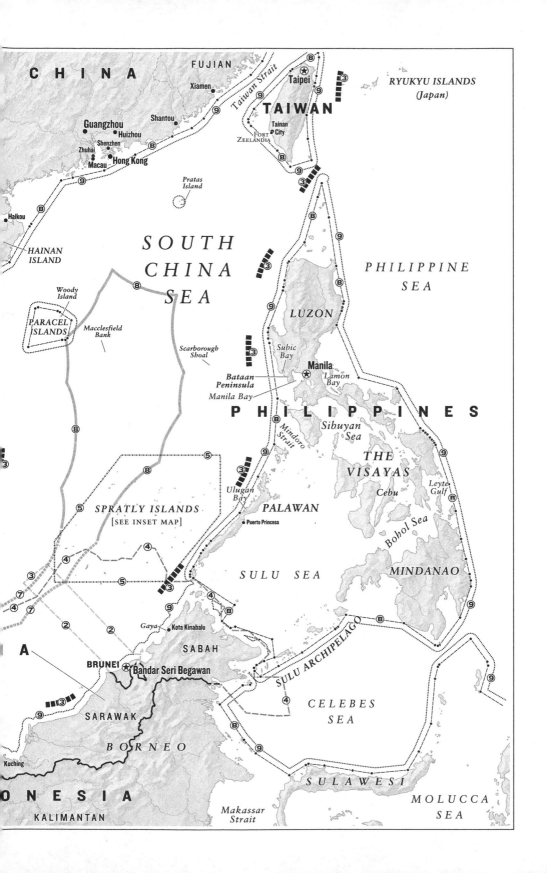

CHAPTER I

The Humanist Dilemma

Europe is a landscape; East Asia a seascape. Therein lies a crucial difference between the twentieth and twenty-first centuries. The most contested areas of the globe in the last century lay on dry land in Europe, particularly in the flat expanse that rendered the eastern and western borders of Germany artificial, and thus exposed to the intensive to-ing and fro-ing of armies. But starting in the last phase of the Cold War the demographic, economic, and military axis of the earth has measurably shifted to the opposite end of Eurasia, where the spaces between the principal nodes of population are overwhelmingly maritime. By maritime I mean sea, air, and outer space: for ever since the emergence of aircraft carriers in the early decades of the twentieth century, sea and air battle formations have become increasingly inextricable, with outer space now added to the mix because of navigational and other assistance to ships and planes from satellites. Hence *naval* has become shorthand for several dimensions of military activity. And make no mistake, naval is the operative word. Because of the way that geography illuminates and sets priorities, the physical contours of East Asia argue for a naval century, with the remote possibility of land warfare on the Korean Peninsula being the striking exception.

East Asia is a vast, yawning expanse, stretching from Arctic to Antarctic reaches—from the Kuril Islands southward to New Zealand—and characterized by a shattered array of coastlines and archipelagoes, themselves separated by great seas and distances. Even accounting for the fact of how technology has compressed distance, with missiles and fighter jets—the latter easily refueled in the air—rendering any geography closed and claustrophobic, the sea acts as a barrier to aggression, at least to the degree that dry land does not. The sea, unlike land, creates clearly defined borders, and thus has the potential to reduce conflict. Then there is speed to consider. Even the fastest warships travel comparatively slowly, 35 knots, say, reducing the chance of miscalculations and thus giving diplomats more hours—and days even—to reconsider decisions. Moreover, navies and air forces simply do not occupy territory the way armies do. It is because of the seas around East Asia that the twenty-first century has a better chance than the twentieth of avoiding great military conflagrations.

Of course, East Asia has seen great military conflagrations in the twentieth century that the seas did not prevent: the Russo-Japanese War (1904–1905); almost a half century of civil war in China that followed the collapse of the Qing (Manchu) dynasty; the conquests of Imperial Japan and World War II in the Pacific, which followed from them; the Korean War (1950–1953); the wars in Cambodia, Laos, and two in Vietnam involving the French and the Americans from the 1950s through the 1970s. What unites all of these conflicts is that each was organic to the formation of a state or empire, or similarly to the process of decolonization. A number of these conflicts were internal, contested by both conventional and unconventional ground forces, where navies played extremely limited roles. The fact that the grand geography of East Asia is primarily maritime had little impact on these essentially domestic wars. (I include Korea in this category:

for the conflict between the North and the South was mainly fought on land, and was integral to the formation of separate states following the long Japanese occupation of 1910 to 1945.) But now the age of national consolidation throughout East Asia lies behind us. East Asian militaries, rather than focusing inward with low-tech armies, are focusing outward with high-tech navies and air forces. Yet as I will explain, they are not likely to reenact in terms of scale the naval conflicts of the Russo-Japanese War and World War II in the Pacific.

The Russo-Japanese War and the Pacific Theater in World War II were the upshots in significant measure of Japanese militarism, for which the seas offered no defense; in fact, the seas were fundamental to the expansion of an island nation that required large stores of oil from distant shores for its rampaging armed forces. But China, now the rising military power in the Pacific, demonstrates far less aggression than did Imperial Japan following the Meiji Restoration: even as China's military (particularly its navy) expands, fascism as in Japan is almost surely not on the horizon in the Middle Kingdom. As for the comparison between China and Imperial Germany prior to World War I that many make, whereas Germany was primarily a land power, owing to the geography of Europe, China will be primarily a naval power, owing to the geography of East Asia. It is this geography, I repeat, that will foster the growth of navies, which, while a worrisome trend in its own right, is still not as worrisome as the growth of armies in continental Europe at the beginning of the last century.

Truly, military power is moving to Asia, but the worst of the twentieth century might be avoided, thanks generally to what the University of Chicago political scientist John J. Mearsheimer calls the "stopping power of water."[1] Water, Mearsheimer explains, is an impediment to invasion because while a state can build a naval force and transport an army across the sea with it, such a state will find it much more difficult to land an army on a hostile shore, and then move it inland to subdue permanently a hostile population.

For example, the Taiwan Strait is only a hundred miles wide, making it one of the narrower waterways in the Western Pacific, but it is still almost four times wider than the English Channel, across which

came the Allied invasion. China may in a decade or so be able to defeat Taiwan in a war, U.S. assistance to Taiwan notwithstanding. But
occupying Taiwan would be far more difficult, and thus will likely
never be attempted. This would not be the case if Taiwan were not an
island with one hundred miles of water between it and the mainland.
So it goes with the maritime distances between Japan and Korea, between South Korea and China, Japan's Ryuku Islands and China,
China's Hainan Island and Vietnam, and so on. With postcolonial
wars obviously no longer on the horizon, China however truculent is
no Imperial Japan, and East Asia's maritime geography argues in
favor of naval competition but militates against amphibious landings
in heavily populated areas.

What will this purely naval competition look like? To find out we
must examine more closely the geography of East Asia.

East Asia can be divided into two general areas: Northeast Asia dominated by the Korean Peninsula, and Southeast Asia dominated by the
South China Sea. Northeast Asia pivots on the destiny of North
Korea, a totalitarian and hermitic state that combines communism
with national fascism. Such a state has dim prospects in a world governed by rampant capitalism and electronic communication. Were
North Korea to collapse, Chinese, American, and South Korean
ground forces might meet up in the peninsula's northern half in the
mother of all humanitarian interventions, even as they carve out territory for themselves in the course of feeding the hungry. Naval issues
would be distinctly secondary. But an eventual reunification of Korea
would bring naval issues to the fore, with a Greater Korea, China,
and Japan in delicate equipoise separated by the Sea of Japan and the
Yellow and Bohai seas. In sum, because North Korea still exists, the
Cold War phase of Northeast Asian history is not over, and thus land
power will come to dominate the headlines in the area before sea
power will.

Contrarily, Southeast Asia is already deep into a post–Cold War
phase of history. That is what makes it so critical. Vietnam dominates

the western shore of the South China Sea. Once the preeminent foreign symbol of domestic turmoil inside America, Vietnam has been—until recent years at least—a capitalist dynamo seeking closer military ties to the United States, in order to balance against China. China, consolidated as a dynastic state by Mao Zedong after decades of chaos, and made into the world's most dynamic economy by the liberalizations of Deng Xiaoping, is now pressing outward with its navy to the First Island Chain in the Western Pacific. Then there is the demographic Muslim behemoth of Indonesia, which, having sustained endless decades of left- and right-wing authoritarian rule during the Cold War, could possibly emerge as a second "India," that is, a vigorous and stable democracy that has the potential to project power through its growing economy. Singapore and Malaysia, meanwhile, move forward economically in devotion to the city-state-cum-trading-state model, through varying blends of democracy and authoritarianism. Therefore, the composite picture is of a cluster of states that, with problems of domestic legitimacy and state building mostly behind them, are ready to advance their perceived territorial rights beyond their own shores. This outward collective push is located in the demographic cockpit of the globe: it is here in Southeast Asia, with its nearly 600 million people, where China's 1.3 billion people converge with the Indian Subcontinent's 1.5 billion people. And the geographical meeting place of all these states is maritime: the South China Sea.

The South China Sea functions as the *throat* of the Western Pacific and Indian oceans—the mass of connective economic tissue where global sea routes coalesce. Here is the heart of Eurasia's navigable rimland, punctuated by the Malacca, Sunda, Lombok, and Makassar straits. More than half of the world's annual merchant fleet tonnage passes through these choke points, and a third of all maritime traffic worldwide.[2] The oil transported through the Malacca Strait from the Indian Ocean, en route to East Asia through the South China Sea, is triple the amount that passes through the Suez Canal and fifteen times the amount that transits the Panama Canal. Roughly two thirds of South Korea's energy supplies, nearly 60 percent of Japan's and Taiwan's energy supplies, and 80 percent of China's crude oil imports come through the South China Sea.[3] Whereas in the Persian Gulf only energy is transported, in the South China Sea you have energy, finished goods, and unfinished goods.

In addition to centrality of location, the South China Sea has proven oil reserves of seven billion barrels, and an estimated 900 trillion cubic feet of natural gas. If Chinese calculations are correct that the South China Sea will ultimately yield 130 billion barrels of oil (and there is some serious doubt about these estimates), then the South China Sea contains more oil than any area of the globe except Saudi Arabia. Some Chinese observers have called the South China Sea "the second Persian Gulf."[4] If there really is so much oil in the South China Sea, then China will have partially alleviated its "Malacca dilemma"—its reliance on the narrow and vulnerable Strait of Malacca for so much of its energy needs coming from the Middle East. And the China National Offshore Oil Corporation has invested $20 billion in the belief that such amounts of oil really do exist in the South China Sea.[5] China is desperate for new energy. Chinese oil reserves account for only 1.1 percent of the world total, while it consumes over 10 percent of world oil production and over 20 percent of all the energy consumed on the planet.[6]

It is not only location and energy reserves that promise to give the South China Sea critical geostrategic importance, it is the territorial disputes surrounding these waters, home to more than two hundred small islands, rocks, and coral reefs, only about three dozen of which are permanently above water. Yet these specks of land, buffeted by typhoons, are valuable mainly because of the oil and natural gas that might lie nearby in the intricate, folded layers of rock beneath the sea. Brunei claims a southern reef of the Spratly Islands. Malaysia claims three islands in the Spratlys. The Philippines claims eight islands in the Spratlys and significant portions of the South China Sea. Vietnam, Taiwan, and China each claims much of the South China Sea, as well as all of the Spratly and Paracel island groups. In the middle of 2010 there was quite a stir when China was said to have called the South China Sea a "core interest." It turns out that Chinese officials never quite said that: no matter. Chinese maps have been consistent. Beijing claims to own what it calls its "historic line": that is, the heart of the entire South China Sea in a grand loop—the "cow's tongue" as the loop is called—surrounding these island groups from China's Hainan Island south 1,200 miles to near Singapore and Malaysia. The result is that all of these littoral states are more or less arrayed against China, and dependent upon the United States for diplomatic and military backing. For example, Vietnam and Malaysia are seeking to divide all of the seabed and subsoil resources of the southern part of the South China Sea between mainland Southeast Asia and the Malaysian part of the island of Borneo: this has elicited a furious diplomatic response from China.[7] These conflicting claims are likely to become more acute as energy consumption in developing Asian countries is expected to double by 2030, with China accounting for half of that growth.[8]

"Paradoxically, if the postmodern age is dominated by globalization," writes the British naval expert Geoffrey Till, then "everything that supports" globalization, such as trade routes and energy deposits, becomes fraught with competition. And when it comes to trade routes, 90 percent of all commercial goods that travel from one continent to another do so by sea. This heightened maritime awareness that is a product of globalization comes at a time when a host of relatively new and independent states in Southeast Asia, which only recently have had the wherewithal to flex their muscles at sea, are making territorial claims against each other that in the days of the British Empire were never an issue, because of the supremacy of the Crown globally and its emphasis on free trade and freedom of navigation.[9] This muscle flexing takes the form of "routinized" close encounters between warships of different nations at sea, creating an embryonic risk of armed conflict.[10]

One high-ranking official of a South China Sea littoral state was particularly blunt during an off-the-record conversation I had in 2011, saying, "The Chinese never give justifications for their claims. They have a real Middle Kingdom mentality, and are dead set against taking these disputes to court. China," this official went on, "denies us our right on our own continental shelf. But we will not be treated

like Tibet or Xinjiang." This official said that China is as tough with
a country like the Philippines as it is with Vietnam, because while the
latter is historically and geographically in a state of intense competition with China, the former is just a weak state that can be intimi-
dated. "There are just too many claimants to the waters in the South
China Sea. The complexity of the issues mitigates against an overall
solution, so China simply waits until it becomes stronger. Economically, all these countries will come to be dominated by China," the
official continued, unless of course the Chinese economy itself unrav-
els. Once China's underground submarine base is completed on
Hainan Island, "China will be more able to do what it wants." Meanwhile, more American naval vessels are visiting the area, "so the disputes are being internationalized." Because there is no practical
political or judicial solution, "we support the status quo."

"If that fails, what is Plan B for dealing with China?" I asked.

"Plan B is the U.S. Navy—Pacific Command. But we will publicly
remain neutral in any U.S.-China dispute." To make certain that I got
the message, this official said: "An American military presence is
needed to countervail China, but we won't vocalize that." The withdrawal of even one U.S. aircraft carrier strike group from the Western
Pacific is a "game changer."

In the interim, the South China Sea has become an armed camp,
even as the scramble for reefs is mostly over. China has confiscated
twelve geographical features, Taiwan one, the Vietnamese twenty-
one, the Malaysians five, and the Philippines nine. In other words,
facts have already been created on the ground. Perhaps there can still
be sharing arrangements for the oil and natural gas fields. But here it
is unclear what, for instance, countries with contentious claims coupled with especially tense diplomatic relations like Vietnam and
China will agree upon.

Take the Spratlys, with significant oil and natural gas deposits,
which are claimed in full by China, Taiwan, and Vietnam, and in part
by Malaysia, the Philippines, and Brunei. China has built concrete
helipads and military structures on seven reefs and shoals. On Mischief Reef, which China occupied under the nose of the Philippine

navy in the 1990s, China has constructed a three-story building and five octagonal concrete structures, all for military use. On Johnson Reef, China put up a structure armed with high-powered machine guns. Taiwan occupies Itu Aba Island, on which it has constructed dozens of buildings for military use, protected by hundreds of troops and twenty coastal guns. Vietnam occupies twenty-one islands on which it has built runways, piers, barracks, storage tanks, and gun emplacements. Malaysia and the Philippines, as stated, have five and nine sites respectively, occupied by naval detachments.[11] Anyone who speculates that with globalization, territorial boundaries and fights for territory have lost their meaning should behold the South China Sea.

China's position vis-à-vis the South China Sea is akin to America's position vis-à-vis the Caribbean Sea in the nineteenth and early twentieth centuries. The United States recognized the presence and claims of European powers in the Caribbean, but sought to dominate the region, nevertheless. It was the Spanish-American War of 1898, fought primarily over Cuba, as well as the digging of the Panama Canal from 1904 to 1914, that signaled the arrival of the United States as a world power. This development, not coincidentally, occurred following the closure of the American frontier, with the last major battle of the Indian Wars fought in 1890. Moreover, it was domination of the Greater Caribbean Basin that gave the United States effective control of the Western Hemisphere, which, in turn, allowed it to affect the balance of power in the Eastern Hemisphere. Perhaps likewise with China in the twenty-first century.

China, by way of its 1,500 short-range ballistic missiles focused on Taiwan and its 270 commercial flights a week to Taiwan, will be able to do an end run around Taiwanese sovereignty without needing to subdue it through a naval invasion. As with the closing of the American frontier, China's effective capture of Taiwan in the years to come will allow Chinese naval planners the ability to finally concentrate their energies on the wider South China Sea, an antechamber to the Indian Ocean in which China also desires a naval presence, in order to protect its Middle Eastern energy supplies. Were China to

ever replace the U.S. Navy as the dominant power in the South China
Sea—or even reach parity with it—this would open up geostrategic
possibilities for China comparable to what America achieved upon its
dominance of the Caribbean.

To be sure, the South China Sea is no Caribbean. In fact, it is more
important. The Caribbean was far from the main sea lines of communication, while the South China Sea is at the heart of them.

Because the South China Sea is where the sea lines of communication
between the Horn of Africa and the Sea of Japan join together, the
state that dominates the South China Sea will be a long way toward
dominating the navigable rimland of the Eastern Hemisphere. Of
course, the opposite is more likely to be the case: no one state will
dominate the South China Sea. Another reason why the South China
Sea is so important is that it is on the way to becoming the most contested body of water in the world.

The U.S. Navy presently dominates the South China Sea. But that
situation will change. The size of the U.S. Navy has come down from
almost six hundred warships in the Reagan era, to the mid–three hundreds during the Clinton era, to under three hundred now. It might go
lower still by the 2020s, because of the retirement of current classes
of submarines and surface warships, cost overruns, and future budget
cuts, the result in turn of massive fiscal deficits. Meanwhile, the Chinese navy, the world's second most powerful naval service, is growing
rather dramatically. Rather than purchase warships across the board,
China is developing niche capacities in subsurface warfare and ballistic missile technology (the DF-21 missile) designed to hit moving
targets at sea, such as a U.S. aircraft carrier. If China expands its
submarine fleet to 78 by 2020 as planned, it will be on par with the
U.S. Navy's undersea fleet in quantity.[12] While the U.S. Navy's submarine fleet is completely nuclear, it requires that feature to sail halfway
around the world, in order to get to East Asia in the first place, even
as China's diesel-electric submarines are supremely quiet and can
hide better, therefore, in the congested littorals of East Asia. At some

point, China is likely to, in effect, be able to deny the U.S. Navy unimpeded access to parts of the South China Sea.

Thus, as China's navy gets stronger—its economy permitting—and China's claim on the South China Sea—as demonstrated by its maps—contradict the claims of other littoral states, these other states will be forced to further develop their own naval capacities and to balance against China by relying increasingly on the U.S. Navy: a navy whose strength has probably peaked in relative terms, even as it must divert considerable resources to the Middle East. Worldwide multipolarity is already a feature of diplomacy and economics, but the South China Sea is poised to show us what multipolarity in a military sense actually looks like. Just as German soil constituted the military front line of the Cold War, the waters of the South China Sea may constitute the military front line of the coming decades.

There is nothing romantic about this new front line. Whereas World War II was a moral struggle against fascism, the Cold War a moral struggle against communism, the post–Cold War a moral struggle against genocide in the Balkans, Africa, and the Levant, as well as a moral struggle against terrorism and in support of democracy, the South China Sea shows us a twenty-first-century world void of moral struggles, with all of their attendant fascination for humanists and intellectuals. Beyond the communist tyranny of North Korea, a Cold War relic, the whole of East Asia simply offers little for humanists. For there is no philosophical enemy to confront. The fact is that East Asia is all about trade and *business*. Even China, its suffering dissidents notwithstanding, simply does not measure up as an object of moral fury.

The Chinese regime demonstrates a low-calorie version of authoritarianism, with a capitalist economy and little governing ideology to speak of. Moreover, China is likely to become more open rather than closed as a society in future years. China's leaders are competent engineers and regional governors, dedicated to an improving and balanced economy, who abide by mandatory retirement ages. These are not the decadent, calcified leaders of the Arab world who have been overthrown. Rather than fascism or militarism, China, along with every state in East Asia, is increasingly defined by the persistence, the rise even, of old-fashioned nationalism: an idea, no doubt, but not one that since the mid-nineteenth century has been attractive to liberal humanists.

Nationalism in Europe during the 1800s denoted a moral community against imperial rule. Now the moral community for which intellectuals and journalists aspire is universal, encompassing all of humankind, so that nationalism, whose humanity is limited to a specific group, is viewed as reactionary almost. (This is partly why the media over the decades has been attracted to international organizations, be it the United Nations, the European Union, or NATO—because they offer a path beyond national sovereignty.) Yet, despite pan-national groupings like ASEAN (Association of Southeast Asian Nations), it is traditional nationalism that mainly drives politics in Asia, and will continue to do so. And that nationalism is leading to the modernization of militaries—navies and air forces especially—in order to defend sovereignty, with which to make claims for disputed maritime resources.

There are no philosophical questions to ponder in this new and somewhat sterile landscape of the twenty-first century. It is all about power; the balance of power mainly. While the language at Asian summits will be soft, the deployment of warships in disputed seas will be *hard*. Military engagements on land involve occupation of civilian populations, which lead often to human rights violations, so that foreign policy becomes a branch of Holocaust studies. But the application of sea power is a purely military matter. Unless shelling on shore is involved, the dead are usually all in naval uniform, and thus there are no *victims* per se. In the early twenty-first century, the South China Sea will continue to be at the heart of geopolitics, reminiscent of Central Europe in the twentieth century. But unlike Central Europe it will not constitute an intellectual or journalistic passion.

The separation of geopolitics from human rights issues, which were conjoined in the twentieth century in Europe, plus the degree of abstraction that surrounds the naval domain in any case, will help make the South China Sea the realm of policy and defense analysts, rather than of the intellectuals and the media elite. Realism, which is consciously amoral, focused as it is on interests rather than on values in a debased world, will therefore triumph. This is how the South China Sea will come to symbolize a humanist dilemma.

The great exception to this line of argument is the environment. The Indian Ocean tsunami of December 2004 took place in the vicinity of the South China Sea and claimed more victims than the Iraq War. Even absent global warming, the normal variations of climate and seismic activity in environmentally fragile areas, combined with continued absolute rises in coastal populations, will virtually guarantee occasional humanitarian disasters around the South China Sea in coming decades. Navies will need to respond. By responding in the grandiose manner that it did to the Indian Ocean tsunami, the U.S. military, led by an aircraft carrier strike group, applied soft power in a way that augmented its hard power. Namely, humanitarian assistance to Indonesia led to resumed ties with the Indonesian military that the United States had not enjoyed for years. The news coverage of the Indian Ocean tsunami indicates how the South China Sea may appear to the world through the media's distorting mirror. The experts will follow naval movements in these waters regularly, while the media will lavish prime-time attention on the region only in cases of natural catastrophe. But even in the midst of such catastrophes, in comparison to twentieth-century Europe, the human rights angle will be muted because while there will be victims, there will be no villains, except of course for Mother Nature. And without villains, moral choice that distinguishes between good and evil cannot operate, meaning that in a philosophical sense there will be comparatively little drama.

The moral drama that does occur will take the form of austere power politics, of the sort that leaves many intellectuals and journalists numb. Imagine the Melian Dialogue from the Fifth Book of Thucydides, but without the killing of the Melian menfolk, and without the enslavement of the children and womenfolk that followed—and that provided for the tragedy in the first place. In this revised Melian Dialogue for the twenty-first century: the Athenians, Greece's preeminent sea power, tell the Melians that while Athens is strong, Melos is weak, and therefore must submit. As Thucydides writes, "The strong do what they can and the weak suffer what they must."[13] Thus, the Melians give in without violence. This will be China's undeclared strategy, and the weaker countries of Southeast Asia may well bandwagon with the United States to avoid the Melians' fate: in other words, power politics, almost mathematical in its abstractions, without war.

The Cold War excepted, the South China Sea presages a very different form of conflict than the ones to which we have become accustomed from World War I to Iraq and Syria. Since the beginning of the twentieth century, we have been traumatized by massive and conventional land engagements on one hand, and dirty, irregular small wars on the other. Because both kinds produced colossal civilian casualties, war, as I've said, has been the subject of humanists as well as of generals. But in the future we just might see a purer form of conflict (at least in East Asia), limited to the naval realm, with little for the intellectual journals of opinion to chew over: like the struggle between the United States and the Soviet Union, but without the prospect of land warfare. This is a positive scenario. For conflict cannot be eliminated from the human condition. A theme in Machiavelli's *Discourses on Livy* is that conflict, properly controlled, is more likely to lead to human progress than rigid stability. A sea crowded with warships does not contradict an era of great human progress for Asia.

But can conflict in the South China Sea be properly controlled? After all, thus far this argument presupposes that major warfare will not break out in the area, and instead nations will be content to jockey for position with their warships on the high seas, while making competing claims for natural resources, and perhaps even agreeing through negotiations to a fair distribution of them. But what if China were, against all evidential trends, to invade Taiwan? What if China and Vietnam—whose intense rivalry reaches far back into history—go to war as they did in 1979, with more lethal weaponry this time? For it isn't just China that is improving its military, so are Southeast Asian countries in general. Their defense budgets have increased by about a third in the past decade, even as European defense budgets have declined. Arms imports to Indonesia, Singapore, and Malaysia have gone up by 84 percent, 146 percent, and 722 percent respectively since 2000. The spending is on naval and air platforms: surface warships, submarines with advanced missile systems, and long-range fighter jets. Vietnam recently spent $2 billion on six state-of-the-art Kilo-class Russian submarines and $1 billion on Russian fighter jets. Malaysia recently opened a submarine base on the island of Borneo, even as China is developing an underground base for twenty nuclear submarines on Hainan Island on the other side of the South China Sea.[14] While the United States has been distracted by land wars in the Greater Middle East, military power has been quietly shifting from Europe to Asia, where authentic civilian-military, postindustrial complexes are being built, with an emphasis on naval forces.

The geopolitics of the South China Sea are simple in at least one respect. This is not a world of complex, shifting, and multipolar imperial alliances to the same extent that Europe was prior to World War I. There is only one so-called indigenous great power threat in these waters: China, which, with its maps, indicates a desire to exert a Caribbean-like control over the region. But China's obsession with territoriality is not unreasonable, given China's own geographical situation and its nineteenth- and twentieth-century history.

The entire northern boundary of the South China Sea is formed by the Chinese mainland. Indeed, China's South China Sea coastline, from the border with Vietnam in the west to the Taiwan Strait in the east, takes in one of China's principal demographic and economic hubs, the province of Guangdong and the megacity of Guangzhou (Canton), near Hong Kong. Then there is China's Hainan Island, which constitutes China's largest special economic zone, and which also dominates the energy-rich Gulf of Tonkin, thus inhibiting northern Vietnam's access to the wider South China Sea.

A map of China shows that a full half of its seaboard is oriented southward toward the South China Sea, with the other half oriented eastward toward the Bohai, Yellow, and East China seas. Thus, China looks south toward a basin of water formed, in clockwise direction, by Taiwan, the Philippines, the island of Borneo split between Malaysia and Indonesia, the Malay Peninsula divided between Malaysia and Thailand, and the long snaking coastline of Vietnam—weak states all compared to China. Like the Caribbean, punctuated as it is by small island states and enveloped by a continent-sized United States, the South China Sea is also an obvious arena for the projection of power by a continent-sized nation, which also to a significant extent envelops it. And just as the South China Sea provides a perfect spatial configuration for Chinese expansion, it is also in objective terms a great area of concern for China, since it is through these waters that the overwhelming share of China's energy imports come from the Middle East by way of the various Indonesian straits. Indeed, by joining the Indian Ocean with the Western Pacific, the South China Sea functions as China's gateway to the entire arc of Islam, from the Sahara Desert to the Indonesian archipelago; the same as the Caribbean Sea provided the east coast of the United States access to the Pacific with the building of the Panama Canal, of which the Malacca Strait is the equivalent. And this gateway is somewhat threatened by piracy and terrorism, linked to the weak states of the Philippines and Indonesia with their sizable Islamic populations. Geography dictates a strong Chinese naval presence in the South China Sea as thoroughly understandable. Functional domination of the South China Sea eases China's path to becoming a truly two-ocean navy: a navy of the Western Pacific *and* of the Indian Ocean. China must focus on Taiwan and the Korean Peninsula only because of challenges of the moment, but the South China Sea beckons as the key to China's geostrategic future.

Yet there is something deeper that propels China forward into the South China Sea and out to the First Island Chain in the Pacific: that is, China's own partial breakup by the Western powers in the relatively recent past, after having been for centuries and millennia a great power and world civilization. One should not gloss over what happened to China in the past 150 years. Unless one is intimately aware of this Chinese historical experience, one cannot comprehend what motivates China today in the South China Sea.

In the nineteenth century, as the Qing dynasty became the sick man of East Asia, China lost much of its territory—the southern tributaries of Nepal and Burma to Great Britain; Indochina to France; Taiwan and the tributaries of Korea and Sakhalin to Japan; and Mongolia, Amuria, and Ussuria to Russia.[15] In the twentieth century came the bloody Japanese takeovers of the Shandong Peninsula and Manchuria in the heart of China. This was all in addition to the humiliations forced on the Chinese by the extraterritoriality agreements of the nineteenth and early twentieth centuries, whereby Western nations wrested control of parts of Chinese cities—the so-called Treaty Ports. By 1938, as Yale historian Jonathan D. Spence tells us in *The Search for Modern China*, because of these depredations as well as the civil war between the communists and the nationalist Guomindang, "the great expanse of territory that had once been a unified empire under the Qing was fragmented into ten separate units." There was a latent fear that "China was about to be dismembered, that it would cease to exist as a nation, and that the four thousand years of its recorded history would come to a jolting end." An attendant horror was that China would return to the situation that had prevailed during the Warring States period of the third century BC; or to the "shifting patterns of authority and alliances that typified China's history" from the third to sixth century AD, and again from the tenth to the thirteenth.[16] China, having survived that nightmare, and having reached a zenith of land power and territorial stability not seen since the Ming dynasty of the sixteenth century and the Qing dynasty of the late eighteenth century, is now about to press outward at sea, in order to guard its sea lines of communications to the Middle East and thus secure the economic well-being of its vast population. China's very urge for an expanded strategic space is a declaration that it never again intends to let foreigners take advantage of it, as they did in the previous two centuries.

———

In helping to manage China's rise in Southeast Asia, we would do well to consider the Vietnam War. The Vietnam War has been periodically compared to the Athenians' ill-fated Sicilian Expedition of the late fifth century BC, described in the Seventh Book of Thucydides' *Peloponnesian War.* Fourteen years elapsed from Athens's first foray into Sicily to its final disaster there: a similar number of years as between the early forays of the John F. Kennedy administration into Vietnam and President Gerald Ford's final withdrawal. The United States was lured half a world away by its Vietnamese allies, besieged as they were by communist forces, just as Athens was lured into Sicily by its local allies there, which were threatened by other Sicilian city-states loyal to Athens's rival, Syracuse, in turn an ally of Sparta. Just as the Kennedy administration began with the dispatch of limited Special Operations Forces to Vietnam, a commitment that grew under the administration of Lyndon Johnson to over half a million regular troops, the Athenian intervention in Sicily began with twenty ships in support of its anti-Syracusan allies, and quickly grew to one hundred triremes, numerous transport ships, and five thousand hoplites, so that the prestige of Athens's entire maritime empire was seemingly dependent upon a military victory in far-off Sicily. Athens kept pouring in manpower. The Sicilian Expedition ended with the annihilation of forty thousand Athenian troops, of whom six thousand survived to labor in the quarries of Syracuse and be sold into slavery. The American intervention in Vietnam ended with the communist North overrunning the South, with the last Americans fleeing by helicopter from the roof of the U.S. embassy in Saigon.

Paralyzed by pessimism and recriminations, it was some time before Athens was willing to resume in earnest the bipolar conflict with Sparta. America, too, suffered a serious crisis of confidence following the debacle in Vietnam, standing by as the Soviet Union and its allies threatened American allies and toppled regimes in Nicaragua, Angola, Ethiopia, and Afghanistan. Now Vietnam looms in America's destiny once again. Once again the Vietnamese are pleading for America's help. This time the pleas are subtle and quiet, and no ground troops are being asked for. This time it is not a war that they want America to fight: it is only the balance of power that they want America to maintain. They want America as a sturdy air and naval presence in the South China Sea for decades to come. Vietnam and its destiny, either as a quasi-vassal state of China or as a staunch resister of Chinese hegemony, offers a telling illustration of what the United States provides the world that is at risk if the U.S. declines; or if the U.S. should ever retreat into quasi-isolationism or be diverted elsewhere.

China's economy is in trouble, we know. But the possibility of a U.S. decline, or at least a very partial military withdrawal from the world, has to be taken as a possibility, too. The American economy is recovering from the worst economic crisis since the Great Depression. Meanwhile, the cost of air and naval platforms is becoming prohibitive. The price of a new *Gerald R. Ford*–class aircraft carrier is $12 billion with no aircraft or other equipment on its deck. The price tag according to the latest design of a *Zumwalt*-class destroyer is close to $4 billion. The F-22 Raptor cost $200 million a plane and the F-35 Joint Strike Fighter $135 million. In addition to the cost of projecting air and naval power around the world—and particularly in East Asia—there is the very real imperial fatigue felt by the American public, and by some influential sections of the defense and foreign policy elite in Washington, following the ruinous cost in lives, diplomatic prestige, and monetary expense of the wars in Afghanistan and Iraq. The Iraq War, a far-flung military adventure like Vietnam, though it may not have ended in ignominious defeat or a similar cost in lives, can, too, be compared in some respects to the Sicilian Expedition. Will the United States lose its nerve this time around in Asia, as happened after Vietnam, and as happened to Athens after the misadventure in Sicily?

Following the Vietnam War, the Cold War with its attendant Soviet threat kept the United States engaged in the world. But now the threat is far more ambiguous. Take the most dangerous power in the South China Sea, China. While the century of humiliation at the hands of the Western powers "is a period etched in acid on the pages of Chinese student textbooks today," writes the Cambridge Univer-

sity historian Piers Brendon, "the Chinese are not necessarily prisoners of their past and they have overwhelming economic reasons to
seek a political modus vivendi with America."[17] But the issue is not as
simple as that. The best rebuttal to Brendon is provided by John
Mearsheimer in *The Tragedy of Great Power Politics,* who explains
that because the international system is anarchic, with no one in
charge—no night watchman—to enforce the rules, there are actually
few status quo powers: for the aim of each great state—democratic or
not, its internal character makes no difference—"is to maximize its
share of world power," and therefore "especially powerful states usually pursue regional hegemony."[18] The implication is that China will
pursue regional hegemony as a matter of course, regardless of whether
or not its political system becomes more open. A faltering economy
may make it only more nationalistic.

In fact, both Brendon and Mearsheimer can be right. China is
likely to seek a political modus vivendi with America, even as it seeks
regional hegemony. China will continue to build an oceanic navy,
with accompanying air and missile capabilities. The geographical
focus of these assets will be on the South China Sea, control of which
allows regional hegemony to be realized. At the same time, Beijing
will work tirelessly in its pursuit of good economic and political relations with Washington. Washington, for its part, will resist the moves
of Beijing toward regional hegemony, even as it works with Beijing on
as many issues as it can. The South China Sea, as much as the East
China Sea and the Korean Peninsula, will provide the center stage for
this tense and contradictory relationship. For the path to Chinese
hegemony in the Korean Peninsula—because of the uncertainties surrounding North Korea's future—is less clear and fraught with much
more difficulty than is the path to Chinese hegemony in the South
China Sea, where China only faces an assortment of comparatively
weak and divided states, of which Vietnam is the strongest. Thus, the
South China Sea, more than any other part of the world, best illustrates, once again, what would be the cost of a U.S. decline, or even
of a partial U.S. withdrawal from its forward military bases. As such,
the South China Sea shows what exactly the United States provides

the world that is now at risk, and concomitantly, what the bad things are that could happen were the world, in an air and naval sense, to become truly multipolar.

Because the United States dominates the Western Hemisphere, and has power to spare to affect the balance of power in the Eastern Hemisphere, the U.S. not only keeps the peace (aside from small wars that erupt here and there), it guards the global commons, that is, the sea lines of communication that allow for international trade. Without the U.S. Navy and Air Force, globalization as we know it would be impossible. The fact that Russia is still constrained in its attempts to seriously undermine the sovereignty of states in Eastern and Central Europe; the fact that the Middle East has so far at least avoided an interstate Holocaust of sorts; the fact that India and Pakistan have not engaged in a full-scale war in decades, and have never used their nuclear weapons; the fact that North Korea merely threatens South Korea and Japan with large-scale military aggression rather than actually carrying it out, is all in large measure because of a U.S. global security umbrella. The fact that small and embattled nations, be it Israel or Georgia, can even exist is because of what ultimately the U.S. military provides. Indeed, it is the deployment of American air and naval platforms worldwide that gives American diplomacy much of its signal heft, which it then uses to support democracy and freer societies everywhere. Substantially reduce that American military presence, and the world—and the South China Sea, in particular—looks like a very different place.

The United States keeps China honest: limiting China's aggression mainly to its maps, so that China's diplomats and navy act within reason. That is not to say that the United States is pure in its actions and China automatically the villain. For example, the United States conducts classified reconnaissance activities on a regular basis against China in the Western Pacific that it would have difficulty tolerating were they directed at its own nearby waters by a rival great power.[19] What the United States provides to the nations of the South China Sea region is less the fact of its democratic virtue than the fact of its raw power, which counters that of China. It is the balance of power between the United States and China that ultimately keeps Taiwan, Vietnam, Malaysia, the Philippines, Indonesia, and Singapore free, able to play one great power off against the other. And within that space of freedom, regionalism, in the form of ASEAN, can emerge as a power in its own right. Yet such freedom cannot be taken for granted. For the tense, ongoing standoff between the United States and China—in which a stalemate ensues on a plethora of complex issues ranging from cyber-war to trade to currency reform to surveillance of each other's military capabilities—might yet shift in China's favor because of the sheer absolute growth of the Chinese economy (even as the rate of that growth declines), coupled with China's geographic centrality to East Asia and the Western Pacific.

Andrew F. Krepinevich, president of the Center for Strategic and Budgetary Assessments in Washington, believes that the nations of the Western Pacific are slowly being "Finlandized" by China, meaning that they will maintain nominal independence but in the end abide by foreign policy rules set by Beijing. He points out that China's People's Liberation Army (PLA) sees U.S. battle networks—"which rely heavily on satellites and the Internet to identify targets, coordinate attacks, guide 'smart bombs' and more"—as its "Achilles' heel." The Chinese, he goes on, have tested an antisatellite missile in 2007, have reportedly used lasers to temporarily blind U.S. satellites, and have been conducting cyber-attacks on the U.S. military for years. This is in addition to the large numbers of ballistic and cruise missiles and other anti-access/area-denial weaponry that the Chinese have been fielding to undermine U.S. forward bases in Asia.[20] According to Mark Helprin, a senior fellow at the Claremont Institute in California, "China is on the cusp" of being able to use conventional satellites and swarms of miniature ones, as well as "networked surface, undersea, and aerial cuing for real-time terminal guidance with which to direct its 1,500 short-range ballistic missiles," in order to hit U.S. aircraft carriers.[21] The aim is not to go to war, but to adjust the disposition of forces so that, as in the case of Taiwan, but writ large across the Western Pacific, the U.S. military increasingly loses credibility as to what it can accomplish. And with that loss of credibility would come the weakening of America's Pacific alliances. Indeed, the Finlandization of Southeast Asia may indicate the dark side of a multipolar military world.

True military multipolarity benefits the state that is most geographically central to the region in question: namely China in East Asia. This is because the military situation being equal, geography and demography provide the edge. In other words, a multipolar Asia in military terms would be a Chinese-dominated Asia. And Chinese dominance in Asia would be very different from American dominance. Because China is not half a world away from the region, but in fact constitutes the region's geographic, demographic, and economic organizing principle, Chinese dominance would naturally be more overwhelming than the American variety. This is to say nothing about China's own authoritarian system, which even though not harsh as many dictatorships go—and far more competent than most—is still less benign than the American model of government, which, in turn, partly determines the American style of empire.

But do not confuse military multipolarity with the balance of power. For the balance of power in Asia requires American military superiority, in order to offset China's geographic, demographic, and economic advantage. One does not necessarily mean the crushing American superiority of recent decades. In fact, the American military position in Asia can afford to weaken measurably, to take into account future budget cuts, so long as the American military retains a clear-cut advantage in key areas over the Chinese military. It is that edge which will preserve the balance of power.

Multipolarity is fine in a diplomatic and economic sense. Clearly, the U.S. position in Asia will ultimately rest to a significant extent on its willingness to enter into new free trade relationships and to join "wholeheartedly" into the region's multilateral economic arrangements, as East Asia remains a main area of growth in the global economy.[22] It is only by enmeshing itself further into the region's trade that the United States will remain self-interested enough to continue to guard the sea lines of communications in the Western Pacific. But complete multipolarity in all spheres would lead to the South China

Sea becoming China's Caribbean, and that, in turn, would put China in a position to dominate both the Western Pacific and the Indian Ocean. In a Eurasian trading system that is principally maritime, it is fine for China to be the first among equals, provided again that the U.S. Navy is there as a balancing power.

The most comprehensive summation of the new Asian geopolitical landscape has come not from Washington or Beijing, but from Canberra. In a seventy-one-page article, "Power Shift: Australia's Future Between Washington and Beijing," Hugh White, professor of strategic studies at the Australian National University and a former Australian government intelligence analyst, describes his country as the quintessential "status quo" power: one that desperately wants the situation in Asia to remain exactly as it is, with China continuing to grow so that Australia can do more and more trade with it, and America to remain "the strongest power in Asia," so as to be Australia's "ultimate protector." But as White says, the problem is that both these things cannot continue to happen. Asia cannot continue to change economically without changing politically and strategically. Namely, if China keeps growing economically as it probably will (though at a significantly slower pace), it will overtake America as the world's wealthiest country (though not on a per capita basis), and naturally will not be content with American military primacy in Asia.[23]

White notes that what has accounted for Asia's decades-long happy situation, which we have all taken for granted, was actually a "remarkable piece of strategic diplomacy" engineered by President Richard Nixon and his national security advisor, Henry Kissinger. Nixon and Kissinger went to Beijing in 1972 and cut a deal with Chinese leader Mao Zedong, whereby "America would stop pretending that the nationalist regime in Taiwan was the government of China. . . . In return, China would stop contesting America's position in Asia and stop supporting communist insurgencies around the region [at least to the same extent]." China also got protection from

America against the Soviet Union, as well as insurance against an economically resurgent Japan. This would a few short years later provide China with the security to liberalize its economy to the great benefit of the entire region. Peace was at hand, and now "left to themselves" the countries of Southeast Asia would consequently boom.[24]

It was China's repudiation of Marxist economics begun under Deng Xiaoping in 1979 that allowed it to finally join the global economy, a century later than countries in the West. Once it did so, the immensity of its population has assured China of becoming among the most powerful economies in the world, thus leading to a security situation in Asia different from the peaceful one that Nixon and Kissinger had wrought.[25]

What does China want now? White posits that the Chinese may desire in Asia the kind of new-style empire that America engineered in the Western Hemisphere, once Washington had secured dominance over the Caribbean Basin (as China believes it should over the South China Sea). This new-style empire in the Western Hemisphere, in White's words, meant America's neighbors were "more or less free to run their own countries," even as Washington insisted that its views were given "full consideration" and took precedence "over anyone from outside the hemisphere." The problem with this model is Japan, which would probably not accept Chinese hegemony, however soft. That leaves the nineteenth-century Concert of Europe model, in which case China, America, Japan, India, and perhaps one or two others would sit down at the table of Asian power as equals. But now the question becomes, would America accept such a modest role, since it has associated Asian prosperity and stability with its own primacy. White suggests that in the face of rising Chinese power, American dominance might henceforth mean instability for Asia. American dominance is predicated on the notion that because China is authoritarian at home, it will act "unacceptably abroad." But that may not be so, White argues.[26]

In other words, in the future, America, not China, might be the problem. We, especially our intellectual and journalist class, may care too much about the internal nature of the Chinese regime. But China's regime could very easily act detestable at home and responsible abroad—another reason why the rise of Asia could alienate humanists of all stripes. As I've noted, America's aim should be balance, not dominance. In any case, because the next four decades in Asia will probably be less secure than the previous four, White suggests that Australia may have to "spend much more on defense and build much more capable armed forces."[27] The same is probably true for all the nations of Asia. The seas will become more crowded with armaments.

What is naval power for? The South China Sea might answer that question for the American public during the first half of the twenty-first century. The U.S. Navy has struggled for some time trying to explain its mission to the American public: to explain why it needs hundreds of billions of dollars for hundreds of warships that the average American never sees—unless he or she lives near a naval base—or even reads about much in the news. To be sure, the last decade saw the headlines dominated by ground forces involved in nasty land wars in Iraq and Afghanistan. The trials and tribulations of the Army obsessed the media: the Marines, too, which, while a naval force designed for amphibious landings, essentially became another ground force for those two Middle Eastern wars. But that may change as those wars come to an end for the United States, and as the continued rise of China leads to a different and less stable security environment in East Asia. And because Asia is primarily a maritime sphere, that will give the U.S. Navy an attractive mission statement that it has seemingly lacked. But the question is, Will the mission statement arrive in time to keep the states of the South China Sea—the heart of maritime East Asia—from Finlandization? John Morgan, a retired vice admiral in the U.S. Navy, worries that America, with defense cuts on the horizon, may be committing a great "maritime mistake," by cutting back on its Navy just at the point in history when the world needs it the most to maintain the balance of power, and thus keep countries like Taiwan and Vietnam free. Militarily defending Vietnam may not seem like something the American public has the appetite for, especially given its twentieth-century history with that country. But it is the freedom that a country like Vietnam may yet come to symbolize that will matter much in America's own future. Again, it is not only our values that matter, but the military might that backs them up.

Truly, in international affairs, behind all questions of morality lie questions of power. Humanitarian intervention in the Balkans in the 1990s was possible only because the Serbian regime was not a great power armed with nuclear weapons, unlike the Russian regime, which at the same time was committing atrocities of a similar scale in Chechnya where the West did nothing; nor did the West do much against the ethnic cleansing in the Caucasus because there, too, was a Russian sphere of influence. In the Western Pacific in the coming decades, morality may mean giving up some of our most cherished ideals for the sake of stability. How else are we to make at least some room for a quasi-authoritarian China as its military expands? (And barring a social-economic collapse internally, China's military will keep on expanding.) For it is the balance of power itself, even more than the democratic values of the West, that is often the best pre-server of freedom. That also will be a lesson of the South China Sea in the twenty-first century—one more that humanists do not want to hear.

CHAPTER II

China's Caribbean

It is a harsh but true reality: capitalist prosperity leads to military acquisitions. States in the course of rapid development do more trade with the outside world, and consequently develop global interests that require protection by means of hard power. The economic rise of post–Civil War America in the late nineteenth century led to the building of a great navy. The culmination of industrial development in Europe at the turn of the twentieth century was an arms race that helped cause World War I. Europe's relative decline in military power in our own era is possible only because Europe free rides off secure sea lines of communication provided by the United States Navy and Air Force. Though China and other Asian states similarly free ride off the policing services provided by American sailors and airmen, their situation is radically different than that of the states of early-twenty-first-century Europe. Asian states have conflicting claims of sovereignty, and lack the integrative mechanisms of a NATO and European

Union. They are also, in many cases, as we saw in the last chapter, congealing as strong and cohesive polities for the first time in their history, and are consequently feeling their oats, so to speak. Their stability on land for the first time in decades and centuries allows them to make territorial claims at sea. Indeed, they are new to modern nationalism rather than sick and tired of it, like the Europeans in the early decades following World War II. And so power politics reigns in Asia. It is not ideas that Asians fight over, but space on the map.

It is the very steepness of Asia's economic rise (and particularly of China's until recently) from the 1970s through the first decade of the twenty-first century that causes its leaders to pound their chests militarily. Whereas it took Great Britain nearly six decades to double its per capita income during its industrial revolution following the late eighteenth century, and America five decades to do the same following the Civil War, China doubled its per capita income in the first decade after its late-twentieth-century takeoff. As a whole, Asia's per capita income rose sevenfold in less than six decades following 1950, reports Asia expert Bill Emmott, a former editor in chief of *The Economist*.[1]

Asia's military rise has followed in tandem with its economic rise. Desmond Ball, professor at the Strategic and Defence Studies Centre of the Australian National University, reports that from the late 1980s to the late 1990s defense outlays rose so dramatically that Asia's share of global military expenditure nearly doubled, from 11 to 20 percent. Asia's share of arms imports increased from 15 to 41 percent of the world total. Because China's economy was not upended by the 1997–1998 economic crisis, its defense budget has increased by double digits nearly every year since 1988, leading to an eightfold swelling in the size of its defense budget over the past two decades.[2] In 2011, China's defense budget rose another 12.7 percent to nearly $100 billion. Though the U.S. defense budget is $708 billion, "the two are headed in opposite directions."[3] Moreover, China's total military-related spending was estimated by the Pentagon to be $150 billion in 2009, and has surely moved higher since.[4] China is now the world's second largest military spender, with China and Japan far ahead of Germany and Russia in military expenditures.[5]

Ball observes that Asian defense expenditures have moved from the stage of "non-threatening" general buildups and modernizations to an "action-reaction" phase, in which the various littoral countries are engaged in a heated arms race, particularly in regards to surface and subsurface warships, ballistic and cruise missiles, and missile defense systems, and all facets of electronic and cyber-warfare. Thus does postmodern nationalism define itself.

Worse, this new Asian arms race and the regional security dynamics associated with it will be "much more complex" than that which obtained during the bipolar Cold War era, notes Ball, with more points of interaction and therefore greater likelihood of miscalculations and attendant instability.[6]

Of particular note is the feverish acquisition of submarines, as surface warships become more vulnerable to offensive missiles. "Submarines are the new bling, everybody wants them," Bernard Loo Fook Weng of the S. Rajaratnam School of International Studies in Singapore told me. Note that submarines are moving, undersea intelligence-gathering factories. Unlike aircraft carriers for example, which in and of themselves constitute statements of national prestige and are useful for a variety of missions, including humanitarian relief, submarines are about sheer aggression, even as the gathering of information in which they engage may serve a stabilizing purpose by providing one state with knowledge about the intentions and capabilities of another. On the other hand, submarine acquisitions introduce a dangerous uncertainty into the military equation, because as soon as they submerge nobody knows exactly where they are. Submarines can patrol in very intrusive ways without announcing their presence.

China has over sixty submarines and will have around seventy-five or so in the next few years, slightly more than the United States. China "is outbuilding the U.S. in new submarines by four to one" since 2000, and by "eight to one" since 2005, even as the U.S. Navy's ASW (antisubmarine warfare) forces have diminished, write James C. Bussert of the U.S. Naval Surface Warfare Center and Bruce A. Elleman of the U.S. Naval War College.[7] Whereas many of China's submarines are diesel-electric and all of America's are nuclear, the latest Yuan-class diesel-electric models are quieter than the nuclear ones, and because the Western Pacific constitutes China's home waters, China's submarines do not have to travel from half a world away to get to the Asian military theater as America's must. The unstoppable buildup of military force by China means paradoxically that China can wait and adopt a benign foreign policy for the moment because time is on its side. By the late 2020s, at the current rate of acquisitions and decommissionings, China will have more warships in the Western Pacific than the U.S. Pacific Fleet.

India, South Korea, and Vietnam are expected to acquire six more subs apiece by the end of the current decade, while Australia will acquire twelve new subs within twenty years, though recent budgetary restrictions may affect this statistic downward. Singapore, Malaysia, and Indonesia will shortly acquire two more subs apiece. Malaysia's defense spending has more than doubled since 2000, with conventional weapons deliveries increasing 722 percent in 2005–2009 compared to the first half of the decade. (Malaysia originally thought of acquiring subs in the 1980s to counter Vietnam, which had just annexed Amboyna Cay in the Spratly Islands, but with Chinese power now looming, it finds another use for them.) Singapore, a tiny city-state at the southern extremity of the South China Sea, is now among the world's top ten arms importers. Meanwhile, Australia was expected to spend a whopping $279 billion in the next two decades on new submarines, destroyers, and fighter planes, again, continued funds permitting. In all, given military modernization programs under way in South Korea and Japan, Asian nations are expected to purchase as many as 111 subs by 2030, according to AMI International, which provides market research to governments and shipbuilders.[8]

South Korea may be the best example of this defense (and particularly naval) craze in the Asia-Pacific region. In 2006, South Korea decided to more than double defense expenditures by 2015, to $1.24 trillion. It is investing in—among other things like submarines and frigates for antisubmarine warfare—six new Sejong-class destroyers, each carrying 128 missiles guided by an advanced Aegis system. Then there are the purchases of F-15K Slam Eagle air-superiority fighters, four Boeing 737 AWACS aircraft, and probably F-35 Joint Strike Fighters. Japan at the end of 2009 green-lighted construction of an entire new generation of large helicopter carriers, the 22DDH, vital for antisubmarine warfare.[9] Asia's arms race may be one of the most underreported stories in the elite media in decades.

All of these Asian navies are dwarfed by that of the United States, but whereas each of them is increasing in size, the number of U.S. warships over the decades will decrease in number. Military multipolarity, as I indicated in the last chapter, will thus eventually follow economic and diplomatic multipolarity. This military multipolarity is a sign of a more liberalized and just world, in which indigenous states, rather than Western empires, have control over their own resources. To wit, China has recently put to sea its first aircraft carrier, in some sense a refitted Russian-Ukrainian "piece of junk" that is more of an amphibious assault ship than an American-sized carrier.[10] American naval officers are not worried about it and they shouldn't be. It will take Chinese crews years and perhaps decades of training to properly utilize carrier strike groups. But were China able to keep up its naval modernization and expansion—a big "if"—by 2050 it would have nine carriers concentrated in the Western Pacific and Indian oceans, by which time the United States would have about the same number for policing the entire globe.

Future projections are obviously dangerous because of the flaw of linear thinking: current trends rarely continue as they have in the past. But given how China has constituted a great world civilization and seen great empires for the overwhelming majority of its history going back thousands of years, it is reasonable to see the last 150 years of weakness as an aberration that is now being rectified. This is likely despite China's decreasing economic growth rates, and despite heightened domestic tension. Moreover, the very launching of an aircraft carrier indicates that China has the ambition to transform its navy from the "sea denial" type—in order to protect its coastline—to the more formidable "sea control" type, which portends a blue-water oceanic force.[11] In fact, in 2012, China launched the fourth of its projected eight new 071 amphibious landing ships that can each carry up to eight hundred troops, hovercraft, armored vehicles, and medium-lift helicopters. "Having a significant fleet of large amphibious assault vehicles clearly suggests a desire for power projection," says Christian Le Mière, a researcher for the International Institute for Strategic Studies in London. (China has also launched a line of 056 stealthy littoral combat frigates.) Moreover, China overtook South Korea in 2010 to become the world's largest shipbuilder, even as its best submarines and surface warships are now armed with advanced air defense weapons and long-range antiship missiles.[12]

China has not yet sufficiently developed and practiced the so-called system of systems necessary for fleet operations, even as it is accelerating training and sustained deployments to gain such experience, says Rodger Baker, vice president and East Asia analyst for Stratfor, a private global intelligence firm. But in the near seas (South China and East China seas), he goes on, China does not necessarily need to engage in coordinated fleet activities to provide deterrence and defense—it can, for example, rely on swarm tactics backed by land-based air and missile assets. China can also use what it calls "combination punches." In late 2012, challenging Japan's de facto administration of the Diaoyu/Senkaku Islands in the East China Sea, China "launched joint combat controls by its navy, air force, and strategic missile corps," in coordination with the threat of economic retaliation, a refusal to attend a major financial conference in Tokyo, and encouraging anti-Japanese protests at home.[13] A fleet need not fight well if it can be used in conjunction with diplomatic and other organs of state to exert pressure on adversaries. (Witness China's emphasis on multiple civilian maritime forces such as coast guards, which can bully neighboring states in the South China and East China seas without eliciting a proportional U.S. response, because the U.S. Coast Guard is absent in the region.)

Keep in mind that China spends only around 2 percent of its GDP, gross domestic product, on defense, whereas the United States spends

4.7 percent.[14] So China is in better shape to keep increasing its military budgets. (Likewise, the dramatic growth of national economies throughout East Asia in recent decades has allowed for these military buildups without much affecting defense budgets as percentages of GDPs.)

Because naval power and air power cannot in terms of strategy be disaggregated, it is particularly symbolic that on January 11, 2011, just hours before then-U.S. secretary of defense Robert Gates met in Beijing with President Hu Jintao, China tested a prototype of its J-20 stealth fighter, designed to rival America's F-22 Raptor, the world's only operational stealth fighter. "Larger than the F-22, with bigger fuel tanks, it will fly higher, faster and with less chance of detection."[15] China has increased the number of its modern, fourth-generation aircraft from fifty to five hundred since 2000, even as it has reduced the size of its overall air force from three thousand fighters to two thousand.[16] This is a perfect illustration of the lesson that military modernization is actually about smaller but more up-to-date force structures. Yes, Asian nations are acquiring a lot of ships and planes: more important, however, is that they are acquiring top-of-the-line items that will mesh with their future space satellite reconnaissance systems, existent missile systems, and electronic and cyber-warfare capabilities.

In particular, China, according to the U.S. Department of Defense, "has the most active land-based ballistic and cruise missile program in the world."[17] China's new land-based antiship ballistic missiles—using information from space-based tracking systems—may threaten U.S. surface warships, particularly aircraft carriers. Though the United States retains the power of massive retaliation, the very idea that its carriers, cruisers, destroyers, and frigates are not as inviolate as they used to be could affect the deployment patterns of America's carrier strike groups. And affecting the behavior of your competitor is the essence of power.

According to Yale professor of management and political science Paul Bracken, China isn't so much building a conventional navy as an "anti-navy" navy, designed to push U.S. sea and air forces away from the East Asian coastline. Chinese drones putting lasers on U.S. warships, sonar pings from Chinese submarines, the noisy activation of Chinese smart mines, and so on are all designed to signal to American warships that Beijing knows about their movements and the United States risks a crisis if such warships get closer to Chinese waters. Because "relations with China are too important to jeopardize with a military confrontation," this anti-access strategy has a significant political effect on Washington. "The strategic impact of China's agility is not so much to tilt the military balance in its direction and away from the United States. Rather," Bracken goes on, "it introduces new risks into the American decision-making calculus."[18]

None of these developments is lost on U.S. military planners. For despite the headlines in North Africa and the Middle East, the United States maintains the preponderant amount of its naval forces in the Pacific, Indian, and Arctic oceans—all in Asia or close to it. Of the eleven U.S. aircraft carrier strike groups currently in existence, six are usually focused on the Pacific and Indian oceans. The U.S. Fleet Marine Force, Pacific, is the largest of the Marine Corps' field commands. The Pacific Air Forces is the largest U.S. Air Force Command. While technically speaking all these American air and sea forces range over 50 percent of the globe, in fact they are primarily focused on balancing against China. For in addition to China's subs and fighter jets, included in its arsenal are seventy-five major surface warships and its new-old aircraft carrier, with plans to acquire four to six additional carriers in the near and mid-term future.[19]

The Pentagon's deployment strategy *against* China (even as it would publicly deny such a characterization) is a fact of life in the Pacific, not really because China has this or that number of submarines, surface warships, and fighter jets, but because China's "sheer size [in terms of geography, demography, and economics] and presence at the very heart of Asia make it a potential threat to virtually all of its neighbors," writes Princeton professor Aaron L. Friedberg. At the same time, Friedberg goes on, "unlike the United States, China has no option to withdraw from the region. This fact alone cannot help but give pause to any smaller nation that might contemplate

defying Beijing's will."[20] To be sure, China, despite "its steadily expanding global involvement," is enveloping Asia.[21] In the words of
U.S. Naval War College professor Andrew S. Erickson, while the
American Navy and Air Force are spread thin around the planet,
"China inherently enjoys theater concentration."[22] This is true not
only militarily but economically as well. Even as China's defense budget has soared, its bilateral trade with the members of the Association
of Southeast Asian Nations jumped by 640 percent during the first
decade of the twenty-first century.[23] In other words, to avoid Finlandization, the countries of the South China Sea must rely on the con-
stancy of U.S. naval and air power in an age of declining American
defense budgets; or on the possibility that China's own economic and
domestic security will itself at some point suddenly deteriorate to the
level where it adversely affects the growth of Beijing's defense budget.
To clarify: it is not China's burgeoning air and naval forces per se, nor
its burgeoning Asian trade patterns per se, but the combination of the
two that threatens the de facto independence of other Asian states,
particularly those in the South China Sea region.

Whereas Northeast Asia enjoys a rough balance of power between
China, Japan, and South Korea (the latter two supported by the presence of the U.S. military) in the South China Sea, China is a much
greater threat because in this rapidly militarizing age of ours the U.S.
military and body politic simply do not have quite the same attach-
ment to countries like Vietnam, Malaysia, and the Philippines as they
do to Japan and South Korea. While the United States has fought
wars in the past in Vietnam and the Philippines, it presently has tens
of thousands of troops stationed in Japan and South Korea. Japan
and South Korea have formidable military-industrial complexes of
their own, far superior to the budding arsenals of the weaker nations
to the south. That is why the South China Sea will be among the most
salient political and moral registers of any future U.S. defense re-
trenchment. Here is where everyone is arming to the teeth, even as
China's military is pulling further and further ahead of every other in
the region.

The South China Sea, to use an alternative geographical definition from the one used in the last chapter, connects the Strait of Malacca in the southwest to the Bashi and Balintang channels and the Taiwan Strait to the north and northeast: that is, it connects the maritime world of the Middle East and Indian Subcontinent to that of Northeast Asia. It is as central to Asia as the Mediterranean is to Europe. If one assumes that the Persian Gulf and Northeast Asia are the two critical areas of the non-Western world that the United States should never let another great power dominate, consider the energy-rich South China Sea, which lies between them, the third. In fact, in geopolitical terms it might arguably be the most critical geographical juncture of the non-Western world; the reason will become apparent shortly.

First, consider how the South China Sea is uniquely crucial to China. As the analyst Mingjiang Li writes, it is a "natural shield" for China's security in the south, China's most densely populated and developed region. A "strong foothold" in the South China Sea gives China a strategic "hinterland" of over a thousand miles stretching to Indonesia, and would thus act as a "restraining factor" for the U.S. Navy's Seventh Fleet transiting the Pacific and Indian oceans. A strong foothold in the South China Sea also helps China's navy break through the straitjacket of the American-dominated First Island Chain in the Western Pacific. Moreover, Chinese observers complain that other competing states have dug over a thousand oil wells in the South China Sea, which exceeds China's own offshore production by several times.[24] Control over the South China Sea's oil and natural gas reserves would make China a little less dependent on Middle East energy.[25]

China claims "indisputable sovereignty" over the South China Sea. "How would you feel if I cut off your arms and legs?" asked Chinese navy commander Wu Shengli at a forum in Singapore. "That's how China feels about the South China Sea," which Chinese officials refer to as "blue national soil."[26]

China's claim to the South China Sea is, in its own words, historical. Chinese analysts argue that their forebears discovered the islands in the South China Sea during China's Han dynasty in the second century BC. They argue that in the third century AD, a Chinese mission to Cambodia made accounts of the Paracels and Spratlys; that in the tenth through fourteenth centuries during the Song and Yuan dynasties many official and unofficial Chinese accounts indicated that the South China Sea came within China's national boundaries; that during the fifteenth through nineteenth centuries the various maps of the Ming and Qing dynasties included the Spratlys in Chinese territory; and that in the early twentieth century during the late Qing dynasty the Chinese government took action to exercise jurisdiction over the Paracels. This is to say nothing of the de facto rights Chinese fishermen have enjoyed in the South China Sea for centuries, and the detailed records they have kept of islands, islets, and shoals.[27]

Then there were the various official maps made by the Nationalist Guomindang government before and after World War II, incorporating South China Sea dry-land formations into Chinese territory. These maps also featured the U-shaped cow's tongue, a historical nine-dashed line that, as Chinese analysts argue, preceded the interpretations of contemporary international law as stipulated in the United Nations' Convention on the Law of the Sea. Nevertheless, as the analyst Mingjiang Li points out, many Chinese experts accept that the historical nine-dashed line does "not translate to full sovereignty over the whole South China Sea." An example of China's willingness to compromise is its 2004 maritime boundary agreement with Vietnam over the Gulf of Tonkin, where China is entitled to 46.77 percent of the Gulf and Vietnam 53.23 percent.[28] However, the Gulf of Tonkin is a special geographical case: a semi-enclosed appendage of the South China Sea where Vietnam and China are in such claustrophobic proximity that it makes sense for China to compromise on the issue, without giving up its claims on the larger sea. Though China seeks dominance, do not assume it will be unreasonable. On the other hand, the cow's tongue cannot be conceded too easily for fear of a nationalist backlash in China.

China is following up its historical claims with military movements. It has relocated its new SSN nuclear attack submarines and SSBN nuclear ballistic missile submarines from Qingdao in the north, across the Yellow Sea from South Korea, to Yulin, on Hainan Island in the heart of the South China Sea, where Chinese subs have been able to roam at will since the 1990s.[29] China has stationed troops of the People's Liberation Army on many of the disputed islands and atolls in the region, where China has built elaborate signal stations.[30] Hainan, in particular, has an extensive electronic military infrastructure in place. By home-porting its newest submarines in Hainan, alongside its extensive communications and intelligence-gathering infrastructure, China, write Bussert and Elleman, is "exerting regional maritime control incrementally."[31] In effect, China is using its land to control the sea.[32] Though far out at sea, too, China is ambitious—as it develops its aerial refueling program to project military power from the sea throughout the South China Sea.[33] Indeed, while the South China Sea fleet is historically the last of China's fleets to modernize, that is rapidly changing as China for the last decade has been sending its newest naval combatants and aircraft to the region. Hainan Island, jutting out in the direction of Vietnam, allows China its most proximate perch on the South China Sea. The new naval base at Ya-long Bay "sprawls across a spacious tract of land" with one-thousand-meter-long piers for surface warships and 230-meter piers for submarines, which will also be serviced by a special submarine tunnel to ward off aerial surveillance. Even as Southeast Asian countries modernize their own air and sea forces, most notably Malaysia—with its new F-15SG fighter jets, *Archer*-class submarines, and *Formidable*-class frigates—they continue to fall behind China.[34]

Actually, there is nothing unusually aggressive about anything China is doing. China is a great demographic and economic power, enjoying the geography of a vast continent with a long seaboard in the tropics and temperate zone. The fact that it seeks to dominate an adjacent sea crowded with smaller and much weaker powers, where there is possibly a plentitude of oil and natural gas, is altogether natural. If it weren't, great power politics over the course of the past few millennia would not have been as they have. University of Chicago political scientist John Mearsheimer offers this challenging assertion: "An increasingly powerful China is likely to try to push the U.S. out of Asia, much the way the U.S. pushed the European powers out of the Western Hemisphere. Why should we expect China to act any differently than the United States did? Are they more principled than we are? More ethical? Less nationalistic?"[35] In sum, unless China is stopped or slowed in its track by a domestic socioeconomic upheaval, the U.S. military will have to make some serious accommodation with a rising Chinese military power, with great political ramifications for the states in the region.

What would be the larger strategic effect of China becoming the dominant military power in the South China Sea? In other words, does the South China Sea represent something existential for the Middle Kingdom? It is at this point where one should bring the American experience in the Caribbean more fully into the discussion, so as to provide historical context for the deployment of all these submarines, fighter jets, and so on. The history of the Caribbean adds another dimension to the current tensions in the South China Sea.

We might call the Caribbean stretching from Florida to Venezuela, together with the Gulf of Mexico, the Greater Caribbean. This Greater Caribbean, which unites North and South America into a single coherent geopolitical system, is roughly the size of the South China Sea—fifteen hundred miles in one direction and one thousand miles in the other. But the two seas have the opposite visual effect on the map: whereas the South China Sea is defined by continental and island masses around it, the Caribbean is defined by the cluster of islands, big and small, in its very center. But as we know, the map is deceptive unless we peer very closely at it: for the South China Sea is indeed filled with many geographical features, however microscopic, even as they hold the key to significant energy resources.

The sugar revolution holds the key to Caribbean history, bringing an increase in trade in goods and slaves. By 1770, every piece of the Caribbean was the colonial possession of some European state. But with the waning of the slave trade and the shift toward an interest in the temperate lands of North and South America, European enthusiasm for the Caribbean dissipated, too. It was this period that saw the emergence of the United States as an imperial force. The spread of the United States across temperate zone North America was as "rapacious" as anything, for example, the Chinese engaged in while fulfilling their own continental destiny.[36] Indeed, when the United States was in an earlier phase of its modern development than China is presently—especially in terms of the political consolidation of its home continent—the United States was already seeking to dominate the Greater Caribbean, which it naturally saw as falling within its geopolitical sphere of interest. That is what the Monroe Doctrine of 1823 was primarily about. By the early nineteenth century, Latin America had largely become free of European rule, and President James Monroe and Secretary of State John Quincy Adams were dead set against European power returning in the form of client states. They wanted, in the words of Naval War College professor James R. Holmes, "to freeze the status quo." Domination of the Greater Caribbean by America meant neither isolationism, nor the subjugation of local peoples, nor the abjuration of international cooperation. Indeed, while the Monroe Doctrine was being promulgated, the U.S. Navy was working with Great Britain's Royal Navy to police the Caribbean, in a joint effort to end the slave trade.[37] Rather than seek to keep European navies out of the Caribbean altogether, President Monroe sought only to keep them from reestablishing footholds on land in the region. The Monroe Doctrine was far more subtle than commonly supposed.

The key geographical fact about the Caribbean is that it is close to America and was far from the great European powers of the age, just as the South China Sea is close to China but far from America and other Western powers. Of all the European powers, the British, with the world's greatest navy and bases in Jamaica, Trinidad, British Guiana, British Honduras, and the Lesser Antilles, were, like the U.S. Navy today in the South China Sea, best positioned to challenge the United States in the Caribbean at the turn of the twentieth century.

But the British did not challenge the Americans, because they knew the latter would fight hard to defend the maritime extension of their own North American continent. (For the same reason, the United States must now be careful of openly challenging China in the South China Sea.) Moreover, while the British were a key economic and military factor in the Caribbean, by 1917, U.S. economic influence over the Caribbean, born of geographical proximity and a burgeoning American economy, surpassed that of Britain—just as China has come to surpass the influence of the United States in Asia. "The American Mediterranean," is what the Caribbean came to be called.[38]

At the turn of the twentieth century, writes historian Richard H. Collin, "the complex confluence of what we generally call modernism— transportation, communication, and industrial technology—transformed the world."[39] And modernism led to all forms of gunboat diplomacy to protect new economic interests, just as postmodernism leads today to an air, naval, and electronic and cyber-warfare buildup in Asia. Modernism also led to the American desire to build an isthmian canal athwart Central America, to link the Greater Caribbean with the Pacific Ocean.

The modern age began in full force in the Western Hemisphere with the outbreak of the Spanish-American War in 1898 in Spanish-held Cuba, which led, in succession, to the American defeat of the Spanish in the Philippines in the South China Sea. The historian Collin writes: "The United States demonstrated to itself and to Europe that it could fight and win a foreign war. With former Confederates fighting side by side with Union soldiers, military unification cemented the political and economic reunion that had already given the post–Civil War United States its awesome" power.[40] The Spanish-American War, which arose partly out of the need to control the Caribbean sea lanes, also meant the death of America's nonhegemonic exceptionalism, as it, too, acquired an empire of sorts. Theodore Roosevelt, who in 1898 led his Rough Riders in a charge up San Juan Hill in Cuba, would a decade later, as a retiring president, be the ruler of Spain's former colonies in the Caribbean and the Pacific, the builder of the Panama Canal, the winner of a Nobel Peace Prize for settling a war between Russia and Japan, and the commander of a twenty-two-battleship navy. Likewise, if China's benign and nonhegemonic view of itself becomes increasingly untenable, it would only be following in America's footsteps. Collin writes, "Eliminating Europe from the New World was the cornerstone of Roosevelt's foreign policy."[41] So will China, according to Mearsheimer, have as a goal of grand, long-term strategy the elimination of America from Asia?

The Roosevelt Corollary to the Monroe Doctrine, issued in 1904, stated that the United States "would interfere with them [the peoples of the Greater Caribbean] only in the last resort, and then only if it became evident that their inability or unwillingness to do justice at home and abroad had violated the rights of the United States or had invited foreign aggression to the detriment of the entire body of American nations." Roosevelt's secretary of war, Elihu Root, specifically rejected the policy of the Grover Cleveland administration that the United States was "practically sovereign" in the Greater Caribbean. Root said, "we arrogate to ourselves not sovereignty . . . but only the right to protect." Root had in mind crises in the Dominican Republic and Venezuela, where bankrupt and outlaw regimes were threatened with intervention by European creditors, who might then convert customs houses into naval bases. Roosevelt, much as he bristled at the irresponsibility of those regimes, was not about to let Europeans take advantage of the situation. Coups and breakdowns also led to American small-scale and large-scale interventions in Panama and Cuba, even as political crises dominated Colombia and the Central American states: many, to varying extents, threatening to invite European interference. Moreover, Roosevelt wanted to prevent "a strong Germany from replacing a weak Spain" in the Caribbean, as Kaiser Wilhelm II built up his naval force in the decade prior to World War I.[42] Just as the Caribbean was the natural maritime extension of the continental United States, it was also the part of America's security environment most vulnerable to European attack. Finally, it was necessary to shape the political environment for the digging of the Panama Canal.

American military deployments were accompanied by economic

hegemony: the guaranteeing of loans known as "dollar diplomacy," and the regulation of the region's currencies by pushing as many countries as possible to adopt the gold standard and make their money readily convertible with the dollar.[43] Later on, the full-scale production of oil in Trinidad and Cuba would add another motivation to American involvement.[44] In the end, the years of the Roosevelt administration marked the culmination of American domination of the Greater Caribbean, which would continue for decades with more American military and economic interventions, notably the nineteen-year American occupation of Haiti that began with a Marine landing in 1915. Theodore Roosevelt accomplished three goals relevant to what China may yearn for today in the South China Sea: he ejected Europe from the Caribbean, even as he moved closer to Europe politically, all the while tempering American power with a deeper understanding of the sensitivities of the peoples of Latin America.[45] Borrowing from Roosevelt, Chinese grand strategists should want to weaken American involvement in the South China Sea sufficiently so as to exercise de facto hegemony over their own Asian Mediterranean, while they maintain cordial political and economic relations with Washington and temper their own power through a greater appreciation of the problems and peoples of Southeast Asia.

Obviously, there are great differences between the American and Asian Mediterraneans. The Caribbean states and statelets of the turn of the twentieth century were rickety, unstable, and volatile affairs; not so the formidable entities around the South China Sea, which, with the exception of the Philippines and Indonesia, are strong states, and in the case of Vietnam, a potential middle-level power if it can get its economy in order. And even the Philippines and Indonesia (the latter on the outskirts of the South China Sea) are demographically massive polities whose political and economic structures, as weak as they are compared to neighboring states, are still far more developed than those of the early-twentieth-century Caribbean. The constant mayhem with its consequent interventions that was a feature of Greater Caribbean political life is barely a factor in the South China Sea.

And yet there is a glaringly obvious similarity. They are both marginal seas that are extensions of continent-sized nations: the United States and China. The United States, according to the mid-twentieth-century Dutch-American geostrategist Nicholas J. Spykman, became a world power when it took unquestioned control over the Greater Caribbean. For the basic geographical truth of the Western Hemisphere, he says, is that the division within it is not between North America and South America, but between the area north of the equatorial jungle dominated by the Amazon and the area south of it. Colombia and Venezuela, as well as the Guianas, although they are on the northern coast of South America, are functionally part of North America and the American Mediterranean. Once it came to dominate the American Mediterranean, that is, the Greater Caribbean, and separated as it is from the Southern Cone of South America by yawning distance and a wide belt of tropical forest, the United States has had few challengers in its own hemisphere. Thus the domination of the Greater Caribbean, observed Spykman, gave America domination of the Western Hemisphere, with power to spare for influencing the balance of power in the Eastern Hemisphere. First the Greater Caribbean, next the world.

Likewise with China in the Asian Mediterranean. Domination of the South China Sea would certainly clear the way for pivotal Chinese air and naval influence throughout the navigable rimland of Eurasia—the Indian and Pacific oceans both. And thus China would become the virtual hegemon of the Indo-Pacific. That would still not make China as dominant in the Eastern Hemisphere as the United States has been in the Western Hemisphere, but, in and of itself, it would go a long way toward making China more than merely the first among equals of Eastern Hemispheric powers, with political and economic energy to spare for influencing states in the Western Hemisphere to a greater extent than it already has, especially in the Southern Cone, but also in the Caribbean. The South China Sea, in other words, is now a principal node of global power politics, critical to the preservation of the worldwide balance of power. While control of it may not quite unlock the world for China as control of the Greater Caribbean unlocked the world for America, the Caribbean, remember—even with the Panama

Canal—has never lain astride the great maritime routes of commerce and energy to the degree that the South China Sea presently does.

So here we have a more prosperous and militarizing Asia, the very essence of capitalistic dynamism, with the Asian Mediterranean as its focal point. In the race for armaments in the South China Sea, China is increasing the distance between it and its neighbors, and so over time may come close to replicating America's achievement in the Greater Caribbean. But such realizations represent only the sharp outlines of the South China Sea region's political, economic, and cultural cartography. To fill in the map with richly painted brushstrokes requires dropping down from thirty thousand feet to ground level in the individual countries themselves.

CHAPTER III

The Fate of Vietnam

The effect of Hanoi is cerebral: what the Vietnamese capital catches in freeze frame is the process of history itself. I do not mean history merely as some fatalistic, geographically determined drum roll of successive dynasties and depredations, but also history as the summation of brave individual acts and nerve-racking calculations. The maps, dioramas, and massive gray stelae in the History Museum commemorate anxious Vietnamese resistances against the Chinese Song, Ming, and Qing empires in the eleventh, fifteenth, and eighteenth centuries: for although Vietnam was integrated into China until the tenth century, its separate political identity from the Middle Kingdom ever since has been something of a miracle that no theory of the past can adequately explain.

More stelae, erected in the late fifteenth century in the Temple of Literature, poignantly rescue the names and contributions of eighty-two medieval scholars from oblivion. In fact, there is a particular intensity about the Vietnamese historical imagination. The depth and clutter of the Ngoc Son Temple (which commemorates the defeat of the thirteenth century Yuan Chinese), with its copper-faced Buddha embraced by incense, gold leaf, and crimson wood, and surrounded, in turn, by a leafy pea-soup lake, constitutes spiritual preparation for the more austere mausoleum of Ho Chi Minh himself. Ho, one of the great minor men of the twentieth century, and one of history's great pragmatists, fused Marxism, Confucianism, and nationalism into a weapon against the Chinese, the French, and the Americans, laying the groundwork for Vietnam's successful resistances against three world empires. Buddha-like gilded statues of Ho punctuate many an official meeting room in this capital. His mausoleum gives out onto distempered, century-old European buildings and churches, once the political nerve center of French Indochina, an iffy enterprise that Paris had bravely, tenaciously tried to prolong following World War II, forcing a war against the Vietnamese that culminated in that signal humiliation for the French: the 1954 Battle of Dien Bien Phu.

French Indochina had also comprised Laos and Cambodia, but just as Hanoi was the region's political capital, Saigon was its commercial capital. Vietnam dominated Indochina, in other words, with Thai and Khmer forces, to name a few, periodically cooperating with China to resist Vietnamese power. In fact, while the United States fought to preserve an independent South Vietnam against the communist North, it was the unified Vietnam that emerged under communist control with America's defeat that would prove a far greater threat to China than it would to the United States.[1] Such is the record of Vietnamese dynamism in the region.

Beyond these old French edifices come the latest, epic struggles against historical fate: Hanoi's screaming, pulsating business district, with its hordes of privately owned motorbikes—the drivers texting on cell phones in traffic jams—and cutting-edge new facades invading an otherwise cruddy-drab jumble of storefronts. This is pre–chain store capitalism, with cafés everywhere—each different in mood and design from the other—offering some of the best coffee in the world, yet no sign of Starbucks. Hanoi, despite all the history, is no outdoor museum like the great cities of Europe. It is still in the ungainly process of *becoming,* closer still to the disheveled chaos of India than to the alienating sterility of Singapore. Vietnamese are now prying their way into the first world, for the sake of themselves and their families obviously, but also in order to preserve their independence against an equally dynamic China.

Hanoi, as it has been since antiquity, remains a city of nervous political calculations: the wages these days of a potential middle-level power—the thirteenth most populous country in the world—with a long coastline at the crossroads of major maritime routes and close to offshore energy deposits. Vietnam is Southeast Asia's "principal protagonist" in the South China Sea dispute, asserting sovereignty over both the Paracel and Spratly islands, "based on historical usage dating back to at least the 17th century," write scholars Clive Schofield and Ian Storey.[2] "If China can break off Vietnam they've won the South China Sea," a top U.S. official told me. "Malaysia is lying low, Brunei has solved its problem with China, Indonesia has no well-defined foreign policy on the subject, the Philippines has few cards to play despite that country's ingenious boisterousness and incendiary statements, Singapore is capable but lacks size."

It's all up to Vietnam, in other words.

Vietnam's arrival at this juncture was gradual. Ngo Quang Xuan, vice chairman of the National Assembly's Foreign Affairs Committee, told me that the critical year for contemporary Vietnam was not 1975, when South Vietnam was overrun by the communist North; but 1995, when relations were normalized with the United States and when Vietnam joined ASEAN, and entered into a "framework" agreement with the European Union. "We joined the world, in other words." He admitted that prior to these decisions, "we had many hard discussions among ourselves." For the truth is, that despite their successive victories over the French and the Americans, the Vietnamese communists, as their officials explained to me in a series of conversations over several weeks, felt continually humbled by events thereafter.

Consider: Vietnam had invaded Cambodia in 1978, liberating that

country from the genocidal madness of Pol Pot's Khmer Rouge regime. Though the invasion was an act of cold-blooded realism—as the
pro-Chinese Khmer Rouge represented a strategic threat to Vietnam—
it had a vast and profoundly positive humanitarian effect. Nevertheless, for this pivotal act of mercy pro-Soviet Vietnam was embargoed
by a pro-Chinese coalition that included the United States, which ever
since President Richard Nixon's trip to China in 1972 had tilted toward Beijing. In 1979, China itself invaded Vietnam, in order to keep
Vietnam from marching through Cambodia to Thailand. Meanwhile,
the Soviet Union had failed to come to the aid of its client state in
Hanoi. Vietnam was now diplomatically isolated, stuck in a debilitat-
ing quagmire in Cambodia, and burdened by backbreaking poverty,
largely as a result of its own militarism. Visiting Hanoi in the 1970s,
Singapore's then prime minister, Lee Kuan Yew, writes that he found
the Vietnamese leaders "insufferable," priding themselves as the "Prus-
sians" of Southeast Asia.[3] But the arrogance, as Vietnamese leaders
told me, didn't last. With severe food shortages and the collapse of the
Soviet Empire in 1989–1991, Vietnam was finally forced to pull its
troops out of Cambodia. Vietnam was now utterly friendless—the victory over the Americans a distant memory. "The feeling of victory in
that war was always muted because there was never a peace dividend,"
a Vietnamese diplomat explained.

"The Vietnamese don't have amnesia regarding the war against
the United States in the 1960s and 1970s," a Western diplomat told
me. "Rather, a certain generation of Americans is stuck in a time
warp." The Vietnamese have not forgotten that 20 percent of their
country is uninhabitable because of unexploded American ordnance;
or, because of the effect of the defoliant Agent Orange, nothing will
ever grow on significant parts of the landscape. It is just that three
quarters of all Vietnamese were born after the "American War," as
they call it—to distinguish it from all the others they have fought
before and since. And an even larger percentage have no usable memory of it.

The students and young officials I met at the Diplomatic Academy
of Vietnam, an arm of the Foreign Ministry, are further removed

chronologically from the American War than baby boomers are from World War II. In a town hall–style meeting with me they were, in fact, critical at times of the United States: but for reasons that had nothing to do with the war. They were upset that America had not intervened against China in the 1990s when Beijing challenged the Philippines' ownership of Mischief Reef, part of the Spratly Islands group in the South China Sea; and that America had not engaged economically and diplomatically more with Burma prior to 2011, so as to prevent that country from becoming a satellite of Beijing. Summarized one student: "U.S. power is necessary for the security of the world." Indeed, one student and official after another at the Diplomatic Academy used the term "balancing power [vis-à-vis China]" to describe the United States. "The Chinese are too strong, too assertive," one female analyst said, "that is why a Pax Sinica is very threatening to us."

Both Vietnam and the United States "share an interest in preventing China . . . from dominating seaborne trade routes and enforcing territorial claims through coercion," writes Professor Carlyle A. Thayer of the Australian Defence Force Academy in Canberra. "Vietnam sees the U.S. presence as a hedge against China's rising military power."[4]

"The Vietnamese," writes David Lamb, who covered the war in the 1960s and returned in the 1990s as the *Los Angeles Times* correspondent in Hanoi, simply "*liked* Americans. . . . They had lost 3 million citizens [one out of ten killed or wounded], been pummeled with 15 million tons of munitions—twice the tonnage dropped on all of Europe and Asia during World War II—and lived through a war that created 7 million refugees in South Vietnam and destroyed the industry and infrastructure of North Vietnam. Yet," he goes on, "they had put the war behind them in a way that many Americans hadn't. Their hospitals weren't full of veterans with postcombat trauma, and they had no national mourning memorials like the Vietnam Wall in Washington. They didn't write books about the war. Veterans didn't gather over beers to talk about it. Schoolchildren studied it as only a brief page in their country's 2,500-year history."[5]

Indeed, the cynicism and exasperation with which quite a few Europeans and members of the American Left perennially view the United States is utterly absent in Vietnam. Encapsulating the general attitude here, Nguyen Duc Hung, a former ambassador to Canada, told me: "just as Vietnamese spread south over the centuries to define themselves as a nation, the Americans spread westward—and it wasn't for gold in California, it was for freedom."

Nevertheless, whereas America has been marginal to the Vietnamese past, China has been crucial. The very term *Indochina* is accurate to the extent that Indian influence is apparent throughout the rest of Southeast Asia, whereas Chinese influence is concentrated for the most part in northern Vietnam. It would take the "prolonged chaos" of the late Tang Dynasty and the subsequent semi-chaotic interlude of the Five Dynasties and Ten Kingdoms of the tenth century in China to allow for an independent Vietnamese state to take shape.[6] "The overwhelming emphasis of official Vietnamese history is on resistance, almost always against China," writes Robert Templer in a pathbreaking book about contemporary Vietnam, *Shadows and Wind: A View of Modern Vietnam*. "The fear of domination has been constant and has crossed every ideological gap, it has created the brittle sense of anxiety and defensiveness about Vietnamese identity."[7] Vietnamese fear of China is profound precisely because Vietnam cannot escape from the embrace of its gargantuan northern neighbor, whose population is fifteen times that of Vietnam. Vietnamese know that geography dictates the terms of their relationship with China: they may win the battle, but then they are always off to Beijing to pay tribute. It is a situation alien to a virtual island nation like America.

Explains another Vietnamese diplomat: "China invaded Vietnam seventeen times. The U.S. invaded Mexico only once, and look at how sensitive the Mexicans are about that. We grow up with textbooks full of stories of national heroes who fought China." Or as a western expert of Vietnam put it: "Think of how touchy Canadians are about America, now imagine if America had repeatedly sent troops into Canada."

The Vietnamese historical hostility to China is, in part, artificially constructed: modern-day Vietnamese emphasize the resistances against medieval and early modern Chinese domination, while downplaying the many centuries of "close emulation" of China and the good relations with it, in order to serve the needs of a strong state identity.[8] Nevertheless, there is little denying the passion with which Vietnamese voice their concern about their neighbor to the north.

Vietnamese identity is unique in that it has been formed "through and in opposition to" Chinese influence, in the words of a BBC report. Vietnam itself began as a southern outpost of Sinic culture. It was forcibly incorporated into China's Han Empire in 111 BC. From that time forward it was occupied by China or under its yoke in tributary status for nearly a millennium, until, as I've said, it finally freed itself near the twilight of China's Tang dynasty in AD 939. Thereafter, Vietnamese dynasties like the Ly, Tran, and Le were great precisely because of their resistance to Chinese control from the north, repelling as they did waves of numerically superior armies, notes the former George Mason University scholar Neil L. Jamieson in *Understanding Vietnam*.[9] The Vietnamese did not always succeed: there was a Ming occupation between 1407 and 1427, evidence of how the late-medieval Chinese never resigned themselves to Vietnamese independence. What clarified the nineteenth century Qing dynasty's acceptance of an independent Vietnam was the French mapmakers' insistence on delineating their own territory of Indochina from that of China.

"Chinese contributions to Vietnam cover all aspects of culture, society, and government, from chopsticks wielded by peasants to writing brushes wielded by scholars and officials," writes Cornell University area expert Keith Weller Taylor in *The Birth of Vietnam*.[10] Vietnamese family names and vocabulary and grammar, as well as artistic and literary styles, reflect deep Chinese influences.[11] Indeed, Vietnamese literature was "impregnated" with the classical Confucian heritage of China. Chinese used to be the language of Vietnamese scholarship just as Latin used to be in Europe: this, despite the fact that along with Chinese, the Vietnamese language has Mon-Khmer and Thai origins. Through it all, Vietnamese peasant culture retained its uniqueness to a greater extent than did the culture of the Vietnamese elite. Among the elite, explains the University of Michigan Southeast Asia expert Victor Lieberman, Chinese administrative norms were "internalized to the point that their alien origins became irrelevant." What helped reinforce the fierce desire of all Vietnamese to be separate from China was their contact with the Chams and Khmers to the south, who were themselves influenced by non-Chinese civilizations, particularly that of India. Precisely because of their intense similarity with the Chinese, the Vietnamese are burdened—as I've said—by the narcissism of small differences, and this makes events from the past more vivid to them.

Vietnamese military victories over China in the north, like that of Emperor Le Loi's near Hanoi in 1426, and against the Chams and Khmers in the south in 1471 and 1778, all worked to forge a distinct national identity, helped by the fact that, up through modern times, China rarely let Vietnam alone. In 1946, the Chinese colluded with the French to have the former's occupation forces in northern Vietnam replaced by the latter's. In 1979, as we know, four years after the United States quit Vietnam, 100,000 Chinese troops invaded. Chinese leader Deng Xiaoping "never lost his visceral hatred of the Vietnamese," writes Robert Templer, and, therefore, devised a policy of "bleeding Hanoi white," by entangling Vietnam in a guerrilla war in Cambodia.[12] Now, because of conflicting Vietnamese and Chinese claims to the South China Sea, China's naval intrusion on the Gulf of Tonkin, and China's covetous attitude toward Vietnam's 1,900-mile seaboard straddling the sea lines of communication that link the Indian and Western Pacific oceans, this has all become operative history; whereas Vietnam's war with America simply isn't: except for one detail, though. Because the Vietnamese defeated the United States in a war, they see themselves as the superior party in the bilateral relationship: they have no chips on their shoulder, no axes to grind, no face to lose regarding a future de facto military alliance with America. Vietnamese harbor relatively few sensitivities about the American War precisely because they won it.

The American War, like the Chinese invasion that followed, and

Vietnam's own invasion of Cambodia that had led to the Chinese invasion in the first place, are all part of a similar history that seems long past. It is a history of ground wars that stemmed, in part, from Western decolonization. Now that land border questions are settled, nationalist competition in much of Asia has extended to the maritime domain; namely to the South China Sea. In fact, Vietnam has a creation myth in which the country was founded by a union between the Dragon Lord Lac Long Quan and the fairy Au Co. Together they produced one hundred sons, fifty migrating with the mother to the mountains and the other fifty migrating with the father to the sea. It is the father's legacy that now seems central to Vietnam's destiny, following decades of rule by the mother.

"Land border issues are no longer important to us compared to the South China Sea," says Nguyen Duy Chien, vice chairman of the National Boundary Commission. Chien provided me with a typical Vietnamese performance that recalled Lee Kuan Yew's 1970s impression of the Vietnamese leadership as deadly serious and "Confucianist."[13] We met in a bare and humble office. Chien wore a drab suit. The meeting started and concluded exactly on time and he filled the hour with a relentlessly detailed PowerPoint presentation that attacked the Chinese position from every conceivable point of view.

Chien began with a summary of the land border situation: two hundred areas of dispute with China had been settled during eight years of negotiation in the 1990s, with demarcation work completed in 2008. "Compared with 314 border markers on the frontier with Qing China [at the turn of the twentieth century], there are now 1,971. The problem is not on land, it's maritime." One third of Vietnam's population lives along the coast, he told me, and the marine sector comprises 50 percent of Vietnam's GDP. Vietnam claims a line two hundred miles straight out over its continental shelf into the South China Sea (which Vietnamese call the "East Sea," as they dispute the word "China" in the name). This complies with the economic exclusion zones defined in the Convention on the Law of the Sea. But as Chien admitted, it "overlaps" with maritime areas claimed by China and Malaysia, and with those of Cambodia and Thailand in the adjacent Gulf of Thailand. Though the Gulf of Tonkin is geographically a thorny area, in which the northern Vietnamese coastline is blocked from the open sea by China's Hainan Island, Chien explained that Vietnam and China have settled the issue by dividing the energy-rich gulf in half, though the mouth of the gulf still has to be demarcated.

"But we cannot accept the cow's tongue—China's dashed line in the South China Sea. China says the area is in dispute. We say no. The cow's tongue violates the claims of five countries."

Chien then showed me a series of maps on his computer, and recounted a long history. "When the Ming emperors occupied Vietnam for a time in the fifteenth century they didn't occupy the Paracels and Spratlys. If these island groups belonged to China, why didn't the Ming emperors include them in their maps? In the early twentieth century," he went on, "why did the maps of the Qing emperors ignore the Paracels and Spratlys if they belonged to China?" In 1933, France sent troops to the Paracels and Spratlys, he told me, implying that the islands, because they were part of French Indochina, now belong to Vietnam. He added that in 1956 and again in 1988, China used "military force" to capture rocks in the Paracels. Finally, he displayed a slide of the Santa Maria del Monte church in Italy, which holds a geographical manuscript from 1850, with one and a half pages explaining how the Paracels belong to Vietnam. His obsession with such details had a purpose, for another map in his PowerPoint showed much of the South China Sea, including the Paracels and Spratlys, divided into tiny square blocks that signified oil concessions that Vietnam might in the future award to international companies.

Said a foreign ministry official: "When it comes to the South China Sea, China's attitude is very worrisome, it is constantly in the minds of our people." Rear Admiral Nguyen Viet Nhien, the deputy commander of the Vietnamese People's Navy, called the cow's tongue "unreasonable." Meeting at naval headquarters in the port of Haiphong—heavily bombed by the United States between 1965 and 1972—Admiral Nhien provided me with another dogged Vietnamese performance. Beside him was a large bust of Ho Chi Minh and a massive map showing all the competing claims in the "East Sea" as he repeatedly referred to it. For forty-five minutes he went on, noting every Chinese military action in the Paracels and Spratlys: in particular the 1974 takeover of the western part of the Paracels from a tottering Saigon government. The cow's tongue, he admitted, was less a Chinese legal claim than a "historic dream" of Beijing's, which, in addition to being a subject of debate itself within Beijing power circles, might eventually be ceded in whole or in part in future negotiations. Nevertheless, the Chinese, by building a blue-water navy and commanding East Asia's economy as they do, might still come to dominate the South China Sea as the United States came to dominate the Caribbean in the nineteenth century. Senior Colonel Dzung Kim Le explained that the very expansion of the Chinese economy—however slowed—will lead to a more pronounced naval presence in the South China Sea, coupled with the desire to exploit energy resources there. By declaring an intention to hold its ground in the face of this emerging development, Vietnam is calling forth a nationalism—in all its unyielding intensity—that was last on display during the period of land wars decades ago.

Vietnamese told me again and again that the South China Sea signifies more than just a system of territorial disputes: it is the crossroads of global maritime commerce, vital to the energy needs of South Korea and Japan, and the place where China could one day check the power of the United States in Asia. Vietnam truly lies at the historic and cultural heart of what Obama administration policymakers increasingly label the "Indo-Pacific"—India plus East Asia.

Nothing better illustrates the Vietnamese desire to be a major player in the region than their purchase of six state-of-the-art Kilo-class submarines from Russia. A Western defense expert told me that the sale makes no logical sense. "There is going to be real sticker-shock for the Vietnamese when they find out just how much it costs merely to maintain these subs." More important, the Vietnamese will have to train crews to use them, a generational undertaking. "To counter

Chinese subs, they would have been better off concentrating on anti-submarine warfare and littoral defense." Clearly, the Vietnamese bought these submarines as prestige items, to demonstrate that *we're serious*. According to this defense expert, the Vietnamese are "freaked out" by the construction of a Chinese underground nuclear submarine base on Hainan Island in the Gulf of Tonkin.

The multibillion-dollar deal with Russia for the submarines includes a $200 million refurbishment of Cam Ranh Bay, one of the finest deep-water anchorages in Southeast Asia, astride the South China Sea maritime routes, and a major base of operations for the U.S. military during the American War. The Vietnamese have stated that their aim is to make Cam Ranh Bay available for use to foreign navies. Ian Storey, a fellow at the Institute of Southeast Asian Studies in Singapore, says that an unspoken Vietnamese desire is that the Cam Ranh Bay overhaul will "strengthen defense ties with America and facilitate the U.S. military presence in Southeast Asia as a counter to China's rising power." Cam Ranh Bay plays perfectly into the Pentagon's *places not bases* strategy, whereby American ships and planes can regularly visit foreign military outposts for repairs and resupply without the need for formal, politically sensitive basing arrangements. U.S. naval platforms—aircraft carriers, destroyers, and resupply and hospital ships—are already visiting Vietnamese ports on a periodic basis. Ngo Quang Xuan, the Foreign Affairs Committee vice chairman, was blunt: "U.S. presence is needed for a free maritime climate in the South China Sea."

A de facto American-Vietnamese strategic partnership was, in effect, announced as far back as July 2010 at an ASEAN Regional Forum meeting in Hanoi, when Secretary of State Hillary Clinton stated that the United States has a "national interest" in the South China Sea, that the United States is ready to participate in multilateral efforts to resolve South China Sea territorial disputes, and that maritime claims should be based on land features: that is, on the extension of continental shelves, a concept violated by China's historic dashed line or cow's tongue. Chinese foreign minister Yang Jiechi called Clinton's remarks "virtually an attack on China." American officials basically shrugged off Yang's comments. There was probably no better indication of just how close Washington had moved toward Vietnam than the initialing three months earlier of a civilian nuclear power deal that will theoretically allow American firms to help build atomic energy plants here.

The fact is, no country is as threatened by China's rise as much as Vietnam. Take the Vietnamese approach to ASEAN. Though the Vietnamese would like ASEAN to be stronger, in order to be a counterweight to China, they are realistic, they told me. They know that the very puissance of nationalism in Asia—as opposed to postnationalism for so many decades in Europe—inhibits the integration of ASEAN's member states. "ASEAN is not even a customs union—which makes it a very low level trading bloc," one official explained. In the plush, red-cushioned elegance of the Foreign Ministry, with its glittering tea sets and oriental-French decor, I was repeatedly counseled on Chinese grand strategy, which is, according to the Vietnamese, to postpone all multilateral discussions with ASEAN of South China Sea disputes while Beijing gets stronger militarily, and, in the meantime, to extract concessions from individual Southeast Asian nations through bilateral negotiations—divide and conquer, in other words. China's navy, Vietnamese defense officials told me, is already larger than those of all the ASEAN countries combined.

But Vietnam is by no means estranged from China and in the arms of the United States. Vietnam is too dependent on (and interconnected with) China for that. As Australian expert Carlyle Thayer explains, Vietnamese-Chinese military ties have developed alongside Vietnamese-American ones.[14] While the United States is Vietnam's largest export market, Vietnam imports more goods from China than from any other country—cotton, machines, fertilizer, pesticide, electronics, leather, a host of other consumer items, you name it. The economy here simply couldn't function without China, even as China, by flooding Vietnam with cheap products, impedes the growth of local manufacturing. Furthermore, Vietnamese officials are impressed with the geographical asymmetry of their situation: as they say, *a distant water can't put out a nearby fire*. China's proximity and the fact that the United States is half a world away means that the Vietnamese have to put up with an indignity such as the environmental destruction that comes with Chinese bauxite mining of Vietnam's lush Central Highlands, a project that like others around the country employs Chinese workers rather than Vietnamese ones. "We can't relocate, statistically we're one province of China," Nguyen Tam Chien, a former deputy foreign minister, told me.

Because of the failure of the Soviet Union to help Vietnam in 1979, the Vietnamese will never again fully trust a faraway power. Beyond geography, the Vietnamese at a certain fundamental level distrust the United States. One official told me simply that the United States is in decline, a condition made worse, he claimed, by Washington's fixation with the Middle East rather than with the rise of China in East Asia. Though such an analysis is self-serving, it may nevertheless be true; or, rather, partly true. Then there is the fear of the United States selling out Vietnam for the sake of a warmer relationship with China: Xuan, the vice chairman of the Foreign Affairs Committee, specifically mentioned Nixon's opening to China as providing the geostrategic context for China's invasion of Vietnam. "It can happen again," shaking his head in frustration. Contradictorily, the Vietnamese want the United States to be more of a coldhearted, realist actor in international affairs just like themselves. "The elephant in the room during our discussions with the Americans is democracy and human rights," one official of the communist government told me. The Vietnamese live in fear that because of Congress, the media, and various pressure groups in Washington, the Americans may one day sell them out the way they have for periods of time other coup-prone and autocratic countries: Thailand, Uzbekistan, and Nepal, for example. The Vietnamese look at the former unwillingness of Washington to balance against China for decades in Burma because of Rangoon's human rights record and bristle. "The highest value should be on national solidarity and independence. It is the nation, not the individual, that makes you free," Le Chi Dzung, a Foreign Ministry deputy director general, told me, trying to explain his country's political philosophy.

In fact, the survival of communist rule in the face of Vietnam's rampant capitalism is partly explained by the party's nationalist credentials, having governed the country during wars against the French, Americans, and Chinese. Moreover, as was the case with Tito in Yugoslavia and Enver Hoxha in Albania, Ho Chi Minh was a homegrown leader not imposed on the country by an invading army, unlike so many other communist rulers. Moreover, the Vietnamese communists have always played up the similarities between Ho Chi Minh Thought and Confucianism, with its respect for the family and authority. "Nationalism builds out from Confucianism," Le Chi Dzung of the Foreign Ministry says. Neil Jamieson writes of "that common Vietnamese quality of 'absolutism,'" an assumption of "some underlying, determinative moral order in the world."[15] This, in turn, is related to the idea of *chinh nghia*, which might be loosely translated as one's social obligation, to one's family and larger solidarity group.

Yet another reason why communism persists here is precisely because its very substance is slipping away, and thus an uprising is for the time being unnecessary; though, of course, there is a price to be paid for insufficient reform. Vietnam is in a situation similar to that of China: governed by a Communist Party that has all but given up communism, and has an implicit social contract with the population, in which the party guarantees higher or sustained income levels while the citizens agree not to protest too loudly. (Vietnam cannot ultimately be estranged from China, for they are both embarked on the same unique experiment: delivering capitalist riches to countries ruled by communist parties.)

Think of it, here is a society that has gone from ration books to enjoying one of the largest rice surpluses in the world in a quarter of a century. Vietnam recently graduated in statistical terms to a lower-middle-income country with a per capita GDP of $1,100. Instead of a single personality to hate with his picture on billboards, as was the case in Tunisia, Egypt, Syria, and other Arab countries, there is a faceless triumvirate of leaders—the party chairman, the state president, and the prime minister—that has delivered an average of 7 percent growth in the GDP annually between 2002 and 2012. Even in the teeth of the Great Recession in 2009, the local economy grew by

5.5 percent. "This is one of the most impressive records of poverty alleviation in world history," says a Western diplomat. "They have gone from bicycles to motorcycles." That to them may be democracy. And even if it isn't, one can say that the autocracies of Vietnam and China have not robbed people of their dignity the way those of the Middle East have. "The leaders of the Middle East stayed in office too long and maintained states of emergency for decades, that is not the case here," a former high-ranking Vietnamese political leader told me. "But the problems of corruption, huge income gaps, and high youth unemployment we share with countries of the Middle East." What spooks the Communist Party here is less the specter of the Arab Spring than that of the student uprising in 1989 in China, a time when inflation was as high in China as it was in Vietnam until recently, and corruption and nepotism were perceived by the population to be beyond control: again, the case with Vietnam. And yet, party officials also worry about political reform leading them down the path of pre-1975 South Vietnam, whose weak, faction-ridden governments were integral to that state's collapse; or to late-nineteenth- and early-twentieth-century China, with its feeble central authority that led to foreign domination. Thus, Vietnamese officials openly admire Singapore: a predominantly single-party *company* state that emanates discipline and clean government, something Vietnam's corruption-ridden regime is still a long way from.

The Singapore model was made explicit for me at the Vietnam-Singapore Industrial Park, twenty miles outside Ho Chi Minh City, or Saigon as it is still called by everyone outside of government officialdom. I beheld a futuristic world of perfectly maintained and manicured right-angle streets where, in a security-controlled environment, 240 manufacturing firms from Singapore, Malaysia, Taiwan, South Korea, Europe, and the United States were producing luxury golf clubs, microchips, pharmaceuticals, high-end footwear, aerospace electronics, and so on. In the next stage of development, luxury condominiums were planned on-site for the foreign workers who will live and work here. An American plant manager at the park told me that his company chose Vietnam for its high-tech operation through a process of elimination: "We needed low labor costs. We had no desire to locate in Eastern Europe or Africa [which didn't have the Asian work ethic]. In China wages are already starting to rise. Indonesia and Malaysia are Muslim, and that scares us away. Thailand has lately become unstable. So Vietnam loomed for us: it's like China was two decades ago, on the verge of a boom." He added: "We give our employees in Vietnam standardized intelligence tests. They score higher than our employees in the U.S."

There are three other Vietnam-Singapore Industrial Parks in the country, whose aim is to bring the corporate, squeaky-clean, environmentally *green,* and controlled Singapore model of development to Vietnam. They are among four hundred industrial parks located throughout Vietnam, from north to south, that all to greater and lesser extents promote the same values of Western-style development and efficiency. The existing megacities of Saigon and the Hanoi-Haiphong corridor cannot be wholly reborn, their problems cannot be wholly alleviated: the future is new cities that will relieve demographic pressure on the old ones. True modernity means developing the countryside so that fewer people will want to migrate to cities in the first place. These industrial parks, with Singapore as the role model, are what will help change the Vietnamese countryside. Because their whole purpose is to be self-contained, they bring infrastructure, such as electricity and water, along with them, as well as one-stop shopping for foreign firms seeking government permits.

Whereas Vietnam was politically unified when the North Vietnamese communists overran Saigon and renamed it Ho Chi Minh City in 1975, only now, through industrial parks and other means of development, is Vietnam becoming economically and culturally unified, through a global standard of production that is connecting Hanoi and Saigon. Because this latest stage of development involves direct input from other Asian tiger economies, Vietnam is becoming increasingly integrated with the rest of the region and thus becoming comfortable with the partial erosion of sovereignty that a future, more robust ASEAN may represent.

"Vietnamese nationalism is aggressive only towards China, an historical enemy, but not towards any other state in the region," Dang Thanh Tam, one of Saigon's leading entrepreneurs, told me. Tam, sitting at an empty desk while operating two smart phones almost simultaneously, embodies the new Saigon, which, because it ceased being a political capital in 1975, has henceforth devoted itself completely to business. Whereas Hanoi is Vietnam's Ankara, Saigon is Vietnam's Istanbul. Tam's Saigon Invest Group represents well over a billion dollars in capital invested in industrial parks, telecommunications, manufacturing, and mining. He has started twenty-five industrial parks all along the country's north–south corridor. "The future," he told me, "is decentralization combined with a more responsive government, and along with a birthrate that stays high in relation to the graying populations of China, Japan, and South Korea."

He continued. "Transparency and accountability are the keys to making Vietnam a middle-level power," the maritime equivalent of Turkey and Brazil, he indicated. "And that, above all, means a dramatic improvement in the legal code." (Indeed, for Vietnam to overcome the economic doldrums that the country has found itself in lately—following decades of growth—dramatic reform on all levels is required.)

Whereas in Hanoi you are told repeatedly how Vietnam hopes to become a regional power and pivot state, in Saigon you get an actual demonstration of it. Everything is on a bigger scale than in Hanoi, with wide streets lined with gleaming designer stores, luxury auto dealerships, and steel and glass towers. There are swanky wine bars and upscale eateries that retain that French-influenced, vaguely naughty edginess of the old colonial French city. The Continental Hotel, the setting for much of Graham Greene's 1955 novel, *The Quiet American,* and a haunt of foreign correspondents during the American War, is—in spite of its spacious white wedding cake aura and neoclassical columns that whisper elegance and scream the past— simply buried amid the new glitz and new brand-name high-rise hotels.

The American GIs' Saigon of nearly half a century ago had 2.5 million people and a $180 per capita GDP; now with a population of eight million, the per capita GDP is $2,900. Saigon has one third of the country's GDP, though only one ninth of the population. One hundred billion dollars eventually will be spent here on a new city center being planned by a Boston firm, featuring a hundred-story building and five new bridges and tunnels. A Japanese firm is building a six-line metro underground system. Officials at the Institute for Development Studies in Saigon told me that they are emphasizing "sustainable" development: a "green" model within a "global-regional" system. Strict zoning will be introduced, as well as limitations on the use of motorbikes and private cars in the various new and old city centers. Yet again, *Singapore, Inc.* is invoked, with talk of an aesthetically sterile "world-class" city, with a new airport and air cargo hub for Southeast Asia, and a bigger capacity seaport.

Hanoi is about geopolitical and military pretensions; Saigon the capitalist prosperity without which such pretensions can never be realized. Greater Saigon must become a clone of Singapore in order for Vietnam to hold its own against China, its historic rival and oppressor. That is the message one gets here.

Of course, Greater Saigon is still a long way from achieving that status. Vietnam is presently in the throes of an economic crisis similar to the one in China: while both communist parties have brought their populations impressive gains in living standards in recent decades, further progress requires deep reforms and political liberalization that will pose greater challenges than ever before.

In the meantime, Vietnam's communist leaders are trying to rely on their Prussianness, their ruthlessly capitalistic economic policies, and their tight political control to maintain their state's feisty independence from China. They know that unlike the countries of the Arab Spring, their nation faces an authentic outside adversary (however ideologically akin), which might help temper the political longing of their people. But like India, they are wary of any formal treaty arrangement with the United States. To be sure, if the necessity of a defense treaty with the United States ever arose, it would indicate that the security situation in the South China Sea region is actually much more unstable than at present. In any case, the fate of Vietnam, and its ability not to be Finlandized by China, will say as much about the American capacity to project power in the Pacific in the twenty-first century as Vietnam's fate did in the twentieth.

CHAPTER IV

Concert of Civilizations?

A boom town of oil and gas revenue erupts out of the compressed greenery; colored glass and roaring steel curves define buildings that are like rocket launch pads located near lakes the hue of algae and mud. I sip a pink cocktail beside a brightly lit rooftop swimming pool at night—glowing balloons float at the surface—and look out at the cityscape. The comic book futurism of Batman and Gotham City comes to mind. Palm trees crowd in on overpasses. Despite the unceasing stacks of high-rises, there is a naked, waiting-to-be-filled-in quality to the landscape of spiky blue-green mountains and coiling rivers: where a hundred years ago tin and rubber were beginning to be extracted in large amounts. This was a time when the capital of Kuala Lumpur was little more than the "muddy confluence" for which it is named. An archipelago of trading posts and river outlets, Malaysia and the Malay world are supposed to conjure up the short stories of W. Somerset Maugham. They don't anymore. Maugham's vast sprawl of uninterrupted, sweaty jungle, with its intimate and heartrending family dramas played out in colonial plantations, is long gone. And yet there is an oppressive fecundity in everything I see. Though it is now other writers to which I must refer as a result of the cutting-edge panorama that lies before me.

Indeed, the upscale malls of Kuala Lumpur, dedicated as they are to fetish and fantasy, raise consumerism to the status of an ideology. Observing the rushing crowds and thick exotica of a mall inside the Petronas Towers—Malay Muslim women, their hair hidden underneath *tudongs* in every primary color, Indian women in equally stunning saris, Chinese women in Western clothes—my whirling thoughts drift in succession to Thorstein Veblen, V. S. Naipaul, Ernest Gellner, Clifford Geertz, and Samuel P. Huntington, philosophers all, though none was classified as such.

In *The Theory of the Leisure Class*, Veblen, one of America's most brilliant and quirky social critics, wrote over a century ago about the consumerist hunger for useless products, brand names, and self-esteem through shopping sprees. He may have coined the term "conspicuous consumption," which he identified with city dwellers because people in close contact with large numbers of other people tend to consume more as a mark of social prestige.[1] I thought the very fact that contemporary Malaysian Muslims conform to Veblen's generalizations about turn-of-the-twentieth-century Americans shows that Muslims are individuals much as everybody else, no different from us. There is no otherness to Islamic civilization, in other words. Of course, this runs counter to what V. S. Naipaul, the novelist and literary traveler, wrote in his 1981 book, *Among the Believers: An Islamic Journey*, in which he noted the "casualness of the Malays" and "the energy of the Chinese. . . . The difference between the old and the new was the difference between Malay and Chinese."[2] That might still be the case, but certainly much less so now than when Naipaul made his observation (as Naipaul himself briefly alludes to in his 1998 sequel, *Beyond Belief: Islamic Excursions Among the Converted Peoples*).[3] There is also Ernest Gellner, the late French-Czech social anthropologist who cast such a microscopic eye on Muslim culture. Gellner observes that

Islam, unlike Christianity, was not born "*within* an empire," that of Rome, but "*outside* two empires, one of which [Eastern Rome, or Byzantium] it promptly overran, and the other [Sassanid Persia] it conquered in the end." Thus Islam, Gellner goes on, "had not corroded an earlier traditional civilization, nor lived on as its ghost. It *made* its own empire and civilization." And as its own "complete and final" civilization, Islam provides—much more so than Judaism and Christianity—an unarguable blueprint for social order.[4] But if that is still the case, how come Veblen made the same observations about Americans in the 1890s as I was making about Malaysian Muslims now? Wouldn't that civilizational *otherness* show up in some way at the mall? What had changed in the Malays? I asked myself.

I was helped in my answer by a passage in the late American anthropologist Clifford Geertz's *The Interpretation of Cultures,* in which he says that while the reality of a foreign culture is not simply a prejudice on the part of the observer, at the same time, there was such a thing as the "basic unity of mankind."[5] Thus, too much of an emphasis on culture and civilization could obscure the reality of human nature itself. And what I was seeing at the mall was human nature unleashed, in the form of naked materialism.

Yet despite the mall's glossy, one-world imagery, different civilizations and races there still were. Geertz himself observes that the Malaysian civilizational confection comprises races that at least in the relatively recent past bore a mutual "suspicion and hostility that would make the Habsburg Empire seem like Denmark or Australia."[6] While that might be an exaggeration, Malaysia does constitute an experiment—particularly as it concerns the acceptance of the ethnic Chinese in this predominantly Muslim region: an experiment that if it is successful, would constitute at least one proof against Samuel Huntington's *clash of civilizations* theory.[7] The mall, at least on one basic level, seemed to ease the concerns of the late Harvard professor.

Of course, one could not tell what was going on in the minds of the shoppers. For the very process of modernization, as Huntington and others have theorized, can also lead to ethnic conflict, as previously isolated groups come into contact with each other as a result of urbanization, strengthening rivalries between them, especially if some groups advance faster than others. To wit, as economic growth here registered 25 percent between the late 1950s and 1970, Chinese and Indian incomes rose faster than those of the Malays, one reason for the intercommunal riots of that era.[8]

But as a friend of Huntington, I knew how fascinated he would have been by this spectacle. For the sight of masses of Muslims, Chinese, and Indians all together signified Malaysia's position "at the heart of the world's trading networks," between the Middle East and China: a place that in the nineteenth century was within three days sail of China and three weeks sail from Arabia. Malaysia, embracing both the Malay Peninsula and the northwestern coast of the island of Borneo, acts as a funnel for the shipping routes of the South China Sea passing into the Indian Ocean. Its once bustling commercial port of Malacca lay at the confluence of two great monsoonal systems: the southwest monsoon bringing ships from the Middle East and the Indian Subcontinent to the Far East, and the northeast monsoon bringing ships from the Far East to the Middle East and the Indian Subcontinent.[9] The "funnel" of Malaysia lay at the point of exchange between these routes and the civilizations they indicated.[10] As such, Malaysia is one of the few places in the world where Chinese ceramics, Islamic coins, and South Indian bronze can be found at the same archaeological sites. The mall was a twenty-first-century demonstration of this historical fact: of Malaysia's location at the developing world's very nerve center. Here was the heart of Asia—and, after a fashion, of the globe. The mall signified the former Third World's newly won postindustrial prosperity, which would not at all have surprised Huntington, who wrote that "fundamental changes" in the "balance of power among civilizations" meant that the power of the West would in relative terms "continue to decline."[11]

Truly, Malaysia is a pulsating demographic and economic microcosm of maritime Asia: a worthy successor to medieval and early modern Malacca, the queen of entrepôts located in the southwest of the Malay Peninsula. Of Malaysia's 28 million people, 60 percent are Muslim Malays and *bumiputras* (indigenous non-Malay and non-Muslim peoples in the Malaysian part of Borneo, such as Ibans, Murats, and Kadazans). The ethnic Chinese, mainly Hokkien from Fujian and other parts of southeastern China, who came as indentured laborers, account for 23 percent of the population. Indians, mainly Tamils from southeastern India, make up another 9 percent. Then there are several million migrants and illegals from poverty-stricken Indonesia and Bangladesh. For Malaysia is the most affluent large state in Southeast Asia, according to the United Nations Human Development Index (2011). Only the statelets of Singapore and Brunei rate higher; the former an enclave dominated by the overseas Chinese, the latter the product of oil wealth.

Wealth translates into urbanization and *embourgeoisement,* and that, in turn, means not only consumerism, but a "negotiated tension" between the races, says Rita Sim of the Centre for Strategic Engagement in Kuala Lumpur. The rush to the cities has not only brought different groups together as participants in a single, materialist global culture, but has also introduced to them such phenomena as global Islam, which drives Muslim Malays apart from the other groups. The visual rebuke to Huntington that I experienced at the mall was a first impression only. As I spent weeks in Malaysia meeting with scholars and other experts, they revealed to me a more complex and intricate portrait of intercommunal relations that actually confirmed Huntington's thesis—at least the more nuanced elaboration of it in his book, which followed the famous *Foreign Affairs* article.[12]

Proximity might have brought a measure of understanding among the communities, but it hadn't necessarily brought harmony. Nationalism can certainly emerge out of multiethnic cosmopolitanism within a defined geographic space; but Malaysia, according to everyone I met here, said it had not quite reached that stage, and thus its diverse peoples might never be able to experience true patriotism. Perhaps Malaysia was too physically and communally varied to be psychologically cohesive—that is, to constitute one solidarity group. There

was the Chinese-dominated island city of Penang in the northwest of
the peninsula, and the veritable Islamic state of Kelantan in the northeast (which, because of its informal ways, allowed gambling and
prostitution). And this was to say nothing of the indigenous non-
Malay *bumiputras* who inhabited the isolated regions of Sarawak
and Sabah. The truth was that communal tensions in this ambiguous
country with a highly ambiguous geography—composed of the
Malay Peninsula and northwestern Borneo—subverted the development of Malaysian nationalism: so that the anti-China sentiment,
which, for example, is apparent in highly nationalist and uni-ethnic
Vietnam, simply does not exist here.

In explaining their relatively benign attitude toward China, Malaysians frequently talk about the intimate relations between the
Ming dynasty and the medieval and early modern port of Malacca.
But the deeper truth is that this country is too subsumed by its own
contradictions to focus on an outside threat, especially one that is
rather vague. A rising China is convenient for ethnic Chinese Malaysians, just as a rising India is convenient to ethnic Indians here. Meanwhile, the majority Malays, because of a certain insecurity linked to
a rising China, have oriented themselves increasingly to a wider Arab-
Muslim world. They have escaped from the China problem, in other
words.

This diffuse, unfocused sense of national identity is helped by the
fact that peninsular Malaysia, never mind Sabah and Sarawak in Borneo, was not united even under the British. The British at the end of
the nineteenth century ruled the Federated Malay States of Selangor,
Perak, Sembilan, and Pahang. In 1946, they added the Straits Settlements of Malacca, Penang, Dinding, and Singapore. This was in addition to the nine Malay sultanates in the archipelago. Every piece of
geography occupied its own silo, remarked Chandra Muzaffar, the
head of a nongovernmental organization here. Identity centered
around the village and town. It was only the British-led military response to a communist guerrilla insurgency that centralized the state
apparatus in the first decades of independence during the early Cold
War period.

But the heart of the Malaysian story as it exists today is the move to the cities, Liew Chin Tong, a member of Parliament, told me. In the 1950s, the different ethnic communities inhabited separate rural settings. Members of one group rarely saw members of another. Politics was delegated to village and town elites, often British-educated, who engaged in political horse trading in Kuala Lumpur. Compromises were made at the top and so the rural era, which lasted into the 1970s, constituted a classic patronage system. In 1969, as Tong told me, Kuala Lumpur was an ethnic Chinese city; the still rural Malays would come only later as a form of affirmative action took hold. The Malays that were in Kuala Lumpur back then often lived in slums, out of sight of the Chinese middle class. But by the second decade of the twenty-first century, 70 percent of Malaysia's population was urban, 50 percent were under twenty-five years of age, and Malaysia boasted one of the highest percentages of Facebook users in the world. Half the country was now middle class, with another 40 percent in either the lower middle or upper middle class, according to the Asian Development Bank.

The country's social transformation centered on the majority Malays. Malay-ness into the late colonial period came to be associated with rural *kampung* (village) life, even as this easy prejudice masked the fact that many Malays were merchants and artisans.[13] Nevertheless, the Malay ideal was still a potent one. In the words of Australian historian Anthony Milner, it summoned up images of archipelagic pirates, *songket* textiles, and the "scattered arrangement of houses (and the ever-present coconut trees)" in a *kampung*. It was a "fragmented and fluid" region, without a central polity, until the emergence of Kuala Lumpur in the last decades of the twentieth century, so that here was an ambiguity linked to the one about Malaysian nationalism later on.[14] Malays had heaps of tradition, helped by their archipelagic location at the confluence of the Sinic and Indian worlds, even as they lacked, or rather were not burdened by, the immense accumulation of a hydraulic, material culture that in nearby Java was symbolized by the great Buddhist monument of Borobudur.[15]

In his definitive study of the Malay world, *Leaves of the Same*

Tree, University of Hawai'i historian and area specialist Leonard Andaya writes that the term "Malayu" is only used when one is confronted by a distinct other, such as the Javanese, Siamese, or the Portuguese. In all other cases, he goes on, Malays "are associated" only with a specific locale, such as "men of Melaka" or "men of Johor." A common Malay identity in Andaya's view was formed less by blood than by a "pattern of interaction" throughout a "voyaging corridor" that stretched across maritime Southeast Asia.[16] Malay identity, indistinct and flexible as it was, thus made itself ripe for its integration with Islam.

It was Indian Muslim traders arriving by sea in the twelfth and thirteenth centuries who are thought to have originally brought Islam to the Malay Peninsula. "The relationship between ethnicity and religion," writes the scholar Joseph Chinyong Liow, "is so intimate that the popular term for having converted to Islam, *masuk melayu,* means having 'become a Malay.'" More than any single factor perhaps, it was the robust seafaring trade that Malay Aceh, at the northern tip of Sumatra, conducted with Islamic kingdoms in India and the Greater Middle East in the sixteenth and seventeenth centuries, bringing Islamic scholars to the region, that cemented Malay identity to Islam long before modern Malaysia was ever thought of.[17] And because the various sultanates in the peninsula now no longer carry the weight they once did, "Islam's role at the core of Malay identity is more salient than ever."[18]

Immense social change tied to urban migration means an encounter with both Western liberal ideas and global Islam. And the encounter with the former encouraged Malays to take refuge in the latter. In Kuala Lumpur especially, with its 1.5 million people, more Muslim women have taken to conservative clothing, including the *tudong.* In the 1970s, men began wearing Arab robes and headgear. Arabic vocabulary took root, especially in formal greetings, like *as-salamu alaykum.* The *dakwah* (Islamic "revivalist") movement grew. Whereas older mosques were built in the local Malay style, in turn influenced by the Indian Subcontinent, newer ones evinced Middle Eastern architecture. *Islam Hadari* ("civilizational" Islam) became a political phrase that sought to unite economic development with Islamization.[19]

Malays now go abroad to study Islamic law at such conservative Middle Eastern institutions as Cairo's Al-Azhar University, and the International Islamic University of Malaysia offers courses in law and economics in both Arabic and English, for Arabs and Iranians both are flocking to Malaysia. Saifuddin Abdullah, the deputy minister of higher education, explained to me that Malaysia is a perfect location for Middle Eastern Muslims. "They can get a modern education in English. The food here is *halal* [permissible according to Islamic law]. Malaysia is relatively inexpensive and the climate is pleasant. We're multicultural and progressive relative to the Middle East. Most Arabs and Iranians want a more liberal version of their own homelands and they find it here."

Professor Abdullah al-Ahsan, the deputy dean of the International Institute of Islamic Thought and Civilization, remarked that Malaysia is the only Muslim country with regular elections going back to 1957, even if it has been a one-party state, dominated by the United Malays National Organization (UMNO). "Malaysia has made an impact. It is a model country in the Muslim world. People go on from our institution to high positions throughout the Middle East." Perhaps Professor al-Ahsan's most famous student was the current Turkish foreign minister, Ahmet Davutoglu, who studied in Malaysia during the first half of the 1990s. Davutoglu's innovative foreign policy toward the Islamic world has made him the brains behind Turkey's awakening as a middle-level power no longer firmly anchored to the West. "It was Malaysia that gave Davutoglu the opportunity to see the outside world"—or rather a version of it that was both cosmopolitan and Islamic. Thus, Davutoglu was able to envision similar possibilities for his native Turkey.

It is important to realize that Malaysia's civilizational Islam has roots that predate the rush to modernizing cities. Khaldun Malek, a Muslim intellectual in Penang, explained to me that Malaysia's organic ties to the Middle East go back to the medieval era, when the predictable monsoon winds, friendly as they were to sailboats, al-

lowed for an Indian Ocean cultural unity that did not have to wait for
the age of steamships. Steamships, in fact, only intensified pan-
Islamism, so that the late-nineteenth-century Islamic modernism of
the Persian Jamal ad-Din al-Afghani and the Egyptian Muhammad
Abduh, with its emphasis on reacting to the challenge of a techno-
logically ascendant West by finding universalist principles within
Islam itself, made its way to the Malay archipelago long before the
urbanization of our own era. Malaysia, through all of these developments, has blossomed as an outgrowth of the Middle East in Asia.
What delimits Islam here, and provides it with moderation on one
hand and insecurity on the other, is the unique fact that this is a society that is 60 percent—not 80 or 90 percent—Muslim. And the re-
mainder of the population is composed overwhelmingly of vigorous
civilizations in their own right.

Sinic civilization in particular is a challenger to Islamic dominance.
Malaysia's Chinese community is arguably the most authentic in the
world, without the deracination that accompanied the Great Proletarian Cultural Revolution in China itself; and without the fierce
Westernization pursued by the Chinese community in Singapore.
Moreover, whereas the Chinese community in Malaysia used to be
characterized by diversity, numbering, for example, Hokkien Chinese
from Fujian in southern China, and locally born Malay Chinese,
known as *Peranakan,* a monochrome and, therefore, potentially nationalistic Chinese identity has now taken root in the big Malaysian
cities—another upshot of globalization. This is comparable to the
monochrome Hinduism that in recent decades has taken root in
India, replacing the various regional and village cults of yore. It was
this monochrome Hinduism that has been the foundation for Hindu
nationalism. The Chinese in Malaysia are very different though, being
a commercial-minded middle-man minority without the same call to
national greatness as the Hindus, despite their identification with
some specific political parties. Yet the potential for Malaysian Chinese to more narrowly identify themselves in ethnic terms exists,
faced as they are with what *The Economist* calls "the sharpening of
ethnic and religious dividing lines" here.[20]

"As a boy, Muslims always came to my house," one Chinese scholar in Kuala Lumpur told me. "Now it is rare to host Muslims in a Chinese home. Even if your dishes and silverware are clean, they contain the residue of pork and thus are not *halal,* and this contaminates your entire house in Muslim eyes." I heard a variation of this story throughout my stay in Malaysia. But a Muslim scholar I know said the observation was true only up to a point: in the past, he explained, elites only dealt with elites, and so Muslims would visit Chinese houses because all were part of the same cosmopolitan circle. But now newly middle-class Chinese are having to deal with newly middle-class Muslims who are fierce about their dietary restrictions.

Chinese and Indians know Malay, but the Malays, whose Islamic fervor is felt mainly in the cities, speak no Chinese and Hindi. Malays are also synonymous with the urban poor—Malaysia's salient problem, as it is for so many developing countries. Tensions abound, in other words, kept in check by an oil-and-gas-fueled consumerism, a plethora of social welfare organizations, and an unemployment rate that is very low by the standards of the developing world—4 percent by some estimates. Crucially, there have been no ethnic riots for over four decades, and despite different ethnic communities living apart from each other as in Sri Lanka and Fiji, there have been no ethnic wars and insurrections as in those places.

And so Malaysia, despite its divisions, constitutes a comparatively successful postcolonial experience, in which millions have—we should not forget—been lifted out of poverty and social mobility enshrined.

The glittering vista of economic and technological dynamism that is contemporary Malaysia did not happen by accident. It is, to a significant extent, the product of one man: Dr. Mahathir bin Mohamad, a medical doctor who was prime minister from 1981 to 2003. The youngest of nine children, Mahathir was born in 1925 in a semirural slum in Alor Setar, in northwestern Kedah state, with its overtones of Islamism, and would not become prime minister until he was fifty-six. From the time of his youth money was a constant problem. In short, he had a difficult upbringing and before achieving power spent decades rising through the hurly-burly of local politics (with all of its discrimination against those from the socioeconomic margins like himself), so that once he had achieved power he was determined to do something dramatic with it. Truly, he constructed his governing worldview on his very personal experiences. During World War II, while he saw cruelty firsthand—the bayoneting of a British soldier by Japanese troops—his overall impression of the Japanese occupation was of Malay "backwardness and incompetence." Soon after the war, while in modern Singapore, the utter lack of sophistication of his fellow Malays was etched deeper into his memory, as he witnessed them in comparison to the more modern and urbanized Chinese and Indians. It was this nose-to-the-ground sensibility about the crudeness of daily Malay life that allowed him to see a "pent-up reservoir of ill-feeling" between Malays, Chinese, and Indians in advance of the intercommunal riots in 1969 that saw hundreds die of wounds from knives, machetes, and crowbars.

Mahathir's rise in politics is ascribed to his ability to capture Malay resentment toward the other, more advantaged ethnic groups. Unlike the Chinese and the Indians, who had vast homelands to which to return, the Malays had nowhere else to go, and yet these *bumiputra,* or "sons of the soil," Malay and not, felt dispossessed in their own land, even as they made up about 60 percent of the population. In his 1970 book, *The Malay Dilemma,* he upheld the indigenous Muslim Malays of the Malacca Strait and the southern littorals of the South China Sea as the "definitive race," whose language non-Malay immigrants like the Chinese and Indians would simply have to learn. Muslim Malays would be in control of the bureaucracy, armed forces, police, judiciary, and other pillars of the state, as well as of the various monarchies. There would be a tyranny of the majority, in other words, something that made the nineteenth-century English philosopher John Stuart Mill worry about new democracies.[21] Indeed, Mahathir's solution to Malay backwardness was "constructive protection," a kind of affirmative action for Malays, in order to gradually bring them up to the developmental level of the other groups. The Malays would have distinct social and economic privileges, but not so many as to make them lazy.[22]

Mahathir spoke openly about Malay slothfulness, passivity, and their negative attitudes toward time, money, and property. Mahathir would transform Malay culture to a similar extent that Mustafa Kemal Ataturk transformed Turkish culture: only while Ataturk attempted to secularize the Turks, Mahathir opted for Islamization. Thus, in a way, Mahathir's achievement was greater: coming to power the year V. S. Naipaul published his book, he proved Naipaul wrong, demonstrating that Islam was not incompatible with economic dynamism and social energy. Under Mahathir, the call to prayer was now broadcast over state-run radio and television and Malay women—in a reverse of Kemalism—covered themselves with "various versions of the veil," even as he used Islam's strict ethical standards to root out cronyism and corruption. By his ability to combine religiosity and devoutness with science and technology, Mahathir made Malaysia, at the far periphery of the Muslim world in Southeast Asia, central to the values debate in the Middle East.

Whereas Singaporean strongman Lee Kuan Yew buttressed local patriotism with secularism, Mahathir buttressed Malaysian patriotism with Islam, whose appeal was limited to the dominant Malays. Saifuddin Abdullah, the deputy education minister, told me that Mahathir "defined moderate Islam for the entire world, by building a modern country with Islamic technocrats. Mahathir knew," Saifuddin went on, "how to be modern without being Western—as he looked toward Japan and South Korea, not just the West." Mahathir in his own person signaled the rise of middle-level powers and of the non-Western "rest" of the globe.

Arabs and Iranians both revered Mahathir for his support for the Palestinians, and his consequent attacks on the Jews and the West. Mahathir was a champion of Muslim Bosnia and against the American invasion of Iraq. His militant Islamist foreign policy was an attempt to give Malaysia more of a national identity. The problem was that his very emphasis on devout Islam inflamed interethnic relations between the Muslim Malays and the non-Muslim Chinese and Indians.[23]

Raising the stature of his own ethnic group constituted only part of Mahathir's sweeping agenda. Mahathir announced his ambition by his heroes: in addition to Ataturk, he admired Russia's Peter the Great and South Korea's Park Chung Hee, great state builders both. During the twenty-two years Mahathir was prime minister, the economy grew by an average of 6.1 percent annually, making Malaysia one of the developing world's fastest growing countries at the time. The emphasis on basic commodities gave way to the production of manufactured goods, which soon accounted for 70 percent of exports. His government poured money into airports, highways, bridges, skyscrapers, container ports, dams, and cyber networks. The "tech-savvy" Mahathir understood how transportation and communications infrastructure would be critical for a nation's success in the twenty-first century. The late Barry Wain, a former editor of *The Wall Street Journal Asia Edition,* writes in his scrupulously objective biography of Mahathir, *Malaysian Maverick,* "With a combination of ruthlessness and dexterity," Mahathir as prime minister "delivered social peace and sustained economic growth, introducing increasing numbers of Malaysians to middle-class comforts, even as significant numbers of non-Muslims (Chinese, in particular) opted to emigrate. Though if they were critical, few were willing to jeopardize their rising living standards, or risk ostracism and worse." As one Malaysian commentator noted, "One of Mahathir's signal triumphs was to have persuaded Malaysian society that 'less politics' and 'more economics,' 'less democracy' and 'greater stability' were the guarantees of continued prosperity." Chandra Muzaffar, the head of a local NGO who had been jailed once by Mahathir, told me that "now there were Malay doctors and lawyers, and a real Malay middle class to go along with the Chinese one. This," he went on, "was achieved without violence and through a functioning democracy." And yet, Mahathir's ruling style was that of a traditional authoritarian. He jailed political opponents and civil society activists alike, allowing no one to question his vision of a modern, high-technology, and industrialized Malaysia.[24]

Mahathir's rule combined an attention to detail with elements of the grandiose. He was anal and visionary, treating his country as though he were still a doctor with a sick patient. He would personally conduct spot checks of drains and public toilets, and record violations in a notebook. He insisted that civil servants wear name tags for identification in case of complaints. Nevertheless, his ability to think big, combined with a rarefied sense of aesthetics, led to the creation of a Japanese-designed, postmodern mega-airport servicing Kuala Lumpur—one of the world's largest and most beautiful such facilities. The spanking-new capital city he built, Putrajaya, adjacent to Kuala Lumpur, with its Persian-cum-Mughal-cum-Malay architecture, and with its rich, turquoise colors and fairy-tale domes, is far more pleasing to the eye than Pakistan's own built-from-scratch capital of Islamabad, with its bombastic Stalinist-cum-Mughal structures. The difference between Putrajaya and Islamabad demonstrates in aesthetic terms the difference between Malaysia and Pakistan: between a healthy Muslim-dominated society and an unhealthy purely Muslim one. The eighty-eight-story Petronas Twin Towers in Kuala Lumpur, built by the Malaysian petroleum giant and designed by the late Argentinean-American architect César Pelli, were for a time the tallest buildings in the world, shaped from the top down like Islamic stars—something insisted upon by Mahathir, ever the micromanager. The towers' shiny steel and glass and spectacle of winking multicolored lights at night bespeak ambition and inspiration on an epic scale.

Mahathir's energy is summed up by the fact that he despised golf, the quintessential game of world leaders, considering it a waste of time. His negatives were profound: he allowed a cult of personality to form around him, he created a system that was long on obedience and short on integrity, despite efforts to hold civil servants to account, and he destroyed political rivals like Deputy Prime Minister Anwar Ibrahim by campaigns of character assassination. His attacks on ethnic Chinese in the 1960s and on World Jewry during the 1997–1998 Asian economic crisis reeked of prejudice and anti-Semitism. He stoked ethnic rivalries, rather than assuaged them. This was rank political calculation on his part: he knew that such attacks would go down well among his constituents. Aware that the Israeli occupation of Palestine was seemingly existential among Malay Muslims, he was a deliberate sensationalist who played the global media for local effect.

Mahathir could be mean and petty, as well as fantastically insecure. After taking power, he confiscated a stunning hilltop mansion, the Carcosa Seri Negara, built in 1904, that served as the British High Commission. The mansion had especial meaning for the British, as it was from this house that Field Marshal Sir Gerald Templer had directed the pathbreaking counterinsurgency campaign against communist guerrillas in the 1950s that has lived on in British military lore. But Mahathir did not want *white people literally looking down on us from on high,* and so he just took the building away.

The Western media wants heroes it can applaud or villains it can vilify. The real world is different. There is no unity of goodness. A great leader can come with hideous faults. That is the lesson of Mahathir. Mahathir put Muslim-dominated Malaysia on the map, giving the somewhat artificially conceived state a national identity, especially within the Muslim world, and as a consequence he pushed back at the West. Malaysia's very dynamism under his rule constituted a part of the epic story behind the West's relative decline.

The style of Mahathir's rule demonstrated that, in the words of the Australian scholar Harold Crouch, "the sharp dichotomy between 'democracy' and 'authoritarianism' does not seem to apply." And this distinctly mixed or "ambiguous" regime has led to a "degree of coherence that has provided the foundation for a remarkably stable political order," despite Malaysia's deep ethnic and civilizational cleavages, and recent political unrest. Mahathir's regime, reflecting a category all its own, became at once "more repressive and more responsive" to people's needs. It solved problems even as it clamped down on dissent. The electoral system grossly favored the government at the expense of the opposition, even as elections were vigorously contested and members of the regime faced stiff fights to keep their seats. Mahathir reduced poverty by half during his tenure. But because of "crosscutting communal cleavages" that threatened stability, the evolution of a modern middle-class structure, liberating in its own right, did not result in full democracy. The regime's dilemma was that the new middle class remained firmly divided along ethnic lines.[25] Again, there was no unity of goodness.

There have been military emergency laws, detentions without trial, and press and trade union restrictions. Nevertheless, as Crouch wrote in 1996, "in a society in which the possibility of violence is ever-present, both the Malay and non-Malay elites, as well as much of the population, tend to value stability more than further democratization."[26] (What argues against interracial violence are the political divisions within ethnic Malay society: between secular and less secular elements.) For beyond the communal splits, there is the unsettling memory of Muslim Malay society being divided among nine sultanates, not to mention the former colonial Straits Settlements of Malacca and Penang and the eastern states of Sabah and Sarawak in Borneo: a politically unstable setup that hampered the Malay independence movement against the British and finds expression in today's highly federalized system.

Malaysia is thus the ultimate postmodern society. "Politically, we don't have a Malaysian identity, divided as we are by communalisms," explained former minister Zaid Ibrahim. "When politicians declare that we do, in fact, have such an identity that in itself is a sign of insecurity. We are merely communities living peacefully and separately." Malaysia, in his view, is already beyond nationalism without having ever experienced it. And the explosion of Islamic and other private schools, along with the teaching of English, creates even more of a global society here.

The military modernization that Malaysia has pursued is less an expression of nationalism than of "keeping up with the Joneses" in regard to Singapore, according to a Malaysian defense official. "It is Singapore's arms purchases that have spurred our own." Malaysians fear that in a war Singapore's air superiority would make Malaysia capitulate in "six to ten hours." Of course, when you ask people here what the motive would be for such Singaporean aggression they have no answer. There is none, and Malaysians know it. Malaysians do not feel under threat. And this, too, dilutes their sense of nationalism.

The military itself splits Malaysian public opinion. The uniformed ranks are filled mostly with Malays, so the armed services are less popular among the Chinese and Indian communities. Likewise, the Malaysian military finds support from the political establishment that governs the country, but is much less popular among the political opposition, which itself is comprised heavily of Chinese and Indians.

Malaysia, unlike hyper-nationalistic Vietnam, wants nothing of the conflict with China, even as it is implicitly protected against Chinese power by fifty visits per year by American warships, up from six in 2003; and by 280 American warship visits per year throughout Southeast Asia. American nuclear submarines have visited Malaysian ports in Borneo. American forces have trained with Malaysians, and the Pentagon has provided Malaysia with tens of millions of dollars of radar equipment for use in the South China Sea under the guise of the global war on terrorism. Bilateral military ties between Malaysia and the United States are extremely close, in fact. The last three chiefs of the Malaysian navy are graduates of the U.S. Naval War College in Newport, Rhode Island. "We are very comfortable with China because we know the United States is there to safeguard the region," the same defense official told me. Thus, America helps give Malaysia the luxury of its national ambiguity.

After Singapore, postnational Malaysia, with all of its Islamic pretensions, is America's most reliable—albeit quietest—ally around the South China Sea (though Vietnam may soon surpass Malaysia in this regard). Malaysia is careful to station its two French-Spanish submarines at Teluk Sepanggar naval base in Sabah, close to the Spratlys, in order to keep China honest. Malaysia's military, particularly its air force, is now doing more contingency exercises in Borneo in order to defend its garrisons in the Spratlys. (Malaysia claims twelve features in the Spratlys, of which it maintains a presence on five rocks, including a landing strip for C-130s on Swallow Reef.[27]) "We emphasize deterrence and readiness vis-à-vis China—we're not looking for a fight," said Dzirhan Mahadzir, a consultant specializing in defense matters. Still, Malaysian military officials have never forgotten that China supported mainly ethnic Chinese communist insurgents in the northern jungles of peninsular Malaysia through the 1970s.

But it is mainly within defense and security ranks that Malaysian nationalism is vibrant. Because domestic challenges and intercommunal complexities may leave too little energy to engage in outside conflict, Malaysia might yet do its bit to mitigate military rivalries in the South China Sea.

"The nation-state is actually a very recent phenomenon here" compared to the sprawling, archipelagic Malay community, which spans different countries, Khaldun Malek, the Muslim intellectual, told me. Indeed, Malaysia was cobbled together within the areas of the Malay Peninsula and Borneo administered by Great Britain: an area south of the kingdom of Thailand and north and west of the Dutch East Indies, which became Indonesia. Malaysia is not a historic state to the degree of China, Thailand, Vietnam, and even Burma with all its ethnic militia problems. This is why, according to Khaldun, Islam has been able to partially replace nationalism.

Such internal weaknesses play into the country's political fragility. "For it is no longer possible to run the country paternalistically," as Mahathir did, says Zaid Ibrahim. The ruling party, UMNO, in power for more than half a century, may well lose future elections. The main competition, he continued, will be between UMNO and PAS (Parti Islam se-Malaysia, or Pan-Islamic Malaysian Party). Indeed, it is the Islamic party, seen as free of corruption, that will loom increasingly larger in Malaysian politics, even as governing majorities are bound to get narrower in a post-UMNO era. "The days of UMNO's two-thirds majorities [which allowed Mahathir the political space to economically develop the country] are over." All this, as the population is harder to satisfy, because now people (thanks to a global media) have the basis of comparison with other peoples. Power must at some point pass to the opposition. And if it does so peacefully, then, rather than discredit Mahathir's rule as experts both inside and outside Malaysia will no doubt claim, it will in a historical sense vindicate his partially unsavory accomplishments.

All these "negotiated tensions" were brought into perspective by my visit to Penang. In the late eighteenth and nineteenth centuries, Arabs, Armenians, Hokkien Chinese, Indians from Gujarat, and Malays from Aceh on Sumatra were drawn to this island off the northwest of the Malay Peninsula, on account of the free trade policy of the British, coupled with the security that they provided. The sea routes from Penang led to Siam and Burma across the Bay of Bengal, and to Fujian in southeastern China across the South China Sea. It was these traders from throughout the East, coalescing in Penang, who helped finance the burgeoning tin mines in the Malay Peninsula at the turn of the twentieth century. Penang was mainly a Chinese affair, though. And in recent decades the Muslim Malaysian government, watchful of the Chinese, and seeking to centralize economic power in Kuala Lumpur as a hedge against separatist tendencies elsewhere, deliberately marginalized Penang, so that the local harbor trade these days is predominantly from within Malaysia.

Trying to recapture this bygone cosmopolitan ambience of previous decades and centuries, I went down to the old quarter of Penang, which is dominated by a sixty-foot-tall, dazzling white clock tower with a Moorish dome—erected in 1897 in honor of Queen Victoria's diamond jubilee. The tower soars into the sky, even as it is utterly diminished by immense new high-rises in the distance. Likewise, the adjacent early nineteenth-century Fort Cornwallis, from which the British ruled Penang, is equally diminutive. But it is old Penang's shuttered and balconied commercial streets, grubby and battered in their single and double stories, with their potted plants and exposed electric wires, that make one realize just how everything was on such a smaller, more intimate scale back then. It took me only little more than half an hour to walk old quarter Penang from one end to the other. Technology, as we know it, was not required to unite this British-ruled city with its mainly Chinese subjects, and thus there was nothing virtual about this community: it was real. But as the distant high-rises made clear, politicians in Malaysia had now to satisfy a mass of strangers living in inhumanly sized apartment blocks. And because politics here has become less personal—less retail—it requires more potent symbolism, and thus it runs the risk of descending into ideology. Thus, in the future, one cannot rule out extremism, whether emanating from the Middle East or elsewhere—one danger that colonialism, eminently practical and often cruel as it was, usually lacked.

How to be a mass democracy in an age of high technology, while existing at the unstable crossroads of different civilizations? Malaysia, in terms of its political development, may turn out to be among the most revealing countries on earth.

CHAPTER V

The Good Autocrat

In the heart of Singapore, along the Singapore River, near to the perfectly engineered design statement that is the Asian Civilizations Museum, stands a diminutive and elegant monument to the late Chinese leader Deng Xiaoping. Deng was arguably among the greatest men of the twentieth century, because he dramatically lifted the living standards of close to a billion people throughout East Asia by introducing a version of capitalism to the Chinese economy. No man in history improved the quality of life for more people in a shorter time than Deng. But Deng elicits mixed feelings in the West. He was a ruthless authoritarian, who was the driving force behind the massacre of perhaps thousands of protesting students at Tiananmen Square in Beijing in 1989. Only in Singapore would he be so openly honored—at so appropriate a measured level, and for the right reasons. "Singapore has raised pragmatism to the level of a philosophy," explained retired local diplomat Tommy Koh, whose idea it was to erect the monument to Deng. Singapore, he told me, stands against the beauty of ideas in favor of what works.

Standing next to the monument to Deng, I looked out at downtown Singapore: a dull grayish and blue-slate corporate park built on the scale of a megacity, the product of a meticulous mind, with sharp puzzle pieces of skyscrapers all neatly fitting together, maddening in their mathematical logic. At work was the abstract genius of the Chinese, who understand the conceptual utility of empty spaces; as opposed to the Indianized Malay mind, which is more at home in the world of thickly colored and deliciously cluttered textiles, with their floral and cartouche patterns (as evidenced by the displays in the nearby museum). But to call Singapore cold and impersonal is too easy a judgment. For everywhere there is civilizing greenery, starting with the dazzling bougainvillea bushes that line the road from the airport. Singapore is the only place in the Indo-Pacific, other than Japan, where traffic stops voluntarily for pedestrians.

At the end of history there is somnolence: that is the lesson of Singapore. Pragmatism carried to the furthest degree may not inspire the Western humanist mind, but it has been the only way for Singapore to survive as a physical speck of a city-state at the southern tip of the Malay Peninsula, whose location is coveted by the great powers. Singapore's inner logic follows from its geographical vulnerability.

Singapore occupies a natural, deep-water port at the narrowest point of the funnel that is the Strait of Malacca—the most important maritime choke point in the world. Throughout history, this little island has been both violated and fought over. The ancestors of the people of Singapore belonged to ethnic and tribal groups that lived off the high seas and especially piracy—Chinese, Indians, Siamese, Riaus, Javanese, and Malays. Singapore always belonged to someone else's empire or kingdom. The fact that it has been an independent city-state since the last third of the twentieth century constitutes something unique in history.

Singapore, according to a senior serving official, emerged as an embattled state purely because of philosophical reasons. It was thrown out of a Malay-dominated federation in the 1960s because Singapore's leaders insisted on a multiethnic meritocracy. Thus, Singapore found itself alone amid a newly constituted and hostile Malaysia, which controlled Singapore's access to freshwater, while a pro-communist Indonesian demographic behemoth was breathing down Singapore's neck.[1] Singapore was as small and alone in its region as Israel was in its; it was no irony that Israel played a large role in training Singapore's armed forces. The Singaporean business model would decades later be an argument in favor of soft power, but some Singaporean officials despise the term. One Singaporean after another told me: *Soft power is only relevant after you have developed hard power.* The Israelis would concur.

Whereas in the West the concept of balance of power is often seen as a cynical term, reeking, as it seems to, of coldhearted realism, Singaporeans equate the balance of power with freedom itself. Because of great powers all around, only a proper balance of power between these large states can allow for the independence of such a small state like Singapore, which, unlike Brunei, has no oil.

"We have no sovereign waters, even as we are located at the world's most critical naval choke point," one serving diplomat told me. "Independent and secure sea lines of communication are an existential requirement for us." Indeed, freedom of navigation in the South China Sea means that maritime trade of $750 billion annually accounts for three times Singapore's GDP, whereas it is only a third of GDP for neighboring states.

But Singapore faces a particular challenge that is best summed up in the language of political science: while China is a geographical fact, the United States at least in Asia is merely a geopolitical concept. Translation: China is close by and therefore threatening; whereas the United States does not necessarily have to be present in the region to the extent that it is were its foreign policy to undergo a fundamental shift. "China is big, we're small," a high-ranking military officer told me. "China says that it is a status quo power. But its economic and military growth for decades changes the status quo." Another lesson of Singapore is that it is helpful to be a little paranoid.

And yet Singaporean officials are relieved by their long memories. They are not really worried about the United States reducing its forces in Asia, despite budget woes in Washington. They remember much darker times: the end of the Vietnam War, when quasi-isolationism in the United States regarding Asia was a real possibility; and the presidency of Jimmy Carter, when an attempt was made to withdraw American forces from South Korea, an idea that struck people in Singapore as—to say the least—wildly naive.

In fact, no foreign policy and security elite in the world struck me as quite so cold-blooded as that of Singapore's. Example: though the Philippines, like Singapore, is enthusiastic about countering Chinese power, the Filipinos, in the Singaporean view, "are emotional and unstable and thereby make the security situation worse." The Singaporeans are more comfortable with serious adversaries than they are with unserious friends. One Singaporean summed it up this way: "At the end of the day, it is all about military force and naval presence—it is not about passionate and well-meaning talk." Typically, everybody I met in the various Singaporean ministries insisted that frank conversations must be off the record: public diplomacy, in their view, is overrated, and is another thing they have no illusions about.

Singapore's independence began less with a declaration of such than with the building of a formidable military. "Spider-Man needs a suit to make him strong; we needed an outsized armed forces," explained a defense official. While Singapore has only 3.3 million citizens, it boasts an air force the same size as Australia's, whose population is 23 million. "Like the Israelis, the Singaporeans believe in air superiority. They pay their pilots well. They have AWACS," a defense official from a neighboring country told me. In addition to its one hundred or so fighter jets, Singapore has twenty missile-carrying ships, six frigates, and, notably, six submarines—an extraordinary number given that far more populous countries in the region like Indonesia, Malaysia, and Vietnam each have fewer. "Nobody can squeeze us through a blockade."

It is not enough that Singapore has these air and sea platforms.

For it is deadly serious about using them effectively. Because Singapore lacks empty space for military training, it regularly has four air squadrons training in the United States, ground troops training in Taiwan, and helicopter crews training in Australia. It allots sixty-five days a year for army maneuvers with leopard tanks. "We will not be hemmed in by our neighbors." Too, Singapore has a conscript military. Said the same defense official: "There are only three developed countries in the world that are very serious about national service— South Korea, Israel, and us."

But the vast latent power of China still unsettles the Singaporeans, so much so that they feel they have no choice but to rely directly on the United States. As another diplomat told me: "We see American hard power as benign. The U.S. Navy defends globalization by protecting the sea lanes, which we, more than any other people, benefit from. To us, there is nothing dark or conspiratorial about the United States and its vast security apparatus."

In 1998, the Singaporeans built Changi Naval Base solely to host American nuclear-powered aircraft carriers and submarines. "We designed the piers to meet the dimensions of American warships," a high-ranking military man here told me, in order to lure American naval platforms to Singaporean waters. "It's kind of like, if you serve good coffee and tea, people will come." Indeed, in 2011 there were 150 American warship visits to Singapore. Then there were the three American littoral combat ships that, it was announced in 2011, would be stationed in Singapore.

Finally, beyond military might, there is the power of diplomacy. Singapore externalizes its security not only through the American navy and air force, but through an alliance like the Association of Southeast Asian Nations. ASEAN is about "socializing other states to a set of core values." Those core values revolve around the independence of small and medium-sized states banding together in the face of a rising great power like China, even though no diplomat in the region will ever say that on the record.

Whenever I met with senior civil servants in Singapore they were accompanied by younger colleagues who were present throughout our conversations. This was in order that the younger generation, as I was told, could learn from "our governing philosophy" and thus "carry on the tradition." In fact, the more visits I made to Singapore, the more it occurred to me that despite their differences and remaining inequalities, the various ethnic groups of this city-state—Chinese, Indian, and Malay—talked and acted alike: as though a philosophical principle could erase ethnic differences. Well, of course, it could. For this was what the United States was all about with its Protestant Creed that American Catholics, Jews, and others subscribed to. But maybe because of Singapore's small size, the expression of the same phenomenon here seemed that much more intense and noticeable. It was as though I were inside a version of Plato's Republic, with a reigning philosopher king.

Indeed, there was a reigning philosopher king, who these diplomats and defense officials kept mentioning and quoting from: who I must now introduce. For he is Singapore's version of Deng Xiaoping. In fact, it was partly from him that Deng got his vision to modernize China.

Just consider: in three decades, Singapore had gone from a malarial hellhole of overpowering smells and polluted, life-threatening monsoon drains to a global economic dynamo that topped businessmen's lists for efficiency and quality of life. The old Singapore was a place of slums, rats, garbage, and stray dogs. The new Singapore was so clean, sterile, and easy to negotiate that I thought of it as beginner's Asia. In the early 1960s, Singapore was as poor as many countries in sub-Saharan Africa; by the 1990s, this city-state, one fifth the size of Rhode Island, had a standard of living higher than Australia's. Credit for the miracle went to one man: an English-educated ethnic Chinese barrister, Harry Lee, who, when he decided to enter politics, changed his name back to the traditional Lee Kuan Yew.

Whenever in the 1990s I sat with influential figures in the Arab and ex-communist worlds, I always posed the question, Who was the greatest minor man of the twentieth century—not someone on par with Churchill or Roosevelt, but a tier below—the kind of man your country needs at the moment? The answer I got was never Nelson Mandela or Václav Havel, but invariably Lee Kuan Yew. Some journalists and intellectuals who had never wielded bureaucratic responsibility over large groups of people, and who preached moral absolutes from the sidelines, disliked him. But Western leaders—Gerald Ford, George H. W. Bush, and Margaret Thatcher, to name a few, each of whom understood the need for moral compromise in the face of implacable, violent forces—rightly held him in awe. Lady Thatcher observed: "In office, I read and analyzed every speech of Harry's. He had a way of penetrating the fog of propaganda. . . . He was never wrong."[2]

In the best short analysis of Lee's career, Australian editor and intellectual Owen Harries writes that Lee's political philosophy was the upshot of his experiences in the 1940s: in the first half of the decade he knew the utter brutality of Japanese occupation; in the second half studying at Cambridge he experienced a civil society established under the rule of law.[3] "The three and a half years of Japanese occupation were the most important of my life," Lee writes in the first volume of his memoirs, *The Singapore Story.* "They gave me vivid insights into the behavior of human beings and human societies, their motivations and impulses." He goes on. "The Japanese demanded total obedience and got it. . . . Punishment was so severe that crime was very rare. . . . As a result I have never believed those who advocate a soft approach to crime and punishment, claiming that punishment does not reduce crime. That was not my experience in Singapore." Lee says he "learnt more" from the Japanese occupation "than any university could have taught me." Nevertheless, at university after the war he also learned much. He and his fellow Singaporean and Malayan students at Cambridge "were enthusiastic about the mature British system, under which constitutional tradition and tolerance allowed fundamental shifts of power and wealth to take place peacefully."[4]

Lee tempered the Japanese fascist penchant for order with the lawful rule of the British to achieve a developmental miracle on this small island that comprises 214 square miles at low tide. Lee tells how he accomplished this in two massive volumes of compulsively readable memoirs. Most political memoirs are dreadful ghost writer–assembled hackwork that are little more than a stitching together of banal justifications. But Lee's two-volume set, *The Singapore Story* and *From Third World to First: Singapore and the Asian Economic Boom,* are contenders for inclusion in Plutarch's early-second-century AD *The Lives of the Noble Grecians and Romans.*[5] Lee's books tell a story that challenges the philosophical underpinnings of the Western intellectual elite, because it implies that virtue is not altogether connected with democracy and that meritocratic quasi-autocracy can in a poor country achieve economic results quicker than can a weak and chaotic parliamentary system.

Lee Kuan Yew of Singapore constitutes a more worthy model of leadership than Mahathir Mohamad of Malaysia. Both men imposed an authoritarian style over newly wrought democratic systems. Yet Lee is without Mahathir's decidedly nasty prejudices and petty meannesses, while harboring a more acute strategic vision that, unlike Mahathir's, goes far beyond the Muslim world. Mahathir is head and shoulders above most other Muslim leaders; whereas Lee, as I indicated, is head and shoulders above most other leaders worldwide in the twentieth century.

At the beginning of the first volume of his memoirs, Lee assesses Singapore's situation as he found it in the 1950s, the time when he established the People's Action Party by combining an English-speaking elite with a broad working-class base. Though located at "the heart of the British Empire in Southeast Asia," with the decline and dissolution of empire, Lee feared that Singapore would become "a heart without a body." As he explains, British defense spending accounted for 20 percent of the city-state's GDP, and created employment for 10 percent of its workforce. Thus, the end of the British Empire would signal Singapore's greatest domestic crisis since the entrepôt was founded in 1819 at the ultra-strategic southernmost tip of the Asian mainland, with deep harbors and sheltered anchorages dominating the Strait of Malacca—where the Indian Ocean ends and the Western Pacific begins in the form of the South China Sea. Seventy-five percent of Singapore's population of two million back then were ethnic Chinese, surrounded at the time by 100 million Malay and Indonesian Muslims. "How could we survive in such a hostile environment?" the young aspiring politician asked himself.[6]

Moreover, the Chinese themselves in Singapore were a feudal community divided by clan and dialect, with the exception of a small group of English speakers to which Lee's family belonged. Within the Chinese community, the dominant political force was the local Communist Party, whose raison d'être was the "latent animosity" that the Chinese population had for its white bosses, which, in turn, led to a communist strategy of provoking confrontation with the British. Then there were the Indian and Malay minorities in Singapore itself. (Singapore, or *Singapura*, is Malay for "City of the Lion.") Malay culture, Owen Harries explains, was "hierarchical, deferential, and characterized by an easygoing cronyism that shaded into corruption." And there was Indonesia, adjacent to Singapore and the Malay Peninsula, where Sukarno, the most anti-Western leader in the Third World, was about to run amok through the manipulation of the largest Communist Party outside of the Warsaw Pact. For Harry Lee, about to become Lee Kuan Yew, it was hard to be an optimist.[7] The only way to survive politically and create a modern polity was through indirect thrusts and maneuvering among hostile forces for years on end, especially in regards to the communists.

For Singapore's ethnic Chinese were in the early years, before the crimes of the Great Leap Forward and the Great Proletarian Cultural Revolution came to light, very proud of Mao Zedong's Red China—even as they despised Western colonialism in the guise of their British occupiers, the same occupiers who, as Lee was painfully aware, provided Singaporeans with jobs. It was Singapore's chronic unemployment that inspired trade unionism, and it was trade unionism that inspired communism. Lee knew that it was the communist threat in both Singapore and Malaya that motivated the British toward the "less unpleasant option" of handing over power to his own People's Action Party in Singapore and to the moderate and traditional force represented by Tunku (Prince) Abdul Rahman in peninsular Malaya.

"In pre-war India, where there was no communist threat, constitutional methods of passive resistance took decades to work," Lee writes in true Machiavellian style. Indeed, with communists and their kindred spirits in power in both China and Indonesia, the British, who could no longer afford an empire, were desperate to hand power to Western-oriented local rulers in Singapore and Malaya, in order to keep the sea lanes open in the South China Sea and in the all-important Strait of Malacca. That meant that the political positions of Lee and the Tunku had to be strengthened by the British, because in the early post–World War II years a democratic system—in Singapore at least—would have likely brought a pro-communist government to power. In the history of the Cold War, Lee's ability and willingness to engage in a "ceaseless ding-dong" with local communists, "exchanging vitriol with them in the press and exercising restraint in the face of provocation by their strikes," while borrowing their mass mobilization techniques like street-sweeping campaigns and the organization of work brigades, constituted a godsend to the West.[8]

It was Lee's very drive, energy, and life force that altered history in this hotly contested theater of the Cold War, roiled as it was by communist insurgencies in nearby Malaya and Vietnam. Amidst the struggle to consolidate power against the communists and maneuvering between Malaya and Indonesia as a prime minister in his late thirties, Lee compelled himself to learn a new language, Hokkien Chinese.

Lee decided early on that his first strategic move would be to identify his political party with "independence through merger" with Malaya. Malaya, with its large stores of tin and rubber, provided Singapore with an economic base and the prospects for a common market to sustain Singapore's industrialization and reduce its unemployment. Furthermore, Singapore shared a common British colonial past with Malaya, and needed it as protection against Sukarno's Muslim demographic Goliath of Indonesia. Malaya, for its part, needed to control Singapore for the sake of a tighter grip on communism in the city-state, even as it desperately yearned to incorporate the budding export dynamo. The problem for Malaya's leader, Tunku Abdul Rahman, was that adding Singapore to Malaya would upset the ethnic balance in favor of the Chinese: to solve the problem, the heavily Malay populations of Sabah and Sarawak on the island of Borneo were, with British acquiescence, added to the federation, thus creating Malaysia in 1963.[9]

The very creation of the federation elicited threats from Indonesia and the Philippines, both of which coveted the northern and northwestern Borneo territories of Sabah and Sarawak, which the Indonesians and Filipinos felt the British had no right to cede to the new Malaysia. Sukarno's Indonesia was especially dangerous. Sukarno, his own economy unraveling by the minute, was warning Great Britain and the United States to get out of Southeast Asia and the South China Sea region, and make way for the axis of Red China, North Vietnam, and neutralist Cambodia. Sukarno's leftist-populist, blood-and-soil appeals to ethnic Malays in both Indonesia *and* Malaysia posed another threat. In order to compete with Sukarno, the Tunku had to adopt a similar strategy of advancing the rights and privileges of ethnic Malays in the new federation, which angered the ethnic Chinese and Indians, the former of which were concentrated in Singapore. Thus did the federation with Singapore begin to come undone.

Sukarno would be toppled in 1967 by the pro-Western Suharto, who would bring order and stability to Indonesia, educating his people and making Indonesia into a budding tiger economy, while his own family would add to—rather than alleviate—the megacountry's rampant corruption. But in the mid-1960s the bad blood between ethnic Malays and Singapore-based ethnic Chinese in the new Malaysia could not be assuaged. Lee had tense negotiations with the increasingly populist Malay leader, Tunku Abdul Rahman, in order to preserve ethnic Chinese rights in the federation, even as Lee fought political battles with Chinese chauvinist groups and pro-communists at home in Singapore. Lee was evidently more ambitious than he lets on in his memoirs. His deep, unstated reason for the union with Malaya was so that he could one day rule Malaysia. Singapore was simply too small a prize for his capability and genius.

Above all, Lee was a man of vision. In the radical 1960s, when Western youth nursed ideas of world peace and connoted centralized power of any kind with evil, Lee saw that "half-digested theories of socialism and redistribution of wealth," when compounded with "less than competent government" in the Third World, would have "appalling consequences" in Asia, Africa, and Latin America. Lee was a Thatcherite and Reaganite before their time, holding off communist forces in Southeast Asia, a key ideological and strategic battleground of the era.[10]

But inside Southeast Asia, Lee just couldn't make the new Malaysia work. He understood that pressures within the Tunku's own ethnic community would force the Tunku to concede to Singapore autonomy only over matters like education and labor. And this would not satisfy Lee's own constituents. Then in 1964 came intercommunal riots in Singapore between ethnic Chinese and ethnic Malays, partly incited by racial propaganda coming from Kuala Lumpur, leaving dozens dead and hundreds wounded. Afterward, in Kuala Lumpur, an ethnic Malay member of Parliament and a future prime minister, Mahathir bin Mohamad, denounced Lee's People's Action Party as "pro-Chinese, communist-oriented, and positively anti-Malay." Mahathir accused Singapore of retaining its multilingualism rather than adopting Malay as its language, which he claimed it should have. To Mahathir, Lee represented a type of Chinese who was "insular, selfish and arrogant," and who could not bear being ruled by Malays, people the Chinese had oppressed for so long.[11]

Finally, the more moderate Tunku told Lee: "You go your way, we go our own way. So long as you are in any way connected with us, we will find it difficult to be friends because we are involved in your affairs and you will be involved in ours. Tomorrow, when you are no longer in Malaysia . . . we'll be friends again, and we'll need each other, and we'll cooperate."[12]

And that is exactly what happened.

Lee concludes the first volume of his memoir from the vantage point of 1965, saying: "I had let down many people in Malaya, Sabah and Sarawak. . . . By accepting separation, I had failed them. That sense of guilt made me break down."[13]

All looked bleak.

"We had to make a living, to persuade investors to put their money into manufacturing plants and other businesses in Singapore. We had to learn to survive, without the British military umbrella and without a hinterland."[14]

So begins the narrative thread in Lee's second volume, which, even more than the first, approximates the lessons of Machiavelli's *The Prince*.[15] As Lee writes, "A soft people will vote for those who promised a soft way out," and because there was no soft way out, Lee determined to forge a hard island race of overseas Chinese with Malay and Indian minorities. Only a hard people could build the "throbbing and humming" industrial, commercial, and communications center he envisioned. He would make a fair society, not a "welfare" society.[16]

Like the Israelis, Lee decided to "leapfrog the region": faced with an initially hostile Malaysia and Indonesia, not to mention hostile communist regimes in China and North Vietnam, Lee's Singapore would link up with America, Europe, and Japan by effusively welcoming multinational corporations, which, at the time, in the radical late 1960s, the "dependency school" of economists were condemning as Western colonialism in disguise. He would give multinationals tax-free status for years on end and control the labor unions to boot, in return for having Singaporeans learn Western technical skills at the new plants. Moreover, he would establish standards of safety, security, infrastructure, service, and even aesthetics—like highways lined with pruned shrubbery—that would attract a professional class of Western engineers and entrepreneurs, who would make Singapore their "base camp" in Asia. Corruption would not be a problem as in other Third World countries. Lee would attack it by simplifying procedures, establishing clear and precise guidelines in business, and making living beyond one's means corroborative evidence in court for taking bribes. English would be the national language, reducing tensions among the various groups who all spoke different tongues and adding another lure to bring in Western banks and companies. Already, in the 1970s, as the oil crisis hit in the United States and the rebellious spirit of the 1960s youth movements was wearing off in the media, glowing reports began surfacing in newsmagazines about Singapore's progress. *Singapore, Inc.,* was in the process of being born. The fact that twenty-first-century Asia is all about *business* had a start in 1970s Singapore.[17]

More so than Mahathir, Lee was manic and meticulous. He demanded maintenance of facilities, and banned spitting, chewing gum, and tobacco advertisements. He chastises the Americans for being far behind in stigmatizing cigarette smoking, because their tobacco lobby was too powerful for too long. Foreign correspondents ridiculed Singapore as a "nanny state." Lee's response is that journalists make fun of his edicts only because Singapore offered them no big scandals, corruption cases, or grave wrongdoing to report. Lee criticizes the Western media for being "cynical" about authority, and points out that a freewheeling press in India, the Philippines, and Thailand have not stemmed raging corruption in those places, while Singapore, with its controlled press, has little corruption and meritocratic government.

Lee is nothing if not feisty. He defends caning as inhibiting crime more than long prison terms. He again refers back to the harsh Japanese occupation, when people were semi-starving but there were no burglaries. Lee's tough love was extended to the Malay minority, whose low test scores in math and science he attacked head-on, by working with Malay community leaders and the media to encourage students to study harder.[18]

Eventually relations with Malaysia would improve dramatically, which Lee credits to Mahathir's decisiveness in overriding grassroots political prejudices at home. Lee, ever the pragmatist, forgave Mahathir his early anti-Chinese racism. In fact, Lee's foreign policy was impossible for any freedom-loving nation to fault. When the Indonesians approached him quietly in 1972 to argue that the littoral nations of Indonesia, Singapore, and Malaysia should take control of the Strait of Malacca, Lee argued that it had been an international waterway for centuries, and that fact was the basis for Singapore's survival, and, inferentially, that of the world system's. Lee, as Lady Thatcher noted, could see through the fog of propaganda and the era's conventional thinking. He writes that only because "Americans were resolutely anticommunist and prepared to confront them [the communist regimes], Nehru, Nasser, and Sukarno could afford to be nonaligned. . . . It was a luxury paid for by Americans."[19] Then there is his total rebuke to the received wisdom in the United States about the Vietnam War:

> Although American intervention failed in Vietnam, it bought time for the rest of Southeast Asia. In 1965, when the U.S. military moved massively into South Vietnam, Thailand, Malaysia, and the Philippines faced internal threats from armed communist insurgencies and the communist underground was still active in Singapore. [Leftist] Indonesia, in the throes of a failed communist coup, was waging . . . an undeclared war against Malaysia and Singapore. . . . Standards of living were low and economic growth slow. America's action enabled noncommunist Southeast Asia to put their own houses in order. By 1975, they were in better shape to stand up to the communists. . . . The prosperous emerging market economies of ASEAN were nurtured during the Vietnam War years.[20]

The Australian strategist Hugh White has written, "Many in Southeast Asia would now agree" with that line of thinking.[21]

Lee's opinions may be hard for some to take, though not as hard as some of the statements made by Mahathir over the decades. The reality of the South China Sea region is different from that of the Middle East: here there really has been such a thing as enlightened authoritarianism, which has built not only civil societies, but those that are economic dynamos and therefore primed to become pulsating democracies.

The stories of Lee and Mahathir would appear less strange to the Western liberal mind if we revisit what some of the West's most liberal thinkers in modern times have actually written about political development. For while their writings do not fully exonerate Lee's and Mahathir's authoritarian tendencies, they do lead us along a path that makes sense of how their regimes have brought progress and stability, and, yes, robust military budgets, to Asia.

In his extended essay *On Liberty,* published in 1859, the English philosopher John Stuart Mill famously declares, "That the only purpose for which power can be rightfully exercised over any member of a civilized community, against his will, is to prevent harm to others."[22] Mill's irreducible refutation of tyranny leads him to—I have always felt—one of the most moving passages in literature, in which he extols the moral virtues of Marcus Aurelius, only to register the Roman's supreme flaw. Mill writes,

> If ever anyone possessed of power had grounds for thinking himself the best and most enlightened among his contemporaries, it was the Emperor Marcus Aurelius. Absolute monarch of the whole civilized world, he preserved through life not only the most unblemished justice, but what was less to be expected from his Stoical breeding, the tenderest heart. The few failings which are attributed to him were all on the side of indulgence, while his writings, the highest ethical product of the ancient mind, differ scarcely perceptibly, if they differ at all, from the most characteristic teachings of Christ.[23]

And yet, as Mill laments, this "unfettered intellect," this exemplar of humanism by the standards of the second century AD, persecuted Christians. As deplorable a state as society was in at the time, Marcus Aurelius assumed that what held it together and kept it from getting worse was the acceptance of the existing divinities, which the adherents of Christianity threatened to dissolve. He simply could not foresee a world knit together by new and better ties. "No Christian," Mill writes, "more firmly believes that atheism is false and tends to the dissolution of society than Marcus Aurelius believed the same things of Christianity."[24]

If even such a ruler as Marcus Aurelius could be so monumentally wrong, then no dictator, no matter how benevolent, can ever be trusted, it would seem. It follows, therefore, that the persecution of an idea or ideals for the sake of the existing order can never be justified. And if we can never know for certain if authority is in the right, even as anarchy must be averted, the only recourse for society should be to choose and periodically replace its forever imperfect leaders.

But for Mill, given the complexity of his thought, it is never so simple as that. While famous for his liberalism, Mill was keenly aware of the shortcomings of democracy. (Principal among his fears was that of the tyranny of the majority.) So indeed there is a catch. As Mill admits earlier in his essay, "Liberty, as a principle, has no application to any state of things anterior to the time when mankind have become capable of being improved by free and equal discussion. Until then, there is nothing . . . but implicit obedience to an Akbar or a Charlemagne, if they are so fortunate as to find one."[25] Mill knows that authority has first to be created before we can go about limiting it. "Order," he writes in *Considerations on Representative Government,* published in 1861, is a prerequisite of "Progress." He further explains: "Order means the preservation of peace by the cessation of private violence."[26]

For without authority, however dictatorial, there is a fearful void, as we all know too well from Iraq in 2006 and 2007. And Lee and Mahathir achieved order in their respective countries without nearly the level of repression practiced by Saddam Hussein. Indeed, to speak of the Iraqi strongman in the same breath as the Malaysian and Singaporean ones is itself a sacrilege.

In fact, no greater twentieth-century proponent of individual liberty than Isaiah Berlin himself observes in his introduction to *Four*

Essays on Liberty, "Men who live in conditions where there is not sufficient food, warmth, shelter, and the minimum degree of security can scarcely be expected to concern themselves with freedom of contract or of the press."[27] In "Two Concepts of Liberty," Berlin allows that "First things come first, there are situations . . . in which boots are superior to the works of Shakespeare; individual freedom is not everyone's primary need." Further complicating matters, Berlin notes, "there is no necessary connection between individual liberty and democratic rule." There might be a despot "who leaves his subjects a wide berth of liberty" but cares "little for order, or virtue, or knowledge."[28] Mill clarifies: in some cases a "civilized government . . . will require to be in a considerable degree despotic." For a people "may be unprepared for good institutions; but to kindle a desire for them is a necessary part of the preparation."[29] That is exactly what Lee and Mahathir did.

To be sure, just as there are good and bad popularly elected leaders, there are good and bad autocrats. And the South China Sea region has surely seen some good ones. When Lee Kuan Yew stepped down as prime minister in 1990, handing his job off to a chosen successor in his own party, he had been elected and reelected seven times, making him the longest-serving prime minister in the world. The democracy he had fostered was a limited one with a strong authoritarian streak. But it worked to prepare his people for something better.

The signal fact of the Middle East in the early years of the so-called Arab Spring was that, for the most part, it encompassed few of those subtleties and apparent contradictions that so define Asia. Middle Eastern societies had long since moved beyond basic needs of food and security to the point where individual freedom could be contemplated. After all, over the past half century, Arabs from the Maghreb to the Persian Gulf experienced epochal social, economic, technological, and demographic transformation; it was only the politics that had lagged behind. And while enlightened autocrats there were, the reigning model was sterile and decadent national security regimes, deeply corrupt and with sultanist tendencies, that sought to perpetuate their rule through offspring—sons who had not risen through the military or other bureaucracies, and thus had no legitimacy. Marcus Aurelius was one thing; Tunisia's Zine el-Abidine Ben Ali, Egypt's Hosni Mubarak, and Syria's Bashar al-Assad quite another. Certainly, the Arab Spring proved much: that there is no *otherness* to Arab and Muslim civilization, that Arabs yearn for universal values just as members of other civilizations do—something that I saw with Malaysian Muslims at the Kuala Lumpur mall. But as to difficult questions regarding the evolution of political order and democracy, the Arab Spring in its early phases actually proved very little. No good autocrats were overthrown. The regimes that had fallen had few saving graces in any larger moral or philosophical sense, and the wonder is that they lasted as long as they did, even as their tumultuous demise was sudden and unexpected at the time.

Yet the issues about which Mill and Berlin cared so passionately must still be addressed. Both men understood that such issues are not easy: though each favored representative government, their nuanced sensibilities stand in opposition to the self-righteous cries of some commentators in the West to topple all autocrats, right now, no matter the circumstances. For in some places in the Arab world, and particularly in Asia, there have been autocrats who can, in fact, be spoken of in the same breath as Marcus Aurelius. So at what point is it right or practical to get rid of these men? For as Berlin intimates, it is not inevitable that what will follow their rule will further the cause of individual liberty and well-being. Care must be taken. Absent relentless, large-scale human rights violations, soft landings for non-democratic regimes are always preferable to hard ones, even if the process takes some time. A moral argument can be made that monsters like Muammar Gaddafi in Libya and Kim Jong-il in North Korea should be overthrown any way they can, as fast as they can, regardless of the risk of short-term chaos.

But that argument quickly loses its appeal when one is dealing with dictators who are less noxious. And even when they are not less noxious, as in the case of Iraq's Saddam Hussein, the moral argument for their removal is still fraught with difficulty, since the worse the dictator, the worse the chaos left in his wake. That is because a bad dictator eviscerates intermediary institutions between the regime at the top and the extended family or tribe at the bottom—professional associations, community organizations, political groups, and so on—the very stuff of civil society. The good dictator, by fostering economic growth, among other things, makes society more complex, leading to more civil society groupings, and to political divisions based on economic interest that are by definition more benign than divisions of tribe and sectarian or ethnic group. A good dictator can be defined as one who makes his own removal less fraught with risk, by preparing his people for representative government. All this is exactly what Lee and Mahathir accomplished. Mill's exhortations in *Considerations on Representative Government* that "the first lesson of civilization" is "obedience," and that freedom "breaks down altogether" without "skilled administration," are the very lessons Lee Kuan Yew learned from the hard knocks of his early life.[30]

While one logical conclusion of Mill's essay is to deny the moral right of tyranny, his admission of the need for obedience to an Akbar or Charlemagne at primitive levels of social development leaves one with the question of where and when, exactly, is the transition point at which society should discard the autocrat. For the difference between the rule of even a wise and enlightened individual like the late-sixteenth-century Mughal Akbar the Great and a political circumstance in which one is only ever pressured against his will when it is a case of preventing direct and immediate harm to others is vast: so vast that Mill's proposition remains theoretical and may never be achieved, since even democratic governments must coerce their citizens for a variety of reasons. Nevertheless, certainly, the ruler who moves society to a more advanced stage of development is not only good, but perhaps the most necessary of historical actors—to the extent that history is determined by free-willed individuals as well as by larger geographical and economic forces. And the good autocrat, I submit, is not a contradiction in terms; rather, he stands at the center of the political questions that we face and will continue to face. The South China Sea region proves it.

Good autocrats there are actually quite a few. For example, in the Middle East, monarchy has found a way over the decades and centuries to engender a political legitimacy of its own, allowing leaders like King Mohammed VI in Morocco, King Abdullah II in Jordan, and Sultan Qaboos bin Said al-Said in Oman to grant their subjects a wide berth of individual freedom without fear of being toppled. Not only is relative freedom allowed, but extremist politics and ideologies are unnecessary in these countries. For it is only in the modernizing dictatorships such as Syria and Libya, which in historical and geographical terms are artificial constructions, and whose rulers are inherently illegitimate, where brute force and radicalism have been required to hold the state together.

It is true, Egypt's Mubarak and Tunisia's Ben Ali did not run police states on the terrifying scale of Libya's Gaddafi and Syria's Assad, even as their economic policies were more enlightened. But while Mubarak and Ben Ali left their countries in conditions suitable for the emergence of stable democracy, there is little virtue that can be attached to their rule. Their countries are stable and are not lacking in institutions for reasons that go back centuries: Egypt and Tunisia have been states in one form or another since antiquity. The economic liberalizations of recent years that Mubarak and Ben Ali engineered were haphazard rather than well planned. Moreover, they promoted a venal system of corruption built on personal access to their own ruling circles. And Mubarak, rather than move society forward toward democracy, sought to move it backward by installing his son in power. Mubarak and Ben Ali were dull men, enabled by goons in the security services. They, unlike Mahathir and Lee, are nothing in the sense of what Mill and Berlin had in mind. In fact, the real story in the Middle East beyond the toppling of these decrepit regimes is the possible emergence of authentic constitutional monarchies in places like Morocco and Oman. Here is where the Middle East begins to look like the South China Sea region.

Both Morocco and Oman, which lie at the two geographical extremities of the Arab world, have not been immune to demonstrations. But the demonstrators in both cases explicitly called for reform and democracy within the royal system, and have supported the leaders themselves. King Mohammed and Sultan Qaboos have both moved vigorously to get out in front of popular demands and reform their systems, rather than merely fire their cabinets. Indeed, over the years they have, in the style of Lee and Mahathir, championed women's rights, the environment, the large-scale building of schools, and other progressive causes. Qaboos, in particular, is sort of a Renaissance man who plays the lute and loves Western classical music, and who—at least until the celebrations in 2010 marking forty years of his rule—eschewed a personality cult.

But such rulers are rare in the Middle East. Truly, the place where benevolent autocracy has struck deep and systematic roots is Asia. Any discussion of whether and how democracy can be successfully implemented might, because of the current headlines, begin with the Middle East, but the answers such as there are, will, nevertheless, ultimately come in Asia. It is in places like China, Singapore, Malaysia, and Vietnam where good dictators have produced economic miracles that, in turn, have led to the creation of wide-ranging personal freedoms, even as these leaders have on a grand scale compelled people against their will. Aristotle speaks of a regime "midway" between oligarchy and democracy, even as he calls democracy the most "moderate" kind of regime, toward which one should strive.[31] Lee and Mahathir may have governed in the spirit of Aristotle, with their mixed regimes that prepared the way to democratic rule.

The ideology by which Asian autocrats both challenge and support the likes of Mill and Berlin goes vaguely under the rubric of Confucianism. Confucianism is more a sensibility than a political doctrine. Even Mahathir, with all of his Islamic pretensions, absorbed elements of it. Confucianism stresses traditional authority, particularly that of the family, as the sine qua non of political tranquillity.

The well-being of the community takes precedence over that of the individual. Morality is inseparable from one's social obligation to the kin group and the powers that be. The Western—and particularly the American—tendency is to be suspicious of power and central authority; whereas the Asian tendency is to worry about disorder. Thus, it is in Asia, much more so than in the Middle East, where autocracy can give the Western notion of freedom a good run for its money. The fact that even a chaotic democracy is better than the rule of a Gaddafi or an Assad proves nothing. But is a chaotic Middle Eastern democracy better than the rule of Chinese, Singaporean, Malaysian, and Vietnamese autocrats who have overseen growth rates in GDP of 10 percent annually for significant periods over the past three decades? Here the debate gets interesting.

Indeed, as I indicated at the start of this chapter, probably one of the most morally vexing realizations in the field of international politics is that Deng Xiaoping, by dramatically raising the living standard of hundreds of millions of Chinese in such a comparatively short space of time—which, likewise, led to an unforeseen explosion in personal (if not political) freedoms across China—was, despite the atrocity of Tiananmen Square that he helped perpetrate, one of the great men of the twentieth century. Deng's successors in Beijing, as repressive of political rights as they have been, have hewn to his grand strategy of seeking natural resources anywhere in the world they can find them, caring not with which despots they do business, in order to continue to raise the living standards of their people. These Chinese autocrats govern in a collegial fashion, number many an engineer and technocrat among them: this is all a far cry from the king of Saudi Arabia and the deposed leader of Egypt, sleepy octogenarians both, whose skills for creating modern middle-class societies are for the most part nonexistent.

Lee Kuan Yew in particular holds out the possibility, heretical to an enlightened Western mind, that democracy may not be the last word in human political development. What he has engineered in Singapore is a hybrid regime: capitalistic it is, even as consultations between various factions are ongoing, but it all occurs in a quasi-authoritarian setting. Elections are held, but the results for decades were never in doubt. Only recently have Singaporeans expressed dissatisfaction at the polls with the ruling People's Action Party.

Of course, Singapore is a city-state with no hinterland. And it is a hinterland—continental in size as in the case of China—that produces vastly different local conditions with which a central authority must grapple. And such grappling puts pressure on a regime to grant more rights to its far-flung subjects; or, that being resisted, to become by degrees more authoritarian. Lee never had to face this challenge. So Singapore will remain an oddity. Elsewhere in Asia, political Confucianism is messier.

Here is the dilemma. Yes, a social contract of sorts exists between these peoples and their regimes: in return for impressive economic growth rates the people agree to forgo their desire to replace their leaders. But as growth rates continue unabated—to say nothing if they collapse or slow down as of late—this social contract must peter out. For as people become middle-class, they gain access to global culture and trends, which prompts a desire for political freedoms to go along with their personal ones. This is why authoritarian capitalism may be just a phase, rather than a viable alternative to Western democracy. Because Singapore is an oddity, we will have to wait until China's GDP growth slows down for years on end, or, failing that, continues, until enough Chinese have more access to global culture: only then can we begin to draw conclusions about whether democracy represents the final triumph of reason in politics.

"Progress includes Order," Mill writes, "but Order does not include Progress."[32] Middle Eastern despots too often supplied only Order; Asian ones brought Progress, too. Leo Strauss, University of Chicago political philosopher of the mid-twentieth century, in his analysis of Xenophon's *Hiero or Tyrannicus,* writes that the tyrant knows all men are his enemies, that the tyrant is deprived of true honor, and that the tyrant cannot abdicate for fear of punishment.[33] Whereas that description fits Middle Eastern despots, it fails in the case of Lee and Mahathir—for whom the population was not hostile and for whom leaving office brought few risks. But Mill also notes that even the best despotisms are only good if they are temporary. Thus, the political future of South China Sea societies will write the final legacies for their generation of enlightened autocrats. If Singapore and Malaysia truly evolve into stable democracies, where the historic governing parties easily cede power to democratic oppositions, then that will signal the final triumph of Mahathir bin Mohamad and Lee Kuan Yew.

CHAPTER VI

America's Colonial Burden

Whenever I think of the Philippines my eyes revert to *The Manila Shawl* by Henri Matisse, painted in 1911 upon the French artist's return from a two-month trip to Spain. Matisse had purchased the shawl in Seville, and draped it around a model whom he depicted in the pose of a flamenco *bailaora*. The embroidered silk shawls were a popular treasure brought to Europe by Spanish galleons sailing from the Philippines across the Pacific to New Spain (Mexico), from where the shawls were shipped to Spain itself. Showy, garish, with glittering splashes of red, orange, and green oil paint in floral designs, Matisse's *Shawl* is the image I associate with the tropical grandeur and sensuality of the Philippine Islands, and with their occupation by Spain, by way of Mexico, for nearly three and a half centuries beginning in 1556.

For the Philippines are not only burdened with hundreds of years of Spanish colonialism, which, with its heavy, pre-Reformation

Roman Catholic overtones, brought less dynamism than the British, Dutch, and Japanese varieties experienced elsewhere in the First Island Chain, but they are doubly burdened by the imprint of Mexican colonizers, who represented an even lower standard of modern institutional consciousness than those from Spain.

Hence the shock the visitor experiences upon arrival here after traveling elsewhere in East Asia: a shock that has never dissipated for me after four lengthy trips to the Philippines within a decade. Instead of gleaming, stage-lit boulevards with cutting-edge twenty-first-century architecture that is the fare of Malaysia, Singapore, Taiwan, and coastal China (not to mention Japan and South Korea); and instead of the beehive pace of human activity evident in Vietnam, whose French Catholic colonizers stayed for less than a hundred years (even as they brought education and development in their wake), the cityscape of the Philippine capital of Manila is, by comparison, one of aesthetic and material devastation.

Bad roads, immense puddles of rainwater because of poor drainage, beggars at stop lights, neon nightclub signs with letters missing, crummy buildings with the look of broken crates bearing no architectural style and none matching with any other, old air-conditioning units sticking out of this and that window like black eyes, jumbles of electric wires crisscrossing the twisted palm trees: these are the visual facts that impress one upon arrival. Amidst the sparkling, watery sunlight diffused through the mist and monsoon clouds there is a near-total lack of an identifying aesthetic. Whether it is the chrome jeepneys with their comic book designs or the weather-stained building facades with their occasional garish colors, there is an amateurish, just-put-together feel to many a surface, as if this entire cityscape—minus the old Spanish Quarter and the upscale malls—is held together by glue. Whereas Vietnamese cities (which have their own economic problems) are frenetic, Manila, despite the dense crowds, is somnolent and purposeless by comparison. Weeds and crumbling cement dominate. The sprawl beyond downtown is not that of suburban houses but of slums with blackened, sheet-metal roofs and peaks of garbage.

Private security guards, whose epaulets and insignias remind me of those in Mexico, guard five-star hotel lobbies and fast food restaurants with sniffer dogs and sawed-off shotguns. The interiors of government buildings are rendered bleak by the dead light of fluorescent tubes. Of course, there is the large and consequential splatter of up-to-date, middle-class shopping centers and chain restaurants. But what becomes apparent after several days is that despite what the guidebooks claim, there really isn't any distinctive Filipino cuisine beyond fish, pork, and indifferently cooked rice. This is a borrowed culture, without the residue of civilizational richness that is apparent at the archaeological sites in places like Vietnam and Indonesia, to say nothing of China or India. And of course, in such a culture, prominent are the luxury, gated communities, inside which the wealthy can escape the dysfunctional environment through life-support systems.

Asian dynamism, born in the 1970s, is something so palpable that it is felt in everything from Chinese and Taiwanese bullet trains, to the manic construction boom of Vietnam and Malaysia, to the perfectly pruned verges of the roads in Singapore. But by the end of the first decade of the twenty-first century, Asian dynamism had, at least so far, bypassed the Philippines.

"This is still a bad Latin American economy, not an Asian one," a Manila-based Western economist told me. "It's true that the Philippines was not much affected by the global recession of 2008, but that's only because it was never integrated into the global economy in the first place. What you have," he went on, is admittedly steady economic growth, lately over 6 percent per year, undermined by population growth of 1.7 percent, unlike other Pacific Rim economies that have churned ahead by almost a third higher that amount for decades, and without commensurate increases in population. Crucially, a "staggering" 76.5 percent of that GDP growth in recent years went to the forty richest Filipino families.[1] It's the old story, the Manila elite is getting rich at the expense of everyone else.

Whereas the Asian tiger economies have strong manufacturing bases, and are consequently built on export, in the Philippines exports account for only 25 percent of economic activity as opposed to the standard Asian model of 75 percent. And that 25 percent consists of low-value electronic components, bananas, and coconuts mainly. The economist pulled out a cheat sheet and rattled off statistics: the Philippines ranks 129 out of 182 countries, according to Transparency International, making it the most corrupt major Asian economy, more corrupt than Indonesia even; according to the World Bank's ease-of-doing-business indicator, the Philippines ranked 136 out of 183; in every list and in every category, the Philippines—with the world's twelfth largest population—was the worst of the large Asian economies.

No one can deny the situation is improving. The World Economic Forum in Switzerland recently moved the Philippines to the top half of its rankings on global competitiveness.[2] Nevertheless, corruption, restrictions on foreign ownership, and endless paperwork make the Philippines the most hostile country in maritime Asia for the foreign investor. No country in Asia, with the possible exceptions of Myanmar, Cambodia, and Indonesia, has weaker, more feckless institutions. The Philippines is where an objective, statistical reality is registered in the subjective first impressions of the traveler.

Perhaps no other large country in the world has seen such a political, military, and economic investment by the United States for decades on end. Perhaps nowhere else has it made so little difference.

America's entry into the Philippines began at dawn May 1, 1898, when Commodore George Dewey's nine ships, having passed Corregidor Island off the Bataan Peninsula under cover of darkness, entered Manila Bay and destroyed a larger Spanish flotilla. Like so many signal episodes in history, Dewey's victory was both the culmination of vast political and economic forces and an accident of circumstance that might easily have not occurred, for it was not instigated by events in the Pacific at all, but by those in the Caribbean, where Spain's repression of Cuba led President William McKinley—urged on by expansionists including assistant secretary of the navy Theodore Roosevelt—to declare war on the Spanish Empire.

The invasion of the Philippines marked the first time that the United States had deliberately set out to conquer a large piece of territory overseas and ended up occupying it. That would not happen again until the invasion of Iraq more than a century later. Though it began with Commodore Dewey's glorious overture, the first major conflict for the United States outside its continental limits descended within a few months into a military nightmare, as well as a domestic trauma of a kind not to be seen again until Vietnam.[3]

Following Dewey's successful entry into Manila Bay, the American military assisted Filipino insurgents in their takeover of the Spanish-run archipelago. But just as they would in Iraq and elsewhere, the Americans wrongly assumed that because local elements welcomed the ouster of a despotic regime, they would automatically remain friendly once the regime was toppled. After the Spanish were defeated, tensions mounted between the new Philippine government headed by a young ethnic Tagalog, Emilio Aguinaldo, and the American liberators, even as Aguinaldo was losing control over his own faction-ridden forces. By February 1899, Philippine anarchy and misplaced American idealism ignited into a full-scale war between American troops and a host of indigenous guerrilla armies.[4]

On July 4, 1902, when President Roosevelt proclaimed the Philippine War over, 4,234 American soldiers had been killed in the conflict and 2,818 wounded.[5] Overall, 200,000 people died, mainly Filipino civilians.[6] Fighting in the Muslim south of the Philippines would go on for years. One could well argue that it was all unnecessary in the first place, a political blunder of the first magnitude by the McKinley administration, in which America's idealism and naïveté led it on a path of destruction and brutality.[7]

The military victory, however messy and brutal, was followed by decades of American rule that the journalist and historian Stanley Karnow calls a "model of enlightenment" compared to European colonialism.[8] Samuel Tan, a Filipino historian who is critical of American policy in other respects, concurs, describing American rule as the historical engine that brought a modicum of modernity to the Filipino masses.[9]

The Americans forbade themselves to buy large tracts of land. They avoided schemes like opium monopolies. They redistributed land to peasants from wealthy church estates, and built roads, railways, ports, dams, and irrigation facilities. American expenditures on health and education led to a doubling of the Filipino population between 1900 and 1920, and a rise in literacy from 20 to 50 percent within a generation.[10]

The Philippines, in turn, affected the destiny of twentieth-century America to a degree that few faraway countries have. Ohio judge William Howard Taft's leadership of the Philippine Commission propelled him to the presidency of the United States. Army Captain John "Black Jack" Pershing, who would head the expedition against Pancho Villa in Mexico and command American forces in World War I, was promoted to brigadier general over nine hundred other officers after his stellar performance in leading troops against Islamic insurgents in the southern Philippines. Douglas MacArthur, son of Army General Arthur MacArthur, came to the Philippines to command an American brigade and returned for a second tour of duty as the indigenous government's military advisor. One of Douglas MacArthur's aides in Manila was a middle-aged major, Dwight D. Eisenhower, who honed his analytical skills for World War II by attempting to organize a Philippine national army. The Japanese victory over General Douglas MacArthur's forces on the Philippines, MacArthur's last stand on Corregidor in Manila Bay before retreating to Australia, the subsequent Japanese atrocities committed against both American and Filipino prisoners of war during the Death March on the nearby Bataan Peninsula, and MacArthur's triumphal return to the Philippines in the battle of Leyte Gulf, all became part of the Homeric legend of World War II that bound Americans to their military, and gave the American and Filipino peoples a common historical inheritance.[11]

This is to say nothing of the deep involvement of American policymakers in supporting Philippine governments with aid and advice ever since World War II, especially the critical role the Americans played in ushering dictator Ferdinand Marcos peacefully from power in 1986. And it wasn't just grappling with Marcos's dictatorship that engaged American officers and diplomats from the 1960s to the 1980s: for there was, too, the task of supporting Manila against communist and Islamic insurrections right up through the present.

Indeed, anyone who doubts that America is, or was, an imperial power should come to the Philippines, where the white baronial U.S. embassy fronting Manila Bay occupies the most beautiful downtown real estate in the same way that British and French high commissions and embassies do in their former colonies; where the Americans have their own hill station for cool weather retreats, like British hill stations in India; where leading local military officers, businessmen, and politicians are graduates of West Point just like the leading personages of former British colonies have been graduates of Sandhurst; and where the country's romantic hero is not a Filipino but the protean figure of Douglas MacArthur, who in the Filipino mind rescued the country from the butchery of the Japanese occupiers.[12]

Imagine Iraq, nine decades hence, if the United States were still deeply involved with the problems there as a reigning outside power. That would be the Philippines. The Philippines was for much of the twentieth century an American colony in all but name, whose pro-American defense and foreign policy has been taken for granted for too long.

Given this legacy, arguably the fate of the Philippines, and whether it eventually becomes Finlandized by China, may say more about America's trajectory as a great power than the fate of Iraq and whether it continues under the sway of Iran. Make no mistake, the Philippines is crucial: it dominates the eastern edge of the South China Sea as much as Vietnam does the western edge and China the northern one. With a population of nearly 100 million, the Philippines is more populous than Vietnam even.

And yet, despite a century's worth of vast annual outlays of American aid, the Philippines has remained among the most corrupt, dysfunctional, intractable, and poverty-stricken societies in maritime Asia, with Africa-like slums and Latin America–style fatalism and class divides. Indeed, the Philippines has been described as a "gam-

bling republic" where politicians "hold power without virtue," dominating by means of "capital" and "crime."[13]

The early-twenty-first-century Philippines, as corrupt as it is, constitutes to a significant degree the legacy of one man, Ferdinand Marcos,
who manifestly represents the inverse of Lee Kuan Yew, and to a lesser
extent the inverse of Mahathir bin Mohamad and Chiang Kai-shek.
Whereas those other men left behind functioning states with largely
clean institutions, primed to become well-functioning democracies,
Marcos left behind bribery, cronyism, and ruin. Marcos and the Philippines, unlike Singapore, Taiwan, and to a smaller extent Malaysia,
were not at all enriched by Confucian values. While those other men
complexify the thinking of the great political philosophers by showing
how restricted authoritarianism in some cases can lead to political
virtue, Marcos represents the greater majority of cases in which authoritarianism leads, well, to crime and political decay. The other three
men were each extraordinary in their own right, whose early life made
them especially attuned to unpleasant truths about their own societies
that needed correcting. They pierced the miasma of convenient ratio-
nalizations to always see the harsh reality that confronted them: especially so in Lee's and Mahathir's cases, less so in Chiang's. That was
their particular genius; whereas Marcos's world became one of self-
delusion. Lee and Mahathir were efficient, corporate-style managers;
Chiang strived for that in his latter years in Taiwan. But Marcos stood
all of that on its head. Listen to arguably America's greatest journalist-
historian of late-twentieth-century Southeast Asia, Stanley Karnow:

> Isolated in his airless palace, Marcos ultimately lost touch with
> reality. His corrupt administration was totally discredited by
> 1985, yet his blind belief in his own invincibility prompted him
> to schedule the election . . . that spelled his doom. . . . He crum-
> bled under the sheer weight of his flagrant mismanagement and
> venality, which bankrupted the country. Emulating the legend-
> ary Khmer rulers, whose sculpted heads peer down from the
> temples of Angkor, he had his bust carved into a hillside of

central Luzon. He contrived a cavalcade of noble, warrior, peasant, artistic, colonial and nationalist ancestors, as if their collective spirit resided in him.[14]

Marcos and his wife, Imelda, did not steal hundreds of millions of dollars during their more than two decades in power: they stole literally billions. Cultural genius is when a leader isolates the strongest attributes of a given culture in order to raise society to a higher level. Lee did this with overseas Chinese culture; Mahathir did it with Malay culture merging it as he did with the disciplinary attributes of global Islam. But Marcos represented the worst of Spain's legacy of absolutism, fatalism, and the pre-Reformation, and thus he did nothing revelatory or interesting with the Philippines, except postpone the day when it might, too, become an Asian tiger.

And yet Marcos is no longer universally hated here, given the directionless malaise of the post-Marcos era. "During the early years of the Marcos dictatorship we dreamed big," one of the country's leading lawyers told me. "Marcos had a real chance to change the culture, there were possibilities. But his sense of power was Javanese: he believed power inhered in his physical person. This was not the Machiavellian sense of power, where virtue is not about charisma, but about deeds and tough choices." Ever since Marcos, this lawyer went on, "our democracy has merely democratized corruption. There is no Confucianism" that accounts for the strong, self-regulating societies of much of East Asia; nor is there the "Islamic discipline" that helps the rest of the Malay peoples in Malaysia and Indonesia. "We are an easygoing culture: we don't embarrass one another; rather than punish we accommodate and look the other way. This is our tragedy." And it is this lack of discipline, so I was told by a group of Filipino journalists, that makes them skeptical about their country's ability to sustain a strong and united front against China.

Such cultural characteristics certainly can change, and they can change dramatically. But it requires the maintenance of good policies, which, in turn, requires exceptional leadership.

———

Beyond Marcos, the Philippines' central dilemma is geographical. Prior to the arrival of Spanish explorer Ferdinand Magellan on the island of Cebu in 1521, the Philippine archipelago did not exist as a coherent political entity. The contrast with a country like Vietnam, whose sense of nationhood goes back millennia, could not be more stark. The Philippine archipelago roughly consists of three island groups that had little in common prior to Magellan's arrival. Luzon in the north is inhabited primarily by Tagalog speakers whose roots go back to Southeast Asia. In the south is Mindanao and the Sulu archipelago, occupied by Muslim Moros who have much more in common culturally and ethnically with the peoples of Malaysia and Indonesia than they do with those of Luzon. This has led to Islamic terrorism and insurgency, met in turn by a counterinsurgency campaign mounted with direct help from the United States. Luzon in the north and Mindanao in the south are tenuously connected by a far-flung island group, the Visayas, which includes Cebu. Securing these 22,000 miles of coastline, beset with internal threats that are, in turn, a product of its ethnic and religious diversity, makes the Philippines particularly vulnerable to penetration by an outside power like China. The Philippines is less a country than a ramshackle empire ruled from Luzon. Indeed, the fact that despite being an archipelagic nation, the Philippine army is three times the size of its navy in manpower, proves just how internally insecure this country really is. Thus, ultimately because of geography, the Philippines has no choice now but to seek the patronage of the United States against China.[15]

It is true that the Philippines closed America's Subic Bay Naval Station in 1992, with Clark Airfield (also on Luzon) closing the same year. But that was before China's naval power became truly demonstrable. Only two years later, China would move to occupy Philippine-controlled reefs in the Spratlys, and from the mid-1990s forward China would undergo a vast expansion of its air and sea forces, accompanied by a more aggressive posture in the South China Sea. China's increasing geopolitical sway over Manila is helped by the fact that China is the Philippines' third largest trading partner. There is also the extreme wealth and influence of China's émigré community in the Philippines.

In fact, the Philippines' prickly nationalism in response to China's military rise is in other ways, too, an expression of its geographic vulnerability. The sea is the country's economic lifeline for everything from fishing to energy exploration. The Philippines imports all of its oil by sea, even as all of its natural gas supplies come from an off-shore field near Manila Bay. Therefore, the potential loss of access to new hydrocarbon reserves in areas of the South China Sea like the Spratlys and Scarborough Shoal, as well as the loss of access to existing fisheries, due to a shift in the maritime balance of power, constitutes a national security nightmare for Manila.[16]

The vulnerability of a near-failed state under China's lowering gaze was at the time of my visit being exploited by Washington in order to resurrect in different form the strategic platform the Americans had here on the eastern edge of the South China Sea for almost a century from 1899 through the end of the Cold War.

My most recent visit to the Philippines in the summer of 2012 came during a period of naval tension in the South China Sea that in the world news was overshadowed only by the civil war in Syria and the European debt crisis. Indeed, the impasse between Philippine and Chinese ships beginning in the spring of 2012 at Scarborough Shoal, 120 miles west of Luzon, demonstrated the "small-stick" self-confidence of China in dealing with a weak and pathetic adversary in the Philippines.[17] Rather than send actual warships, Beijing dispatched over several weeks more than twenty lightly and un-armed maritime enforcement vessels, equivalent to coast guard ships, to the scene. China had thus signaled that it viewed sea power as a "continuum" constituting a range of options, for even merchantmen and fishing boats can lay mines and monitor foreign warships. (In fact, China, as Naval War College professors James Holmes and Toshi Yoshihara maintain, is turning out state-of-the-art coast guard cutters "like sausages," and its nonmilitary maritime enforcement services are taking delivery of decommissioned naval vessels.) Using vessels at the soft end of the continuum reinforced Beijing's message that it was merely policing waters it already owned, rather than claiming new ones in competition with other navies. And no one should be in any doubt that Beijing had the ability to quickly ramp up its sea power in the vicinity. Facing off against China's nonmilitary ships was the pride of the Philippine navy, a 1960s hand-me-down from the U.S. Coast Guard, renamed the *Gregorio del Pilar*.[18] The very mismatch was poignant, the signature of China's growing might and the abject failure that was the modern Philippine state, whose lack of naval capacity was an outcome of its own social and economic failure. Certainly, what sparked the intense, emotional reaction among Filipinos against China was the knowledge that written into Chinese naval behavior at Scarborough Shoal was a large dose of condescension, something that was deeply humiliating.

The Scarborough Shoal affair made it obvious to the Filipinos—if it wasn't obvious by then—that they needed a substantial military alliance with the United States. This would be in keeping with over a century of recent history, but was new considering the estrangement of the two countries during the post–Cold War. Just as the U.S. Navy had left Cam Ranh Bay in Vietnam under humiliating circumstances in the 1970s and was now being invited back, the U.S. Navy had left Subic Bay in Luzon in the early 1990s and was now being invited back. "The only leverage we have is the alliance with the United States, and that alliance itself is asymmetrical to the Americans' advantage," remarked Professor Aileen Baviera of the University of the Philippines. Other countries in the region were coming to a similar conclusion.

From the Americans' point of view, the current Philippine president, Benigno Simeon Aquino III, constituted a window of opportunity. He was the son of Benigno Simeon Aquino Jr., the popular politician whose assassination in 1983 had sparked the revolt against Marcos. Unlike the other Filipino presidents since Marcos's ouster, the younger Aquino was seen as neither corrupt nor ineffectual. Aquino was a nationalist who wanted to root out corruption and alleviate poverty through oil and gas revenues in the South China Sea. *Good luck with that,* you might say. Nevertheless, U.S. officials felt they had to exploit his tenure, for *who knew what kind of crook might replace him.* "Let's institutionalize a new relationship while he's still in power," one American official told me.

The American military, despite the closings of the Cold War legacy bases at Clark and Subic, had in fact already intensified its relationship with the armed forces of the Philippines following 9/11. Because the Sulu archipelago in the southern Philippines was a lair of Islamic terror networks loosely affiliated with al Qaeda, several hundred American Special Operations Forces deployed there and in southern Mindanao in 2002, executing a counterinsurgency strategy that over a few years reduced Jemaah Islamiyah and Abu Sayyaf to low-end criminal irritants. The challenge then became getting a weak and corrupt Roman Catholic government to the north in Manila (that is, in Luzon) to channel development assistance to its often forgotten Muslim extremities close to Borneo. This lack of Philippine government will and capacity was also behind the longtime, chronic insurgencies of the Moro Islamic Liberation Front in southern Mindanao and the Communist New People's Army in other parts of the mountainous archipelago. But with the Sulu island chain still politically and militarily fragile, even as the number of American special operators was being reduced from six hundred to 350 and the number of transnational terrorists classified as high-value targets diminished to a handful, Washington now had to convince the Philippine government to reposition its military from being an inward-looking land force to one focusing on external "maritime domain awareness," in order to counter China. "The insurgencies took up 90 percent of our defense efforts for many years, and they are still not over," said Raymund Jose Quilop, the assistant secretary for strategic assessment in Manila.

With so much focus on land forces, in terms of air and sea forces there was now very little to work with. For example, again, given that air power cannot be disaggregated from sea power, the Philippines had one or two C-130 transport planes that could actually fly, and

maybe seven OV-10s, a close air support platform that was truly ancient. Maybe the Filipinos had four fighter jets that were operational.
The Philippines was at a "starter-kit" level in American military eyes.
Moreover, the Americans could not transfer reasonably up-to-date
defense technology to Manila because there was no cyber or operational security to speak of here. Thus, the buzzword among American
military experts for the Philippines had become "minimum-credible-
defense." As one American officer put it to me: "They don't need to
go toe-to-toe with China. The Filipinos merely need a dog and a fence
in their front yard so the Chinese will hesitate before trespassing on
them." When the Americans rushed the decommissioned 1960s U.S.
Coast Guard cutter to be converted to the pride of the Philippine
navy, much of the world laughed. But the Americans were dead serious. As one told me: "We just raised the Filipinos from a World War
II navy to a 1960s one. That's progress." The Americans had thought
of selling the Filipinos a late-1980s frigate, but with a turbine engine
it was judged to be too complex for them to maintain. Thus, Washington was encouraging Manila to invest in less sophisticated frigates
from Italy, and in small patrol boats from Japan (which the Filipinos
have received). Modern navies and air forces, because of the technological mastery, security precautions, and sheer expense required, are
litmus tests for the level of development of national cultures, and the
level reached by the Philippines was low. And yet the government in
Manila was serious about changing that record, as witnessed by an
additional $1.8 billion it recently targeted for defense: a significant
amount in a country that size.

And so the Americans were augmenting the modest improvements
in Philippine naval capacity with the visit to Subic and other Filipino
ports of one hundred U.S. warships and naval supply ships per year,
including submarines. The Philippines, for its part, was upgrading
harbor repair facilities so as to encourage even more American naval
visits. Moreover, the chairman of the American Joint Chiefs of Staff,
the American Pacific Fleet commander, the commander of Pacific
Command, and of the Marine Forces/Pacific were all traveling out
from Washington and Honolulu to Manila on official visits. On the

civilian side, a slew of deputy cabinet secretaries were also passing through Manila from Washington. The idea was to give the Philippines enough political and military cover so as, in the words of one American official, to prevent the Philippines from becoming to China what Ethiopia was to Italy in 1936: ripe for violation. Subic Bay, like Cam Ranh Bay in Vietnam, was not about to become a full-fledged American base again; rather, the Americans envisioned a regular "rotational" presence of their naval forces through Philippine (and Vietnamese) ports. Meanwhile, there was talk of dredging Ulugan Bay on the western Philippine island of Palawan—fronting the South China Sea and close to the Spratlys—as a future naval base.

Nevertheless, China showed few signs of backing down. During one of my visits the Chinese actually announced plans to build a one-mile runway on Subi Reef, only a few miles from Philippine-controlled features in the vicinity of the Spratlys, even though Subi was underwater during high tide. The truth was, that pushing the Philippines around served a purpose in nationalistic circles in Beijing that pushing Vietnam around just didn't. Hating Vietnam was a default emotion inside China and therefore did not advance any Chinese official's or military officer's nationalistic bona fides; whereas, because the Philippines was a formal treaty ally of the United States, bullying the Philippines telegraphed that China was pushing back at the United States. And this was easy to do because of the Philippine military's own lack of capacity. By fortifying the bilateral military relationship with Manila, Washington was upping the ante—that is, intensifying the struggle with China.

All of these hard, difficult-to-admit truths constituted the background to my conversations at the Foreign Ministry in Manila, where, amid loud and uncertain air-conditioning, grim fluorescent lighting, and mellow accents of Filipino officials wearing pressed white barongs, I heard arguments that were realistic and defiant, even as they demonstrated weakness. The law protects the weak by being impartial, but the international system was Hobbesian in the sense that there was no Leviathan to punish the Unjust; and thus international law was at the moment secondary to geopolitical realities. The Filipino officials I interviewed understood all this.

"The real issue here is the creeping expansion of Chinese naval power," began Henry P. Bensurto Jr., secretary-general of the commission on maritime affairs, as he outlined for me all the activities of the Chinese on the various reefs and atolls in the greater Spratlys close to the Philippine mainland. The Chinese, he said, were probing, placing buoys, and planning to garrison any speck of dry land they could find in what he called the "West Philippine Sea." Names such as Woody Island, Reed Bank, Douglas Bank, Sabina Shoal, and Bajo de Masinloc (Scarborough Shoal) peppered his speech. "China," he went on, "will continue to raise tension, then reduce it through diplomacy, then raise it again, so that at the end of the day they will have eaten all of your arm: they want joint development in places where their claims are absolutely baseless." Near the end of his PowerPoint presentation, he said, "The more militarily capable China becomes, the less flexible it will be." Whereas the Philippines was strategic in the eyes of both America and China, from the vantage point of his own country, geography was a nightmare. The Philippines had 7,100 islands to protect within its archipelago, where 70 percent of the towns were close to the coast. The sea was everything, and the South China Sea was coveted by China the way "the Black Sea is coveted by Russia." Technology was not going to help: because of the cost of air transport, tens of thousands of ships were going to continue to pass into the "West Philippine Sea [South China Sea]" in decades to come, making this body of water nervous with warships and war gaming. He concluded with an appeal to international law—the ultimate demonstration of weakness.

Gilberto G. B. Asuque, assistant secretary for ocean concerns, was more blunt: "It's our continental shelf, and they want our oil and gas, it's that simple. We have to show the world that China cannot put everything in its pocket." Behind this emotional talk, uncharacteristic for diplomats, lay a severe vulnerability. The Philippines had little oil and gas of its own. It had dug 263 wells over the past thirty years, while Malaysia and Indonesia had dug four hundred wells each every year. Exxon had given up its rights in the Sulu Sea because there was insufficient hydrocarbons there. The gas field near Manila Bay was relatively small. In 2011 the Philippines launched fifteen energy exploration blocks forty miles west of Palawan—that is, 575 miles southeast of China and 450 miles east of Vietnam. Yet all these blocks fell within China's nine-dashed line, and China was claiming two of the fifteen blocks as its own already. "We're almost 100 million people and our energy reserves are under-explored and contested," one official complained.

Undersecretary Edilberto P. Adan, the executive director of the presidential commission on visiting forces agreements, spoke softly and sadly about the deterioration of American-Philippine military relations during recent decades, and what it had cost the Philippines. In the days when Clark and Subic were permanent American bases, he said, the Philippines received $200 million annually in military assistance from Washington. After the bases were closed, the figure went down to "zero." In the mid-1990s, when China began its "creeping incursions" into the South China Sea, the result by 1999 was a new status of forces agreement that awarded the Philippine military $35 million in annual aid from Washington. "We wish for a deeper defense relationship with the United States, and have put $1.5 billion towards our own military budget, though that is much less than the cost of just one of your submarines." He mentioned that during my visit the Philippines approved a status of forces agreement with Australia: a major development, as it showed Manila was now willing to allow forces from another Pacific country to regularly rotate through its territory. Again, it was all about China. "Since 1995 when the Chinese occupied Mischief Reef, their intentions have not changed: only now they have the muscle to back it up.[19] We need," he went on, "U.S. naval assets here to replenish, refuel, and to loiter in our waters. The model is Singapore [and Vietnam]: if you build facilities for the Americans, they will come." He noted that despite the country's dysfunction, nationalism ran deep here: the Filipinos had fought the United States in a bitter irregular war at the turn of the twentieth century, and then fought equally as hard alongside the United States against Japanese occupiers in World War II.

With China finally emerging after nearly two centuries of domestic turmoil and pushing outward into maritime Asia, the Philippines needed to draw the Americans in once again, it seemed. There was a school of thought among local officials here—both civilian and military—that believed naval brinkmanship on the Philippines' part would force Washington into a more confrontational stance toward Beijing to the strategic benefit of Manila. But the Obama administration in 2012 warned Manila specifically against that approach. Certainly, it was not in the American interest for China to dominate the South China Sea. But neither was it in the American interest, given its many financial and other equities with Beijing, to be dragged into a conflict with China because of the hot-blooded, combustible nationalisms of countries like the Philippines and Vietnam. Former chief of staff General Benjamin Defensor, told me that for this very reason, "the United States would not come to our aid" beyond a certain point. The Philippines was better off employing restraint and an appeal to world opinion, he and others said, if only because the new threat from China did not erase the internal security challenges Manila continued to face, particularly in the Muslim south of the country.

It was clear to me that Philippine defense and security officials felt besieged: besieged by China; besieged by the various, low-level internal rebellions in the country; and in a larger, albeit vaguer sense, by the country's own cultural intractability.

In fact, such intractability extended to the highest political echelons. As Carolina G. Hernandez, a political scientist at the University of the Philippines, told me: "There have been very few leaders in the Philippines who have thought strategically. Democracy with its single, six-year presidential terms has not helped. Our leaders simply cannot think beyond that time frame. Colonialism [by the Americans]," she continued, "because it creates dependency, also inhibits strategic thinking. Frankly, we have no external defense capability.

Between the defeat of the [communist] Huk insurgents in the early 1950s and the rise of the [communist] New People's Army in the late 1960s, there was a space for us to build up a credible defense. But it was not done."

So after 115 years, the American experience with the Philippines still encompassed the same dreary challenge: how to stabilize and prepare to defend a vast and teeming country that can barely look after itself.

That challenge presented itself to me in vivid terms during my visit to Puerto Princesa, the main city of Palawan: the long and thin, spear-shaped island in the western Philippines that juts out into the South China Sea, close to the Spratlys. The Spratlys were named in 1843, after Richard Spratly, the master of the British whaler, *Cyrus South Seaman,* between 1836 and 1844. But the Filipinos call the island group "Freedomland," or Kalayaan, the name given to these atolls and other features by the Philippine adventurer and fishing magnate Tomás Cloma in 1956, after he and several dozen of his men took possession of them. Although Kalayaan is by and large uninhabitable and difficult to reach, there is a mayor of Kalayaan, Eugenio Bito-onon, whose office is in Puerto Princesa.

Puerto Princesa is an overgrown village: a winding rash of corrugated iron stalls offering everything from fruit to auto parts that constitutes a break in a thick pelt of broccoli-dark greenery—dominated by coconut palms, banana leaves, and flowering trees—soaked from heavy rains during many months of the year. The mayor's office lay behind one of the markets in a ratty building with an iron grille. His small office was full of flowcharts relating to provisions needed for the hundred or so inhabitants of Pagasa, or Thitu Island, the largest feature in the Spratlys. Pagasa boasts a runway just short of a mile in length that juts out beyond the island on land reclaimed by Japanese occupiers during World War II. The mayor resides in Puerto Princesa because Pagasa is cut off by monsoons and typhoons for periods of weeks and months. Moreover, as he told me, the runway is potholed and it can take days in heavy seas in the small boats he had available to reach the island.

The mayor drove me through the forest on muddy roads to the headquarters of the Philippine military's Western Command, located by mangrove swamps at the edge of the Sulu Sea. Like military bases throughout the developing world, this one was far neater and cleaner than almost any other habitation in the area, with well-maintained, straight rows of palm trees, and spare offices filled, like the mayor's, with stacks of seemingly organized paperwork.

"We need all-weather aircraft from the States," a Filipino officer remarked as soon as I entered one office. He was talking to an American naval lieutenant junior grade from Gulfport, Mississippi, who was there helping to arrange a marine exercise between the two countries a few months hence. I was immediately brought in to see Philippine Marine Lieutenant General Juancho Sabban, the commander of Western Command. He told me that not only were communications difficult with the very island group his forces had to defend, but the surrounding seas were in many areas uncharted, which meant captains were essentially sailing blind. This may have led to a Chinese navy frigate running aground on Hasa-Hasa Shoal only sixty miles west of southern Palawan just before my visit. "The bad weather, the primitive conditions, give us a comparative advantage over the Chinese, who in these waters cannot use their superior naval assets effectively." In a subsequent brief, he and other officers ticked a long list of Chinese territorial violations "on Kalayaan in the West Philippine Sea": three fighter jets crossing into Philippine airspace here, a navy ship illegally spotted there. The pattern, they told me, was of an increasing frequency of violations closer and closer to Palawan itself. Again the refrains:

"We need more planes and ships."

"We need more airstrips."

"We need more cyber capabilities."

One young officer: "The most important thing for us to do as a nation is to explore for oil and gas in the West Philippine Sea, because we are the poorest country in the Western Pacific."

Another young officer: "China is building en masse medium-sized tanks for deployment on ships in order to invade Palawan [the Philippines proper]."

Here was paranoia mixed with humiliation helped by the fact that the Chinese had just placed the Spratlys, along with the Paracels and Macclesfield Bank, under a new civilian jurisdiction, called Sansha, with its own mayor. So now there were two mayors for the Spratlys, or Kalayaan, and the Chinese one had many more resources.

An hour's drive through mountainous jungle brought me from the Sulu Sea coast of Palawan to the South China Sea coast. I beheld Ulugan Bay: a billowing, ashen blue veil bordered by virginal forests and some of the worst roads I had experienced anywhere in the developing world. The only sound was of leaves swooning in the wind. The naval station was just a few whitewashed buildings in a clearing. Philippine Naval Forces West had moved here the year before and was still landscaping. According to one vision, this was an eco-traveler's paradise. According to another it was a parking place for U.S. warships. "Ulugan Bay: that's the future," I had heard one senior American official say matter-of-factly. Here was a massive and sheltered body of water on the South China Sea within thirty-six hours sail to the Spratlys, almost half the distance as Subic Bay. This was already the home port of the *Gregorio del Pilar*, the 1960s cutter that was the flagship of the Philippine navy. For environmental reasons dredging was not allowed: dredging that would be necessary were, say, American destroyers or aircraft carriers to crowd and deface the pristine picture before me. It might be that Ulugan Bay constituted an opportunity for military planners just too strategic to leave it in the hands of environmentalists. War and military competition were not only unfortunate, but unaesthetic.

The only thing that could save Ulugan Bay was lack of money, I realized. Dredging and port development were frightfully expensive. The Philippines certainly lacked the funds. But so did the Pentagon given the current budget crisis in Washington.

Every human instinct made me hope that this magnificent coast would remain exactly as it was. But so much depended on China. For the moment, China's continued prosperity was leading, as was normal, to military expansion. But would the Chinese economy continue to grow? For Chinese military expansion was leading the United States Navy, in particular, into a closer embrace of the Philippines. Colonial-like dependency lived on.

CHAPTER VII

Asia's Berlin

"The China seas north and south are narrow seas," writes Joseph Conrad. "They are seas full of everyday, eloquent facts, such as islands, sand banks, reefs, swift and changeable currents—tangled facts that nevertheless speak to a seaman in clear and definite language."[1]

The Pratas Islands, an atoll formed by three islands, only one of which is above water, are such eloquent facts. Called Dongsha, the "East Sand" Islands, by the Chinese, the lone habitable island is a pincer-shaped spit of land well under two miles long and a half mile wide—and that's including the lagoon. Actually, it is little more than a five-thousand-foot runway, just slightly above water, guarding the northern entrance to the South China Sea, nearly equidistant between Taiwan and mainland China: and yet it is still the South China Sea's largest island. The runway and two piers are serviced by the Taiwanese coast guard and assorted technicians, totaling about two hundred personnel. There are also a few ecologists. The hibiscus, screw pines, low coconut palms, silk trees, and seagrass—measured against the limitless ocean—express the moral clarity that is the register of extreme natural beauty. If only men lacked the instinct to fight over every scrap of ground.

It is said that the emperor Wu during the Han dynasty two thousand years ago established sovereignty over features in the South China Sea. The Pratas were specifically written about during the Jin dynasty over a thousand years ago, and consequently we have the Chinese claim. Because Taiwan and the mainland are still in dispute over who represents the real China, the Pratas as well as all the other island groups in the South China Sea (in addition to Macclesfield Bank and Scarborough Shoal) are issues of contention between them. The cow's tongue or U-shaped line was a Guomindang concept, and thus is adhered to by Chiang Kai-shek's successors in Taiwan.[2] It originally had eleven dashes. Later when the mainland Chinese signed an agreement with the Vietnamese over the Gulf of Tonkin, the two dashes by the Gulf were removed and it became a nine-dashed line. Each of the dashes, according to both the Chinese and the Taiwanese, represents the median line between the islands within the South China Sea and the large landmasses comprising the sea's littorals.[3] The purpose of the dashes, says Professor Kuan-Hsiung Wang of the National Taiwan Normal University, is to claim ownership of the islands and their offshore waters within the cow's tongue, rather than ownership of the whole South China Sea itself. The Pratas are a perfect example of a claim by both the Chinese on the mainland and on Taiwan.

The Japanese occupied the Pratas during World War II. In 1946, Chiang Kai-shek's naval forces as representatives of the Republic of China—this was before the victory of Mao Zedong's communists on the mainland—landed on the Pratas and legally claimed them the following year. Taiwan has administered the one island above water during high tide ever since, and in the 1980s built the current facilities—thereby putting facts on the ground.

I arrived in the Pratas on one of the periodic Taiwanese military flights. I stepped out of the deafening noise and dingy darkness of an old camouflaged C-130 Hercules after sixty-five minutes in the air and encountered the intense, oppressive sunlight and religious quiet that are the signature elements of the features of the South China Sea. The tropical abundance stunned me: there are 211 species of plants, 231 species of birds, as well as 577 species of fish. It was flowers, greenery, and a vast panel of ocean in every direction.

The local coast guard commander gave me a tour. I saw the radar and weather stations, the two piers with their twenty-ton coast guard patrol boats, the four desalination units, and the four rumbling generators equipped with diesel fuel that arrives every twenty-five days by naval supply ship from Taiwan. A statue of Chiang Kai-shek with a walking stick and broad-brimmed hat stands sentinel over the flora. The Taiwanese built the Da Wang temple here in 1948, with all of the gaudy deep red colors for which Chinese temples are famous. It was dedicated to a general from the Han dynasty of middle antiquity known for his determination and fighting skills. Finally, I was taken to a large pillar with Chinese characters, meaning "Defense of the South China Sea." I had seen everything on the island in under an hour.

The Taiwanese occupation was concentrated on the runway, around which everything else on the island was jammed. This runway gave Taiwan some strategic depth against the mainland. It is unclear just how much oil and natural gas may be located under the seabed in this particular northern region of the South China Sea, so the Taiwanese occupation was for the time being in defense of nearby abundant fish stocks. Could wars start over this? I doubted it. The future of war, at least from the vantage point of the South China Sea, so far had more to do with nationalistic posturing in a noisy global meeting hall than with actual fighting—with spectators throughout the planet in attendance thanks to electronic media. Every nation in the region wanted new warships, but no one really wanted to escalate the conflict into actual fighting beyond occasonal skirmishes.

"The coast guard runs the island," the local commander told me, and is ready to expel Chinese and Vietnamese fishing boats from coastal waters. (The same holds for Itu Aba, the largest of the Spratlys, which Taiwan also occupies with 140 coast guard personnel.[4])

"But we have quite a few legislators in Taipei who want to deploy the marines and the navy here, to show that Taiwan means business."

Indeed, it was because of the seriousness of Taiwan's claim to the Pratas—and consequently Taiwan's desire to communicate that fact to the outside world—that I was finally permitted on the island. It had taken two attempts and many emails between ministries in Taipei to get me here. In other words, while journalists flatter themselves that they bear witness to history, that is mainly true in the case of land wars, which the media can more easily get to. In the case of the South China Sea, should incidents or hostilities commence in deep water or on tiny spits of land in the midst of it, the media may be dependent on reports from ministries in the respective capitals as to what happened.

It also occurred to me that precisely because there was nothing here, these so-called features were really just that—microscopic bits of earth with little history behind them and basically no civilians living on them. Thus, they were free to become the ultimate patriotic symbols, more potent because of their very emptiness and henceforth their inherent abstraction: in effect, they had become logos of nationhood in a global media age. The primordial quest for status still determined the international system. Take the Spratlys, which were not ultimately strategic from the point of view of the Chinese, who were thus able to let the controversy over them fester. Meanwhile, a naked rock like Scarborough Shoal, for example, acquires totemic significance in the eyes of Filipinos. In May 2012, they staged demonstrations the world over in support of their claim to it, as vessels from the Philippines and China engaged in a tense standoff alongside the feature. The Pratas represented nothing in and of themselves, outside of Taiwan's occupation of them. The same for Itu Aba and Sand Cay in the Spratlys. Thus, did the Taiwanese beat their chests.

And so we come to Taiwan, that stubborn, inconvenient fact disturbing the peace of Asia. Unlike North Korea, Taiwan's vibrant democracy and civil society are completely in sync with the values of the twenty-first century. Nobody expects Taiwan to collapse or go away like they do North Korea. Yet mainland China is adamant about incorporating Taiwan into the Chinese state, however long that may take. Thus we have the Western Pacific's most elemental conflict.

Taiwan is the cork in the bottle of the South China Sea, controlling access between Southeast Asia and Northeast Asia, the two security and conflict systems of the Pacific Rim.[5] But Northeast Asia is dependent upon the South China Sea because most of the former's energy comes from the latter's sea lines of communication. Former U.S. assistant secretary of state of East Asia and longtime Asia hand Paul Wolfowitz once told me that Taiwan is "Asia's Berlin." Like the Cold War–era city, Taiwan represents both an outpost of freedom in comparison to mainland China, as well as the bellwether for the political and military situation throughout the Western Pacific. Were Taiwan's de facto independence ever to be seriously compromised by China, American allies from Japan to Australia—including all the countries around the South China Sea—would quietly reassess their security postures, and might well accommodate themselves to Chinese ascendancy. More hinges on Taiwan than the fate of the island itself and its 23 million inhabitants.

And Taiwan, like Cold War–era West Berlin, is undoubtedly feisty. The occupation of the Pratas and Itu Aba proved it.

Yet in the capital of Taipei, as in Singapore, I have a bout of cognitive dissonance. I stare at an antiseptic, angular cityscape—skyscrapers rising like bamboo shoots—from where I take a gleaming high-speed rail train to the south of the island, the engine's very power pressing at my back. Smart shops and liquid crystal screens flashing Chinese characters are everywhere, once again, consumerism and efficiency raised to the status of a foundational creed. Intellectually speaking, I know it has often been such wealth that fuels a weapons boom in the first place. But my instinct tells me that I am wrong: people this prosperous just don't go to war. They have too much to lose.

Nevertheless, the two realities I have encountered almost everywhere in the region are shopping malls and submarines. The malls are packed with shoppers from Taipei to Kuala Lumpur, even though, as one analyst in Singapore had told me, *submarines are the new bling* as far as the area's defense ministries are concerned.

Complimentary coffee and cakes are served; such service is unknown on American trains. As soon as I finish, a hand removes the cup and wrapper. Asia's efficiency has often struck Westerners as extreme. Imagine such efficiency applied to war, I thought. Large-scale war here would be horrific because it would be an outgrowth of Confucian Asia's very dynamism as a whole.

I am headed south to see a Taiwanese historical landmark. The background is the following:

For hundreds of years, Taiwan was better known as Formosa, short for "Ilha Formosa," which means "Beautiful Island" in Portuguese. In the first two decades of the sixteenth century, Portuguese navigators made numerous forays in the Indo-Pacific. Among the most notable was the voyage of the merchant Tomé Pires, dispatched by the viceroy of Malacca to open trade with China. On one of these expeditions, perhaps one led by Fernão Mendes Pinto, the Portuguese traveled along the island's lush western coast. The name "Taiwan" itself, spelled in various ways, is said to mean "foreigners" in the local aboriginal tongue, and Dutch colonists in the third decade of the seventeenth century picked it up as a constantly repeated word in the natives' conversation. Seventy percent of modern Taiwanese have aboriginal blood, which is ethnic Malay in origin. Taiwan, in addition to being an offshore extension of China and the southernmost extension of Japan's Ryuku Island chain, also represents the northernmost extension of Southeast Asia, hence the link to Malaysia.[6] In geographical terms, to say nothing of political ones, Taiwan is the linchpin and organizing principle of the Western Pacific. Taiwan was central to the security of late-nineteenth-century French Indochina, even as its de facto independence is key to the integrity of the Taiwan Strait that guarantees Japan's trade routes, and even as its repossession by Beijing is necessary to end the century of humiliation that the mainland suffered at the hands of foreign powers. Taiwan impinges on every sub-theater in Asia.

In antiquity and the Middle Ages, mainland China's contacts with Taiwan were intermittent, with expeditions made during the Wu, Sui, and Tang dynasties. With the geographical drama of Chinese history playing out on land—in which the agricultural cradle of Chinese civilization was constantly in a struggle to subdue and manage the pastoral tablelands to the north, west, and southwest—national energies were in a comparative sense turned away from the sea. However, this did not prevent seaborne activity in the form of pirates and fishermen from plying the Taiwan Strait, or prevent the development of a bluewater fleet in the ninth century. The early Ming dynasty explorer Zheng He is best known for his voyages in the Indian Ocean, but some of Zheng He's ships may have visited Taiwan. A warlord-pirate, Cheng Chih-lung, whom the Ming emperor had dispatched to contain the Dutch in the Taiwan Strait region (so that the imperial armies could concentrate on fighting the Manchu invaders from the northern plains), settled many thousands of settlers from famine-stricken Fujian province in Taiwan. Thus began the mainland's organic connection with the island.

But it is Cheng's son, Cheng-kung, or Koxinga, who really is at the heart of the historical interaction between the mainland and Taiwan. Koxinga, educated in the Chinese classics and a patron of high culture, was a warlord general and admiral extraordinaire, able to fend off the political pressures of both the dying Ming and rising Manchu-Qing dynasties. He came to Taiwan from Fujian on the mainland with four hundred ships and 25,000 troops. It is Koxinga who, in 1662, after a successful siege of the Dutch fort of Zeelandia on Taiwan's southwestern coast, allowed the Dutch to leave for Batavia (Jakarta) in Indonesia with all their possessions, "with drums beating, their banners flying, their guns loaded, and the fuses lit." Such was his wisdom and generosity. Koxinga, who died young at thirty-nine, before he might have become corrupted by absolute power, is "deified" both on the mainland and on Taiwan as the "ideal Chinese prince," proof that a warlord could be more enlightened and better educated than a formal head of state. On the mainland, he is revered as a nationalist hero who expelled the Western colonialists and forged forevermore the mainland's claim to Taiwan, governing as he did on both sides of the strait. On Taiwan itself, Koxinga is seen as the "original ancestor," who forged an independent identity for the island. There are sixty temples dedicated to his worship. In light of the island's evolution as a democracy, and the half century of Japanese occupation from 1895 to 1945, the fact that Koxinga epitomizes progress and had a Japanese mother constitutes further proof here that he spiritually belongs to a free Taiwan.[7]

Koxinga was succeeded by his son, Cheng Ching, who ruled in the enlightened manner of his father, leading Taiwan to many prosperous years in commerce and agriculture. However, it all proved short-lived, as a succession battle was set off upon Cheng's death, and Taiwan became a backwater of the Qing Empire for the next two hundred years. "Taiwan is nothing but an isolated island on the sea far away from China, it has long since been a hideout of pirates, escaped convicts, deserters and ruffians, therefore, there is nothing to gain from retaining it," said one report to the Qing emperor. But the emperor chose otherwise, annexing Taiwan to keep it from falling back into the hands of the Dutch. As historian Jonathan Manthorpe writes, Taiwan was brought into the empire in 1684 but treated as a place "of no consequence."[8]

The Qing dynasty expanded and contracted, beginning a drawn-out decline in the mid-nineteenth century, much like Ottoman Turkey during the same period. In 1895, a dynamic Japan, internally powered by the Meiji Restoration, grabbed Taiwan, seeing it as a stepping-stone to Southeast Asia and the South China Sea, as well as key to the control of the Yellow and East China seas. Though the Japanese occupied Taiwan for fifty years, they were not subsequently hated on the island like they were elsewhere in East Asia, which fell under Japanese fascist rule in the 1930s and 1940s, for the regimentation and demonstrations of racial superiority were coupled with clean government and the development of institutions that fostered Taiwanese modern identity, as well as making the Taiwanese the most highly educated people in Asia. Compared with the decrepitude of the late Qing dynasty and the plunder and thuggery of Chiang Kai-shek's Guomindang at least in its early years, the experience with the

Japanese was more than tolerable. The Japanese brought medicine, agriculture, roads, and railways: order and modernity, in other words.

Taiwan was the only place in Asia where the defeat of the Japanese fascists did not in the short run necessarily lead to better government. So repressive was Chiang Kai-shek's rule at first that the Americans might have deserted him had it not been for the Korean and Vietnam wars, a time when Washington was afraid of Taiwan falling into communist hands; Taiwan also proved to be a geographically convenient staging base for bombing North Vietnam as well as a rest and recreation center for U.S. troops. The result, starting in the 1950s, was massive U.S. economic aid, which, coupled with a successful land reform program, resulted in a light industrial revolution as farmers now had the money to invest in small factories. The high level of education that had been the fruit of Japanese occupation, combined with American money and a regime that while not democratic, was not communist or totalitarian either, was the vital mix that would eventually make for one of the Third World's most successful democracies beginning in the 1990s. Together with rapid development came Taiwanization: a distinctive flowering of island culture in the arts, media, and universities that featured the rise of a local dialect, Minnan, and the fading of Mandarin, which the Guomindang had brought from the mainland.

Taiwan's 1996 presidential election proved a coming-out party not only for democracy here, but for the naked assertion of American military power. In the run-up to that election, mainland China's regime resorted to missile tests and a mock invasion in the area of the Taiwan Strait as a way to show force—the Taiwanese, in the midst of the hurly-burly of a presidential campaign, should not get any ideas about declaring independence! President Bill Clinton responded by sending not one, but two aircraft carrier strike groups, the *Independence* and the *Nimitz*, into nearby waters. Suddenly Beijing looked impotent, and saw that a massive defense buildup on its part would be necessary if American air and naval hegemony were ever to be checked in the Western Pacific. So began China's rapid acquisition of submarines, fighter jets, and antiaircraft and antiship cruise missiles, as well as electronic listening posts—thus would China impede the American Navy's access to coastal Asia without aircraft carriers of its own. America's response has been undeniable. Whereas in the past, 60 percent of its naval forces had been oriented toward the Atlantic, by 2005, 60 percent were oriented toward the Pacific.[9]

The confrontation will continue to have a long life span. For China simply will not budge. Leaders in Beijing know that Japan colonized Taiwan at the same time that Great Britain took Hong Kong, that Portugal took Macau, and other Western powers and Russia took Treaty Ports and other Chinese land. Later on, at the conclusion of the Chinese civil war, Chiang Kai-shek set up the Republic of China on Taiwan as a rival government for all of the Middle Kingdom, and was recognized as such by the United States and many other countries until Nixon and Kissinger's diplomacy in 1972. In Beijing's eyes, therefore, the return of Taiwan is essential in order to erase this entire humiliating history.[10]

But here in the south of the island there is a local history distinct from that of the mainland, providing Taiwan with a foundation myth. Fort Zeelandia—which I had come to see, the purpose of my train journey—consists of three levels of walls made of brick that the Dutch brought from Batavia, the modern-day Jakarta, in Indonesia. The bricks and lime are mottled with age and graced with frangipani and pollarded banyan trees alongside them, with bronze Dutch cannons all about. Banyan limbs even climb up the fort walls themselves creating a beautiful calligraphy. The fort was actually refurbished by the Japanese occupation forces in honor of its conqueror's—Koxinga's—Japanese mother. Statues of Koxinga are ever present here in Tainan City, where the heavy, humid air and sleepy ambience is evocative of Southeast Asia. It is clear by the statues of Chiang Kai-shek that he saw himself as the new Koxinga, who also came from the mainland.

Fort Zeelandia no longer stands sentinel against the sea, but is surrounded by narrow downtown streets, the product of reclaimed land, so that much of its magic is lost. And yet, to judge by the hordes of Taiwanese young and old passing through its bastions, the fort retains its power as a symbol of a history unique to the island. It leads one to pose the question, Just how strong now is Taiwanese identity? Given how prosperous they have become, would Taiwanese actually fight and sacrifice for their independence from the mainland, if it ever came to that? Or would they allow themselves to be subsumed by Beijing, if only their freedom and not their living standards were compromised? The diplomats and defense officials I met in Taipei are trying to craft a strategy so that these questions never need to get answered.

Henry C. K. Liu is the deputy director general of Taiwan's National Security Council. As an upper-middle-level official, it is at his rank—as I knew from Washington—that the real work and thinking of any administration gets done. "The longer we survive," he told me, "the more likely that political changes will happen in mainland China itself." *We can buy time, it is all about playing a weak hand well* was what I heard throughout Taipei. In the meantime, Liu said, "we must try our best to maintain the status quo" through creative diplomacy and hard military power. "We can only try, through our own defense capabilities, to make those on the mainland see that the use of military force is unthinkable." He quoted Sun Tzu, the great Chinese philosopher of antiquity, that "the greatest strategy is never having to fight."

Liu had his worries. How reliable was the United States over the long term? The wars in Iraq and Afghanistan had been a shock for Taiwanese officials. Though they officially supported the American military efforts, they were chilled by just how much events in the Middle East had diverted the United States from its responsibilities in Asia. Then there was the inexorable march of Chinese military power itself, which might through the combination of such assets as land-based missiles, submarines, space-based surveillance systems, cyber-attacks, over-the-horizon radar, unmanned aerial vehicles, and small craft disguised as commercial vessels create an anti-access bubble complicating the American military's ability to approach the Chinese mainland, including the Taiwan Strait.[11] Finally there was an awareness that three quiet and predictable decades in Beijing—ever since Deng Xiaoping's consolidation of power—were giving way to more political turmoil on the mainland. Indeed, things were about to get more interesting for Taiwan.

It was even possible that despite the hopes for political liberalization in Beijing, the current group of elite communist technocrats constituted the friendliest government on the mainland that Taiwan was going to get at least in the short run. As Professor Szu-yin Ho of Taipei's National Chengchi University explained to me: "Democracies may not fight each other, but that may not be true of a country in the early phases of democratization." For the loosening of central control in Beijing could unleash more unruly and nationalistic forces, as each new party and faction competes to be more patriotic than the next one. This was Taiwan's nightmare. "The benign period on the mainland may be ending," Professor Ho said.

In fact, as he argued, the Communist Party establishment in Beijing needed Taiwan for its own economic policies. For the People's Republic of China measured itself against Taiwan the same way Malaysia measured itself against Singapore. It was the competition that the Taiwanese economic model offered that spurred Beijing's rulers to want to improve living standards for their own people.

The real danger for Taiwan, I posited to Professor Ho, was Finlandization by China. The combination of 1,500 land-based missiles aimed at Taiwan from the mainland, even as hundreds of commercial flights a week linked the mainland with the island, meant that Taiwan would quietly be captured by China without the latter needing to invade. But he strongly disagreed. He pointed out that Finland's independence during the Cold War was compromised by the Soviet Union because the two nations shared a long land border, enabling Soviet intimidation. Vietnam, too, has a significant land border with China so it also can be Finlandized. "But we have the Taiwan Strait," he explained, which as narrow as it is nevertheless is almost five times as wide as the English Channel. Ho and I then both recalled University of Chicago Professor John Mearsheimer's theory of the "stopping power of water."[12] Navies could land on beachheads, Mearsheimer wrote, but sending a land force inland to permanently occupy a subject population across the seas was exceedingly difficult. And so China's military would continue to both enlarge and improve, with more and better submarines, surface warships, and fighter jets—and better-trained crews to man them. A day might even come in the foreseeable future when the United States Navy and Air Force would be unable to deter an attack on Taiwan. But Beijing would still have the problem of occupying the island. And that problem would persist even in the face of a new correlation of forces in the Western Pacific, in which American military unipolarity gave way to a bipolar order with China.

Might Taiwan become like Hong Kong, a part of China that was nevertheless allowed a large degree of self-governance along with a singular identity? Again, the answer was no. Ho explained that besides Taiwan's island geography, Taiwan had another advantage that Hong Kong lacked: "political symbolism," which was the product of a specific nation-building myth. The Guomindang had waged an epic struggle against Mao's communists and lost, and then retreated across the sea to Taiwan, where, with all hope seemingly gone, it built a dynamic society. Hong Kong was merely a trading post with no such story to inspire a local defense.

Lastly, Taiwan survived through feverish, innovative diplomacy. It may have had diplomatic relations with only about two dozen countries thanks to Chinese intimidation, so that many serving foreign diplomats around the world perforce avoid the island altogether. But Taiwan assiduously cultivated past and future diplomats in many countries, knowing that they still wielded influence in their respective capitals. It constantly invited journalists like myself for visits where intensive rounds of one-on-one meetings were offered. More isolated than the Israelis, the Taiwanese were less bitter about it. No one in Taipei had chips on their shoulder. It was a place you instantly liked. And the Taiwanese were sly: such charm was part of their strategy.

"In the Melian Dialogue," Ho said, paraphrasing Thucydides, "the Athenians told the inhabitants of Milos that *the strong do what they can and the weak suffer what they must.* But that brutal law of nature does not operate to the same extent in a globalized world of intense interconnectivity, where Taiwan is not alone and therefore not as vulnerable as Milos was."

Yet with all the smiles, courtesy, small gifts provided me, and talk of the "soft power of persuasion," there was a tough, inflexible, and steely edge to Taiwanese policy.[13] Andrew Yang, the vice minister of national defense, had a massive map in his office of Taiwan, the Taiwan Strait, and the nearby mainland. He pointed out a wide, semicircular arc reaching deep into the mainland that constituted the air defense identification zone over which Taiwan conducted twenty-four-hour surveillance. "We have been doing this for decades. Our mantra is air defense and sea control. There will be no blockades, no amphibious landings to our detriment. If they bomb our runways, our fighter jets will use our superhighways." One of his aides pointed out to me the fewer than a handful of places on the Taiwanese coast where the mainland Chinese could attempt amphibious landings. "They have few options because of geography. If they tried, they would have the same horrible experience of U.S. Marines assaulting Japanese-held islands in the Pacific in World War II. We will be the defenders, and the defenders have the advantage."

Referring to a 2009 study by the RAND Corporation, suggesting that by 2020 the United States might no longer be able to militarily defend Taiwan, Yang called the report "too much arithmetic." It left out the intangibles of just what would be required to conquer the island. Again, there was a reference to Mearsheimer: holding a beachhead and then moving large forces inland is just plain hard. Then there was the North Korea factor, which few spoke about these days in connection to Taiwan. It was the Korean War of 1950–1953, and China's epic military involvement in it, that saved Taiwan from an invasion by the mainland at a time when Chiang Kai-shek's new regime was at its most vulnerable. If over the next quarter century the regime in Pyongyang falters, in whatever way, China would be too tied down with problems in the Korean Peninsula to even contemplate an invasion of Taiwan.

Of course, there were many other scenarios short of an actual invasion in which China could overwhelm Taiwan, thus forcing a political capitulation of sorts by Taipei. For example, a protracted campaign of Chinese cyber-warfare aimed at Taiwan's power grids and other infrastructure could undermine morale on the island. Yang understood all this, yet continued to talk about indigenous air defense, Patriot missile batteries, Taiwan's desperate need for the United States to retrofit its F-16A/B fighter jets, as well as sell Taiwan the more powerful F-16C/Ds. What Taiwan really required, he told me, was the new vertical launch F-35Bs, thereby undermining China's strategy of bombing the island's runways. He and other officials complained to me about their thirty-five-year-old F-5s, which were quite literally ready for museums.

The numbers were daunting, with the mainland's armed forces increasingly outpacing those of the island. Taiwan had 430 fighter jets; mainland China thousands, with seven hundred of them assigned to coastal areas near Taiwan. But with Taiwan's economy growing at only 3 to 5 percent annually in recent years, Taipei in any case was having trouble paying for arms purchases, and that's if it could arrange them in the first place. Most countries would incur Beijing's wrath by selling Taiwan weapons and transferring the latest military technology to Taipei. Even the United States had exquisite diplomatic calculations to make: just how much could Washington sell Taipei— and what quality of hardware and software could it pass on to the Taiwanese military—without fundamentally damaging its relations with Beijing, with which it had far more equities at risk.

The Taiwanese, Yang told me, also needed more underwater mines to deter Chinese amphibious ships from approaching the island, as well as new submarines to replace their 1970s subs from the Netherlands. But who would sell it to them? The United States manufactured only nuclear-powered subs; not the ultra-quiet diesel-electric ones in which Taiwan was interested. As far as third countries were concerned, again there was the problem of incurring Beijing's ire. Meanwhile, the Taiwanese legislature had recently levied funds to field a squadron of Hsun Hai fast patrol boats, the kind that could hide in caves and shelters around the island's rough coast, in order to conduct independent operations in "wolf packs" against enemy shipping.[14] It was a decidedly mixed picture, if not a bit dreary, as far as Taiwan's defense was concerned. What Taiwan wanted and what it had were two different things. But through it all, the message I got was that Taiwan would remain just militarily formidable enough to make any kind of armed intervention from the mainland fanciful.

And yet, the question remained:

Given Beijing's seemingly inexorable air and naval buildup in the Western Pacific, was there a point where Taiwan—though not as geographically vulnerable as Finland during the Cold War—would still have to politically accommodate the mainland more than it already was doing? Could the Chinese in the future be able to exercise an invisible veto power over who is elected to run Taiwan? Could certain prospective candidates and ministers be excluded from office because they are judged too hostile to China? In other words, Beijing could have a larger and larger vote in future Taiwanese elections. The United States undermined China's attempt at intimidation during the 1996 Taiwanese elections through a show of force. But China's own growing capabilities make that less likely in the future. With 40 percent of Taiwanese exports going to the mainland, was Taiwan's de facto independence already slipping away?[15] Taiwanese president Ma Ying-jeou was presently upholding the status quo with his dictum: no unification with the mainland, but no declaration of independence by Taiwan. Yet would China, in the face of its rising military power, always have to be satisfied with that?

The most vivid symbol of national and cultural pride in Taipei is the National Palace Museum. The thousands of objects here represent the material inheritance of Chinese dynasties stretching back to early antiquity. In 1948, as Chiang Kai-shek's Guomindang contemplated defeat at the hands of Mao's communists, items from the Palace Museum in Beijing, the rare books from the Beijing Central Library, and artifacts from the Institute of History and Philology at the Academia Sinica were selected for removal by air and sea to Taiwan. By 1949, almost 250,000 objects had arrived on the island in crates. It represented only about a fifth of the masterpieces in Beijing, but it was the "cream of the collection."[16] The inventory wasn't completed until 1954, with a new museum sturdily built into a pitch-dark green mountainside, and completed in 1965. The ownership of much of the material legacy of an entire civilization—however outrageous the theft from the mainland—coupled with the signal fact of Taiwanese democracy, provides Taiwan with a certain legitimacy that its lack of diplomatic relations with the outside world cannot take away.

You can travel throughout the mainland and not get such a compressed and comprehensive insight into what, aesthetically, constitutes China as you can in this museum in Taiwan. Busloads of tourists from the mainland flock here to see what wonders their own culture has wrought.

I gaze at the time line of Chinese dynasties reaching back to the Bronze Age: Shang, Zhou, Han, the Three Kingdoms, Qin, Sui, Tang, Northern and Southern Sung, Yuan, Ming, Qing—multiple phases of fragmentation with intermittent periods of unity. I observe the magnificent bronze vessels of the Shang that convey awe and reverence to the gods and ancestors; the jade animals, dragons, and phoenixes of the Han emperors; Tang figurines; the mathematical simplicity of Sung pottery, in which a few spare lines can create an aura of vastness; rich imperial Yuan portraits reflecting the nomadic origins of these Mongols; cobalt blue and white Ming vases, and the faint, feathery elegance of Ming landscape painting; Qing vases with Indian motifs testifying to the territorial immensity of this empire. I learn that there are few things as beautiful as a Chinese box inlaid with coral, jade, and turquoise; or as beautiful as a vase with a hundred deer painted on it; or a simple basin with celadon glaze; or ink painted on silk.

This museum is a political statement: *that by virtue of our possession of these objects we in Taiwan are the real China, and we will change the mainland before the mainland changes us.*

———

Taiwan begins and ends with the legacy of Chiang Kai-shek, who, along with his son, Chiang Ching-kuo, orchestrated the immense transfer of this material cultural inheritance in the first place. Chiang Kai-shek is as crucial to Taiwan as Lee Kuan Yew is to Singapore, and more so than Mahathir bin Mohamad is to Malaysia.

But Chiang is a far more problematic figure than Lee, and a far more pivotal one in terms of the history of the twentieth century. While Lee built tiny Singapore, Chiang lost China to Mao. The escape of Chiang's forces to Taiwan and the subsequent building of a new political order on the island flow from that stark fact. The Chiang Kai-shek memorial complex in Taipei, with its seventy-meter-tall memorial hall made of white marble, topped by a blue-glazed upturned roof in traditional Chinese style, and with two sets of eighty-nine granite steps leading down to vast gardens, towering ornamental gates, and gargantuan pavilions, represents a degree of vanity and grandiosity that one does not associate with the corporate and businesslike Lee. Honor guards stand vigil before a huge, Lincoln-esque statue of Chiang, even while his legacy has dimmed on the island itself, as Taiwan evolves into something dissimilar from its mainland Nationalist past. Indeed, it was Chiang's son, Ching-kuo, who played more of a role than his father in transforming Taiwan into a prosperous democracy.

Nevertheless, Chiang Kai-shek is a totemic figure when it comes to the South China Sea. For the South China Sea is about more than just competition for blue territory on the map, which may or may not have much extractable oil and natural gas. The South China Sea is also first and foremost about the destiny of China, the geopolitical hinge on which war or peace in the region rests. No figure besides Mao Zedong himself has determined China's destiny in the twentieth century as much as Chiang Kai-shek. Mao looks worse and worse from the vantage point of the second decade of the twenty-first century, owing to the tens of millions who died through his policies (as well as because of the post–Cold War realization that communism was as much an evil as fascism). But in recent years the reputation of Chiang has improved somewhat among scholars. And this revisionist treatment of Chiang is revealing about the future of China.

Chiang Kai-shek and my interest in him is also a lesson in how travel involves surprises. The surprises stem not only from what you see but from what intellectually sparks your interest at the moment, leading you, in turn, to read and reread books you never thought you would. So it was with myself and books about Chiang Kai-shek, which followed from my fascination with Taiwan, and led me to some intrepid historians.

In 2003, Jonathan Fenby, former editor of the London *Observer* and the Hong Kong *South China Morning Post,* published a rather revisionist biography, *Chiang Kai-shek: China's Generalissimo and the Nation He Lost.* Fenby partially challenges the received wisdom about Chiang, that he was a corrupt and inept ruler, who dragged his heels on fighting the Japanese despite all the aid he got from the United States during World War II, and who lost China to Mao because he was the lesser man. Fenby notes, in passing, that had Chiang not been kidnapped for a few days in 1936, he would have been in a political circumstance to launch an offensive against the communists right there and then when they were still weak, and the twentieth-century history of China might well have been different.[17]

Then, in 2009, Jay Taylor, former China desk officer at the U.S. State Department and later research associate at the Fairbank Center for Chinese Studies at Harvard, followed up with a stronger revisionist biography of Chiang, *The Generalissimo: Chiang Kai-shek and the Struggle for Modern China,* which more so than the Fenby book took apart many of the preconceptions about the founder of Taiwan. Both authors, Taylor especially, blame the unduly negative image of Chiang on the journalists and State Department foreign service officers who covered China during World War II. The pivotal character in this story was the wartime American military commander in China, Army Lieutenant General Joseph W. Stilwell. Stilwell quite simply hated Chiang, calling him "Peanut" behind his back, and passed on his bile to the journalists and foreign service officers, who, courted by Stilwell, naturally took the American general's side. Taylor mentions *Time*'s Theodore H. White, *Newsweek*'s Harold Isaacs, and the *New*

York Times's Brooks Atkinson in this regard. It was they especially who began a legend that poisoned Chiang's reputation for generations to follow.

Indeed, Theodore White writes in his memoir that Stilwell "wanted us to know that from the day of Pearl Harbor on, 'this ignorant son of a bitch has never wanted to fight Japan. . . . Every major blunder of this war is directly traceable to Chiang Kai-shek.'" Actually, what really turned White against Chiang was his coverage of the Honan famine in 1943, when he saw how Chiang's soldiers were, by collecting grain as taxes, literally starving masses of peasants to death. Another factor was the glowing reports that journalists such as White were filing about the communists, including Mao and his number two, the "suave, engaging" Zhou Enlai, with whom, as White admits, he "had become friends." The "wine of friendship flowed," White recalls about his relationship with Zhou. White admits from the vantage point of 1978—three and a half decades after the war—that in Zhou's presence he had "near total suspension of disbelief or questioning judgment. . . . I can now see Chou for what he was: a man as brilliant and ruthless as any the Communist movement has thrown up in this century." Then there was the heady experience of actually meeting Mao himself in his northern China lair in Yan'an during World War II. "What scored on my mind most was his [Mao's] composure," White writes. "There was no knee jiggling as with Chiang Kai-shek. . . . The indelible impression was . . . a man of the mind who could use guns, whose mind could compel history to move to his ideas." About Chiang, White writes of his "rigid morality . . . animal treachery, warlord cruelty and an ineffable ignorance of what a modern state requires." It would have been better had Chiang been removed from the Chinese leadership early enough in the war, White says.[18]

Historians Jay Taylor and Jonathan Fenby go a significant way toward dismantling the worldview of White and his colleagues.

Taylor's book, published by Harvard University Press, is particularly trenchant, given what we in the West think we know about Chiang. Precisely because Taylor (and Fenby, too) do not engage in a whitewash, after finishing their books we feel that we *know* Chiang from the inside, rather than through a Western journalistic prism unduly influenced by Stilwell.

Taylor admits that Chiang (unlike Mao) "had little charisma and was generally not liked by his peers. . . . He was an inhibited man . . . a staid seemingly humorless individual who had a terrible temper." More crucially, Chiang from early on, as a result of his studies, was consciously Confucianist, a worldview that emphasized political order, respect for family and hierarchy, and conservative stability. It is this belief system that has ultimately triumphed—whether admitted to or not—throughout much of East Asia and in China itself, accounting for the region's prosperity over recent decades, even as the communism of Mao and Zhou Enlai has been utterly discredited.[19]

Besides Confucianist thought, Chiang in his early years was also deeply influenced by the culture of Japan, which to Chiang embodied "disciplined efficiency," from the train system to education to manufacturing. Japan's fierce modernism infected Chiang with the need to fight corruption. But here he encountered fierce resistance, like when Nationalist army commanders rejected Chiang's calls to centralize military financing. Chiang, according to Taylor, "soon realized that he had to give the fight against corruption much lower priority than that of retaining cohesion and loyalty among his disparate supporters . . . both civilian and military. He had no choice." Chiang has often been accused of tolerating corruption, but the alternative in the warlord age in which he operated was to become an extremist ideologue, like Mao. Chiang was far from perfect; but neither was he as deeply flawed as his detractors, applying the standards of the West to a chaotic early-twentieth-century China, demanded. "Craftiness and suspicion are the usual marks of successful political leaders in Chiang's circumstances," Taylor explains. No doubt, years of warfare in the 1920s and early 1930s established Chiang as an exceptional military commander, maneuvering multiple army corps over thousand-mile fronts, without tanks, maps, and trucks, and with only a few rail lines, often in circumstances of personal bravery. He used bribery and divide-and-rule tactics against the warlords, even while, "as an expression of rote neo-Confucian self-cultivation," Chiang complained in his diary of his personal shortcomings.[20]

A map of China during this period establishes the formidable circumstances facing Chiang, as well as his considerable achievement: the whole of central and coastal China divided into massive puddles of warlord control, over which Chiang slowly, painstakingly, established a very tenuous primacy. And he did it without foreign aid, unlike Mao's communists. He was paying for weapons and training from Germany, even as there is no evidence in his statements or in his diary that he ever subscribed to Hitler's fascist ideology, according to Taylor. Under Chiang, says Taylor, the power and authority of the central government was greater than at any point since the mid-nineteenth century, while the rate of illiteracy among government troops diminished over these years from 70 to 30 percent. Fenby concurs, pointing out that Chiang's Nationalist ascendancy in parts of the country "was a time of modernization such as China had not seen before . . . there was a flowering of thought, literature, art and the cinema," and the repression used by the regime was not comparable to what the communists would later unleash. Without Chiang, Fenby writes, "the odds would have been on a continuation of the warlord era, and the fragmentation of China into eternally conflicting fiefdoms." It was Chiang who kept in check pro-Japanese elements in his administration, which on their own might have allied China with Japan, opening up an attack on the Soviet Union from the east while Hitler attacked from the west. After the fall of Nanjing to the Japanese in 1937, Taylor writes, "Chiang Kai-shek issued a proclamation as rousing as that which Churchill would give twenty-one months later and with some similar imagery."[21]

Stilwell missed all of this. "In Stilwell's mind," writes Taylor, "Chiang had no values; no skills in government or generalship; no real interest in the modernization and welfare of China . . . no human qualities worth noting. . . . For Stilwell, life was categorical, nuances nonexistent." While American officials, influenced by Stilwell, believed Chiang wanted to avoid fighting the Japanese in order to store arms to fight the communists later on, during the 1941–1942 Burma campaign Chiang's troops suffered eighty thousand killed and wounded, whereas total American casualties around the world at that point were 33,000. By the end of fourteen years of war with Japan, China would sustain three million military casualties, 90 percent of them Chiang's troops. Meanwhile, Mao's communists were pursuing the very strategy Chiang was accused of: avoiding major military entanglements with the Japanese in order to hoard their strength to later fight the Nationalists. But this did not prevent foreign service officers like John Paton Davies and John Stewart Service, who were working for Stilwell, from describing Mao's communists as "agrarian democrats" and "much more American than Russian in form and spirit." Mao would go on to kill tens of millions of people—sixty million perhaps—in government-induced famines and other atrocities, which in absolute terms—along with the Mongol Conquests of the thirteenth century—counts as the second largest man-made carnage in history after World War II.[22] What these foreign service officers and journalists overlooked was that Mao's talent for creating a mass organization—the very thing that Chiang distrusted, according to Fenby—made Mao's movement more dynamic, and thus more impressive to Western visitors, but also more dangerous should that mass organization pivot in a totalitarian direction.[23]

Chiang would be proven right in his assessment, made near the end of World War II, that rather than agrarian democrats, Mao's forces would prove to be "more communistic than the Russian communists." Indeed, the Great Leap Forward and the Great Proletarian Cultural Revolution would both occur within a quarter century of that statement. And yet Chiang's Guomindang army failed utterly to meet Stilwell's expectations, and thus remained the corrupt, inefficient force that went on to be vanquished by Mao. Barbara Tuchman, Stilwell's sympathetic biographer, may have caught the imperfections of Chiang best by labeling him a master of "plots" who "governed for survival," rather than for social change, even as among the Nationalists there was—as one Chinese academic put it—"no one better in sight." Chiang's seeming "infuriating absence of conscience" in the eyes of the Americans was, in part, Tuchman says, a consequence of

Chiang's resentment at China being treated as a minor theater in the war, with most of the aid and attention going to Europe.[24]

Tuchman grasps what Stilwell didn't. "The Kuomintang military structure could not be reformed without reform of the system from which it sprang," but China was not "clay in the hands of the West." Or as Fenby puts it, Stilwell "was behaving as if he were in a stable democracy, where a professional army is answerable to an elected government, fenced off from interference in politics." Nobody understood China and Chiang's tragedy as much as Chiang himself. In what Taylor calls his "remarkably candid" assessment, penned in January 1949, following the communist takeover of the mainland, Chiang wrote, "we are in a transitional period where the old system has been abolished but the new system is yet to be built." He implies that the blame falls with the incoherent and fractious system he himself had managed, in turn a product of the warlord era.[25]

Upon arriving in southwestern Taiwan in July 1949, Chiang proclaimed a reorganization of his party that stressed enlightened authoritarianism; that is, dictatorship plus good, responsive governance. His formerly mainland Chinese Nationalist security services arrested ten thousand indigenous Taiwanese and executed more than a thousand, as part of a vast repression that characterized the early years of his rule. At the same time, all financial matters were centralized in the hands of the military, thus eliminating many forms of graft. To further curtail corruption, Chiang ordered banks to provide information on all individual and company accounts to the tax authorities. Chiang also promulgated a wide-ranging land reform program, emphasizing a sharp reduction in rural rents, which immediately benefited the Taiwanese. This was only part of a shift to progressive policies that also included reformist political appointments. Chiang's policies were often cruel and tough, but combined with the many examples of progressive governance, they earned political support in the United States to protect Taiwan from a communist invasion from the mainland, especially as Chiang's land reform program stood in stark contrast to

Mao's revolutionary land confiscations, which led to over a million deaths in the early 1950s alone—even before the Great Leap Forward. It was in this period where one really saw the vast gulf between Mao's utopian Marxist-Leninist precepts and Chiang's Confucian ones: rarely was the gulf wider between one form of dictatorship and another.[26]

Chiang had a motive for this combination of disciplined, iron-fisted rule and enlightened social and economic policies. It was to prepare Taiwan for a possible invasion by the mainland communists on one hand, and build American support for Taiwan on the other. Chiang breathed easier the moment he heard the news in June 1950 that North Korean troops had crossed the 38th Parallel and invaded South Korea, in a decision backed by mainland China. Chiang knew that with Mao's focus now on the Korean Peninsula, Taiwan was probably out of danger. He was right. It was the Korean War that forced President Harry Truman to consider the defense of Taiwan a paramount U.S. interest in the Pacific.

Taiwan's path from that point forward was toward prosperity and eventual democracy. Meanwhile, China today becomes less and less autocratic and less and less centralized, having long ago discarded Mao's Marxism-Leninism in all but name. Mao lives on as a nationalist icon mainly. If China continues in this liberal direction, and forges closer economic and cultural ties with Taiwan, Chiang Kai-shek may yet turn out to be a more important historical figure than Mao Zedong.

CHAPTER VIII

The State of Nature

I am situated by a frozen lake, with gray pagodas and upward-curved roofs in the distance visible through the Beijing smog. There is the sickly sweet smell of coal burning. I walk inside a traditional tea house, filled with porcelain, rice paper paintings, lime wood furniture, and a massive red Turkish carpet. In other words, I am in a world of elegant and traditional aesthetics: a world with which sophisticated global elites are comfortable. This is China as seen through the pages of an expensive coffee-table book. My companions are members of an internationally renowned foreign policy institute in Beijing. The atmosphere is convivial. We talk to each other across a geopolitical divide, but actually less so across a cultural one, since we are all similarly educated, all frequently visit each other's countries, and all consequently seek out compromise. Everyone here is equally worried about the stability of the North Korean regime and about the direction of both the American and Chinese economies. There is a discussion about how we can get our two countries' navies to better cooperate. The get-together reminds me of how richly developed United States–China relations are. Millions of Americans and Chinese have visited each other's countries, tens of thousands of American businessmen pass through Beijing and Shanghai. Chinese political elites send their children to be educated at American universities. This is not the Cold War between the United States and the Soviet Union, when I was a lonely American in East European capitals. "Containment" is a word from a previous era, one that simply does not fit the American security approach to China, I tell myself.

But that evening I am somewhere else in the Chinese capital. Rather than in a realm of quiet elegance, I am now in a loud and tacky new hotel under sharp and glaring lights. There is a lot of fake gold and plastic. I eat dinner with two members of a Communist Party foreign policy think tank. They are badly dressed and speak through an interpreter. They tell me that the Japanese national character has not changed since Pearl Harbor. They defend the nine-dashed line that asserts China's claim to virtually the entire South China Sea. They claim the right for China's navy to protect its sea lines of communication across the Indian Ocean to the Middle East. The Vietnamese are unreasonable, they tell me. They warm up to me only after I provide a short disquisition about how much I am aware of the territorial violations inflicted upon China by the West and Japan in the late nineteenth and early twentieth centuries. Yes, here I could be back in Cold War Eastern Europe.

As different as the American relationship with China from the Cold War one with the Soviet Union, the fact remains that China and the United States are two great powers with competing interests in the Western Pacific, and while the experts one meets at Beijing's universities and institutes seem reassuringly flexible—members, as they are, of the global elite—they are not in power: and those that are in power are less flexible. Though, of course, the situation is far more complicated than that. For even within the ranks of China's navy, there are significant voices for moderation alongside tougher assessments.[1] Beijing is indeed rich in differences of opinion. However, throughout Beijing, one is inundated with the nostrum, *While China only defends, the United States conquers.* The South China Sea is the nub of the issue. Hard-liners and soft-liners alike in Beijing—deeply internalizing how China suffered at the hands of Western powers in the recent past—see the South China Sea as a domestic issue, as a blue-water extension of China's territoriality. One night at a seminar I conducted for Chinese students, one shy, quivering young man blurted out: "Why does the United States meet our harmony and benevolence with hegemony? U.S. hegemony will lead to chaos in the face of China's rise!"

This is vaguely similar to a Middle Kingdom mentality, in which China must defend itself against barbarians. Indeed, the South China Sea and its environs are China's near-abroad, where China is harmoniously reasserting the status quo, having survived the assault upon it by Western powers. But because the United States has come here from half a world away in order to seek continued influence in the South China Sea, it is demonstrably hegemonic. Likewise in the Indian Ocean, where China has legitimate commercial and geopolitical interests, while America's interests, again, are merely hegemonic. It is the United States, so the reasoning in Beijing goes, "that attempts to keep Asia under its thumb and arrogantly throws its massive power projection capacity around." Because Washington is seen as the "agitator" of South China Sea disputes, it is the United States, not China, that needs to be "deterred."[2] After all, China dominated a tribute system based on Confucian values that defined international relations in East Asia for many centuries, and resulted in more harmony and fewer wars than the balance of power system in Europe. So the West and the United States have nothing to teach China in regard to keeping the peace.[3]

These are different worldviews informed by different geographical points of reference. They may have no ultimate resolution.

Thus, we are back to containment, the wrong word that unfortunately harbors a great truth: that because China is geographically fundamental to Asia, its military and economic power must be hedged against to preserve the independence of smaller states in Asia that are

U.S. allies. And that, in plain English, is a form of containment. A confident, businesslike official at the Foreign Ministry in Beijing understood completely the dilemma, when he half warned me: "Don't let these small countries [Vietnam, the Philippines . . .] manipulate you." China understands power, and thus it understands the power of the United States. But it will not tolerate a coalition of smaller powers allied with the United States against it: that, given the Chinese historical experience of the past two hundred years, is unacceptable. As for the nine-dashed line, as one university professor in Beijing told me: sophisticated people in government and in the foreign and defense policy institutes here recognize that there must be some compromise down the road, but they need a political strategy to sell such a compromise to a domestic audience, which harbors deep reservoirs of nationalism. In the meantime, the Chinese have doubled down on the nine-dashed line, establishing a prefecture of two hundred islets encompassing two million square kilometers of the South China Sea, with forty-five legislators to govern it.

It may be, in fact, that the nationalism on display among the two Communist Party members I met at the hotel was a low-calorie version of what lies in store for China if the party itself weakens or fractures in the face of an unruly process of democratization and socioeconomic upheaval, aggravated by an overheated, debt-ridden domestic economy. No one can predict the future, but the early phases of transition to democracy often bring nationalism to the surface, unless democratization comes after the earlier establishment of bourgeois traditions, like in the case of former Warsaw Pact Central Europe; or after the complete defeat and subsequent occupation of a country—and delegitimization of extreme nationalism—as in the case of post–World War II Germany and Japan. The idea that China will suddenly be less nationalistic if it were only to become less autocratic has relatively few historical precedents. The current crop of dull, technocratic, and collegial party leaders in Beijing may constitute the most reasonable regime in the field of foreign policy that China may have for some time to come.

Of course, China will be in a state of continued upheaval, if only because the vast economic expansion overseen by the Communist Party in the last thirty-five years has created a more complex society that requires both urgent reform and new institutions that a one-party state can no longer provide. But do not necessarily equate domestic disharmony and severe economic troubles with a weaker posture in China's maritime near-abroad. The *Financial Times* columnist Gideon Rachman has noted that China optimists and pessimists may both be right: China's domestic upheaval could eventually strengthen Chinese power, in a vaguely similar way that the American Civil War produced the conditions for the United States to lead the industrial world.[4] Big changes certainly lie in wait for China. Icons could be smashed and rebuilt. The gigantic poster of Mao that hangs before the upturned yellow roofs of the Forbidden City is there because, despite killing as many as sixty million Chinese, Mao unified China after a century of imperial decrepitude and civil war. Thus, he appeals to the nationalist element in China. The internal debate on Mao is yet to come. But whatever way the debate eventually turns out, it is likely to be integral to China's political development along its path to greater power. And while China will be further integrated into a twenty-first-century global civilization—anchored to a significant degree by legal norms—do not altogether discount China's historic view of its own, vast geographical sway.

To wit, in 1754, the king of Java, well beyond the southern extremity of the South China Sea, requested that his lands be formally incorporated into those of China and its population entered into the Qing dynasty registers. But the Qing emperor, Qianlong, replied that this was not necessary, because—"at least in his eyes"—the lands and people of Java were "already within the compass of Our enlightened government."[5] Thus, from a Chinese historical vantage point, Beijing's dominance of the South China Sea and even the Java Sea is altogether natural.

Aristotle writes, in a manner that recalls Shakespeare, that conflicts arise "not over small things but from small things."[6] Claims and incidents, however petty they may seem to outsiders, if they are tied to the vital interests of those in positions of authority, can lead to war. The fact that archives from China's twelfth-century Sung dynasty and from Vietnam's seventeenth-century Nguyen dynasty refer to the Spratlys augments both China's and Vietnam's claims to those barren islands, the great majority of which lack freshwater: claims that on some future morrow the two nations may be willing to violently enforce. "War is normal," intones America's preeminent academic realist, the late Kenneth N. Waltz of Columbia University. And interdependence, which is synonymous with globalization, can mean more war, Waltz goes on, because highly similar people whose affairs are closely intertwined will occasionally fall into conflict. Moreover, "in the state of nature, there is no such thing as an unjust war."[7] The South China Sea reflects a state of nature in that legal claims are in contradiction with each other and thus provide little basis for cooperation, even as calculations of power, tied partly to the movement of warships, provide the foundation for how the various states interact. This does not mean that war will break out in the South China Sea, or even that it is likely to break out. But it does mean that war there remains a possibility against which all regional powers must always be on guard.

Alleviating the state of nature requires a new security order. A message of both Machiavelli's *Prince* and *Discourses on Livy* is that the founding of a new order is the most difficult thing in politics.[8] Indeed, the old order of American military unipolarity in the waters of the Western Pacific is slowly fading. Meanwhile, the United States demands a new order built on international legal norms that its warships will continue to enforce, even as Washington has not signed the 1982 United Nations Convention on the Law of the Sea. But rather than an international order dominated by American warships, China now demands a regional order that it, as the dominant indigenous power, will do the most to maintain. Because Chinese naval power is rising, the situation is in serious flux.

—

Truly, the map of the South China Sea is a classic document of geopolitics, in that geopolitics constitutes the influence of geography
upon human divisions.[9] It is a relatively shallow sea where the im-
pediments to energy exploration are more political than technological. But the fact that it is a cartographic symbol of conflict does not
prevent it from being captivating. This map clarifies a space dense
with ships and shipping lanes: sixty thousand vessels each year pass
through the Strait of Malacca, including tankers holding more than
thirteen billion barrels of petroleum.[10] The fetching names of many of
the places in dispute are derived from the names of vessels wrecked
on the islets, reefs, and shoals in question. With all of its *features*—
islands and rocks, many of which disappear under high tide—and all
of its broken and unbroken lines denoting various kinds of claims of
sovereignty, the map is dizzying in its complexity. The Spratlys alone
constitute 150 features, only forty-eight of which are above water all
of the time.[11] And it is true that the claims are so numerous and so
often overlapping with other claims that the idea of a solution pales
beside the more realistic hope of just managing the status quo to the
benefit of all, so that all can pursue oil and natural gas exploration in
the face of absolute rises in population that may help drive energy
prices upward. But that will be difficult. For example, the Philippines'
Malampaya and Camago natural gas and condensate fields are in
Chinese-claimed waters. Vietnam and China have overlapping claims
to undeveloped energy blocks off the Vietnamese coast. China has announced that a potential new source of natural gas—frozen methane—
was discovered on the seabed near the Paracels, in an area that China
disputes with Vietnam. The claims just go on like this.[12]

Of course, the importance of hydrocarbons in the South China Sea
should not be overestimated. South China Sea reserves are unlikely to
affect the continuing divergence between demand and domestic production in China: nor would they allow Taiwan to become a net exporter. Vietnam, Malaysia, and the Philippines will remain energy
importers no matter how much oil and natural gas they are able to
extract from the seabed. Brunei, for that matter, is already a large net
exporter of oil. So in terms of the larger dynamics of energy in the

region, little is likely to change. The South China Sea will grow in importance less because of the hydrocarbon resources it holds than because of the increased amounts of imported oil and natural gas passing through its sea lanes.[13]

But it isn't just oil and natural gas that matter. South China Sea fish stocks may account for as much as one tenth of the global landed catch.[14] Chinese fishing boats operating in disputed waters are accompanied by vessels from China's Bureau of Fisheries Administration, in order to assert Chinese jurisdiction in the South China Sea.[15]

Nevertheless, despite all of these complications and provocations, the legal situation of these waters can be simplified, at least somewhat: stare at the map long enough and some basic facts stand out.

The heart of the drama revolves around historic claims to three archipelagoes: the Pratas in the north, the Paracels in the northwest, and the Spratlys in the southeast. The Pratas are claimed by China but controlled by Taiwan. In any case, there is little argument that these are Chinese islands. China and Taiwan actually agree to a significant extent on the South China Sea, except that China does not consider Taiwan a party to the claims because in Beijing's eyes Taiwan is not a state: so the argument has really to do less with the South China Sea than with the future of de facto Taiwanese independence vis-à-vis China.

The Vietnamese have a strong claim to the Paracels, but the western part of this archipelago has been occupied by China since Beijing took control of it from a failing Saigon government in 1974, near the end of the Vietnam War. The Chinese and Vietnamese have, in fact, solved their disputes in the Gulf of Tonkin: a tribute partly to solidarity between the two countries' communist parties and their pragmatism. But the dispute over the Paracels and other places makes the contest between China and Vietnam the centerpiece of the South China Sea conflict zone.

Then there are the Spratlys, which have been claimed by the Philippines only since the 1950s, within a polygon-shaped line known as the Kalayaan Island Group. Nearby is Reed Bank, completely submerged, but vociferously claimed by the Filipinos, who are confident of large deposits of oil and gas in the area. Unlike the Vietnamese claims to the Paracels, which the Chinese privately respect and worry about, the Chinese don't respect Philippine designs on the Spratlys. Whereas Vietnam is a tough and battle-hardened warrior state, the Philippines, to repeat, constitutes a semi-failed entity with weak institutions and an extremely weak military—and the Chinese know all this. Even so, China has to keep its aggression against the Philippines in check because the Philippines is a treaty ally of the United States.

Vietnam, Malaysia, and Brunei all, too, claim features in the Spratlys, though Malaysia only issued its maps in 1979. Up until 2009, the drama was all about who owned the islands. Then Vietnam and Malaysia made a joint submission to international bodies basing their claims beyond their exclusive economic zones, or EEZs, which according to the 1982 United Nations Convention on the Law of the Sea extended two hundred miles straight out from their coasts. For the Law of the Sea treaty is actually about land, not water, since your claim under the treaty is based on the location of your coastline. The land dominates the sea—that is the Law of the Sea's underlying principle. Your coastline gets you two hundred miles into the ocean plus extra if there is a continental shelf involved, but a claim based on ownership of an island gets you only twelve miles out. Brunei, for example, with a coastline on northwestern Borneo less than fifty miles long, claims Louisa Reef and Rifleman Bank almost midway across the South China Sea in the direction of Vietnam. Vietnam and Malaysia also made claims based on the Law of the Sea and guess what: China was cut out of the Spratlys, which come within Vietnam's and Malaysia's EEZs; not to mention the EEZs of the Philippines and Brunei. The Law of the Sea only gets China to the Pratas and the Paracels, not to the Spratlys, where the largest energy deposits are thought to be. And as far as the Paracels are concerned, China could be doomed there to a twilight struggle with a truculent Vietnam, which may have the stronger legal claim.

In other words, once the Law of the Sea came into play, China's cow's tongue—or historic nine-dashed line—suddenly had little legal meaning or rationale. Because of the geographical configuration of the littoral states, everyone else's EEZs get them possession of shallow archipelagic areas near coasts thought to contain energy deposits, whereas China's EEZ extending southward from its coastline gets it comparatively little beyond deep blue water, with exceptions including Pratas Island, Macclesfield Bank, and Scarborough Shoal.

Well, the Chinese say that they have authentic historic claims, while the Law of the Sea only came into being in 1982, and is therefore only part of the story. (Though China ratified the Law of the Sea treaty in 1996, it does not really adhere to it; whereas the United States adheres to it, but hasn't ratified it.) In 2009, Chinese officials put out for the first time a map with the nine-dashed line and began interfering with other countries' survey ships. In 2011, the Chinese made a submission to the United Nations actually making a claim of a full two hundred nautical miles around each of the Spratly Islands.[16] Suddenly, such claims, coupled with China's ongoing military expansion, made everyone fearful of rising Chinese power.

The United States got involved ostensibly because it sought to protect a legal, rules-based order enshrining freedom of navigation, which the nine-dashed line appeared to threaten. In fact, the real problem that the Americans have had with China was its expanding submarine base at Hainan Island in the northwestern corner of the South China Sea, which is home to both the latest diesel-electric submarines as well as nuclear ballistic missile subs. Largely because of that base, and because China's deployment of more and more submarines threatened American power projection in the region, the United States pushed back in the guise of strengthening ties to the smaller littoral countries, offering to mediate these nettlesome maritime disputes in 2010. In 2011, the United States announced a "pivot" to the Pacific from the Middle East.[17] The American fear wasn't about China's naval acquisitions per se, or about China questioning the legal order per se, but about the combination of the two.

Stepping back a bit, one legal expert in the region told me that it is possible to cut all kinds of deals to ease these disputes, if not completely solve them. For example, China could be granted extensive fishing privileges in the deep-water middle of the South China Sea, in exchange for some leeway on the nine-dashed line and thus on the EEZ claims. The real problem is that all sides, with the partial exception of Malaysia, are guilty of playing domestic politics with their claims. And by energizing the nationalistic elements in each country, reaching a compromise becomes more difficult. If you left the South China Sea issue to the experts and to the elites in the region, the various disputes would have a better chance of being solved than if you involved large populations in a democratic process, compromised as they are by their emotions. Again Aristotle: "law is intellect without appetite."[18] Because the masses have "appetite," peace is more likely to reign if they are left out of the equation.

But even with the law, even if China makes its peace with the Law of the Sea convention, and even if the United States were to sign the convention, peace must ultimately be maintained by a balance of power.

It would be healthier for the American-Chinese relationship—the most important bilateral relationship in the world—if Asian states themselves helped balance against rising Chinese military power, rather than relying overwhelmingly on the United States. The most obvious mechanism for that is a strengthened Association of Southeast Asian Nations. ASEAN is ascending. To be sure, ASEAN is not at the level of integration of the European Union (EU), which is united by a common form of government—democracy—giving it a philosophical, and hence political, raison d'être. Moreover, China maintains the ability to exploit divisions within ASEAN. Nevertheless, ASEAN—its democracies and quasi-democracies both—has been over the course of the decades gradually pulling together because of the challenge of a rising China, and also because the individual member states themselves have been evolving into more capable bureaucratic instruments in their own right, able to project power for the first time in their histories. ASEAN's 600 million people produce a combined gross domestic product of $1.7 trillion, greater than that of India (which in less than two decades will be the world's most populous nation).[19]

ASEAN will likely never be as cohesive as the EU was at the height of its harmony and power projection capabilities in the first two decades after the Cold War. But neither will the United States–China relationship be as tense and fraught with ideological animosity as that between the United States and the Soviet Union. China and the United States have starkly different strategic orientations, obviously. And the fact that China still seems to be a rising power militarily can make it particularly ruthless. Still, we can hope that maritime Asia, and the South China Sea in particular, in the twenty-first century will evince a far more nuanced balance of power arrangement than continental Europe in the twentieth. And because, I repeat, with the exception of diminishing American ground troop contingents in Japan and South Korea, the theater of operations will be on the water rather than on dry land, the chances of conflict will be somewhat diminished.

Nevertheless, keep in mind that increased force posture by area navies means more activities at sea, increasing the risk of incidents that can lead to war.

The United States and ASEAN will not constitute the only hedges against a rising China: so, too, will a new webwork of relationships emerging bilaterally among the Asian countries themselves, along the navigable rimland of Asia in the Western Pacific and Indian oceans. At least nineteen new defense agreements were signed between 2009 and 2011 in this region. Vietnam, in particular, became the locus of a whole new set of partnerships that linked Hanoi with India, South Korea, Japan, the Philippines, Malaysia, Singapore, Indonesia, and Australia.[20] And many of these countries have made a similar set of arrangements with each other. The further that this development goes, the lighter will be the burden on the United States to provide for the region's common security.

However, Washington should be under no illusions. All of these states, with the exceptions of South Korea, Japan, and Australia, lack the operational capacity to mount a serious challenge to a growing and improving Chinese military. And even these three militaries evince nowhere near the capability of the American one, while only Australia and Vietnam have usable combat experience in recent decades. Moreover, as China's military capacity in the air, sea, and cyber domains increases, it will seek to "enforce more fully" its ostensible rights against neighboring states in the maritime domain.[21]

Thus, the idea that the United States can reduce its commitment to the Western Pacific, while sitting back and letting the indigenous states themselves bear more of the burden, may be feasible in the long run, but not in the short run. In the short run, a weaker American commitment to the region might result in the states on China's periphery losing heart and bandwagoning instead with China. Because this would be an insidious development, rather than a clear-cut and demonstrable one, it is particularly dangerous, and not worth risking. And given that not only liberal internationalists and neoconservatives, but also traditional realists such as offshore balancers, believe it is important for the United States to maintain a balance of power in the Eastern hemisphere, accepting an imperium over much of the hemisphere run by Beijing would be irresponsible.

And there is another thing. Assuming that China itself does not implode or even partially implode from an internal economic crisis, the serious reduction of American air and sea power—with its stabilizing effect on the region—would cause countries such as China and India, and China and Russia, to become far more aggressive toward each other. This would occur even as countries such as Japan, South Korea, and Vietnam bandwagon with China: altogether a perilous situation, that, even if it did not lead to hostilities outright, would have a negative impact on world financial markets. In this scenario, *the world America made,* to steal a phrase from the scholar Robert Kagan, would go a long way to being undone.[22]

In fact, as Kagan would wish, the opposite is still the case. Roughly half of America's dozen or so aircraft carrier strike groups are nominally assigned to the Pacific, even if two of them have been doing regular duty in the Persian Gulf recently. And U.S. naval domination of China remains immense. Just consider: against America's six nominal aircraft carrier strike groups in the Pacific, China has maybe one. The United States deploys twelve guided missile cruisers in the region, China has none. The United States has twenty-nine guided missile destroyers there; China has eight advanced ones. But as I've indicated earlier in this book, China is catching up. By the latter half of the next decade it will have more warships than the U.S. Navy in the Western Pacific. And it is catching up where it counts: in subsurface warfare, increasingly the future of naval activity. China's eventual parity with the United States in terms of the size of its submarine fleet has two aspects. First, it will take the Chinese at least another generation to operate underwater platforms with the skill required to challenge American crews. Second, countering this, is China's "familiarity" with the very shallow waters of the South China and East China seas. Writes Jonathan Holslag, a Brussels-based expert on the subject: "Complex thermal layers, tide noise and the influx of water from rivers make it very difficult to detect pre-positioned submarines. Conventional diesel-electric submarines," of the kind China has, he goes on, "are ideal for navigating in such environments, and apart from the new *Virginia*-class, older U.S. or Japanese types lack the sophisticated detection capacities that are needed to operate in these areas." Moreover, China is likely to deploy its submarines in conjunction with large-scale use of sea mines, complicating U.S. Navy efforts.[23] (This is all in addition to China's civilian fleet, which, in fact, acts as an adjunct to its military one. For example, Beijing will have added thirty-six new vessels to its maritime surveillance service in 2013 alone.[24])

China's ultimate tactical goal is to dissuade the U.S. Navy from entering the Taiwan Strait in times of war, thus compromising America's ability to defend Taiwan. This will be accomplished by deploying silent conventional submarines in the shallow waters near Taiwan, as well as a large fleet of small surface combatants.[25] The question to ask is not, Will China ever be able to defeat the United States in an air-sea war? For the answer to that is clearly no, for the foreseeable future. Rather, the question is, Will China ever be able to deploy air-sea power asymmetrically to undermine the aura of U.S. dominance in the Western Pacific? And the answer to that is, very possibly.

But it won't just be a matter of subtle, high-tech asymmetry at sea, but also of a more conventional ambition for an oceanic, blue-water navy. To wit, on six occasions by the end of 2010, the Chinese navy passed the First Island Chain off the Asian mainland and entered the Pacific Ocean proper.[26] Indeed, in 2001, when University of Chicago political scientist John Mearsheimer published *The Tragedy of Great Power Politics,* in which he asserted that China would pursue great power status in political and military ways much as rising powers have done throughout history, China's air and naval capacity was only a fraction of what it has now become. Again, it seems that only major economic (and therefore, social) upheaval inside China it-self—of the kind that stops increases in defense spending—can now contradict Mearsheimer's vision.[27]

Nevertheless, this need not lead to war. As M. Taylor Fravel, a political scientist at the Massachusetts Institute of Technology, ex-plains: The very buildup of military power by China means that par-adoxically China can wait and not use force.[28] For as each year passes, China's naval position strengthens. Beijing's goal is not war—but an adjustment in the correlation of forces that enhances its geopolitical power and prestige.

But what if a severe economic crisis does ignite a downward trend in Chinese military procurements, or at least a less steep growth curve? This is also something to seriously consider!

Indeed, in order to assuage public anger at continued poverty and lack of jobs, China's leaders might, for the sake of a political effect, ask the military to make sacrifices of its own. Over time, this could shake the foundations of the Eurasian maritime order, though not nearly as much as the collapse of the Berlin Wall shook the founda-tions of the European continental order.

Stalled Chinese defense budgets would reinvigorate a Pax Ameri-cana from the Sea of Japan to the Persian Gulf, despite the debacles of the Iraq and Afghanistan wars, and despite the U.S. military budget crunch. The U.S. Navy would own the seas as though World War II had just ended. Japan, which continues to modernize its air force and navy (the latter is several times larger than the British Royal Navy), would emerge as an enhanced air and sea power in Asia. The same goes for a future reunified Korea governed from Seoul, which, in the event of a weakened China, would face Japan as a principal rival, with the United States keeping the peace between the two states.

Turmoil in China would slow the economic integration of Taiwan with the mainland. With so many ballistic missiles aimed at Taiwan from the mainland and so many commercial flights per week between the two Chinas, U.S. military aid to Taipei is less and less designed to defend Taiwan than to postpone an inevitable unification of sorts. But the inevitable unification of sorts might not happen in the event of a prolonged economic and political crisis in Beijing. A likelier scenario in this case would be for different regional Chinas, democratic to greater or lesser extents, more loosely tied to Beijing, to begin to emerge. This, too, translates into a renewed Pax Americana, as long as U.S. defense cuts don't go too far.

And what if China's economic crisis does not seriously affect its defense acquisitions? Then the South China Sea would be where the effects of gradual American decline, in a geopolitical sense, are most keenly felt. China's geographical centrality, its economic heft, and its burgeoning air and naval forces would translate into some measure of Finlandization for Vietnam, Malaysia, the Philippines, and Singapore in the event of large-scale U.S. defense cuts. But internal disarray in China, combined with modest U.S. defense cuts that do not fundamentally affect America's Pacific forces, could unleash the opposite effect. Emboldened by a continued American presence and a less than dominant Chinese military, countries such as Singapore and Australia, who already spend mightily on arms relative to the size of their populations, could emerge as little Israels in Asia. Vietnam, meanwhile, with a larger population than Turkey or Iran, and dominating the South China Sea's western seaboard, could become a full-fledged middle-level power in its own right were Beijing's regional grip to loosen and Vietnam able to get its economic house in order.

India, like Vietnam and Taiwan, would gain most from a profound economic and political crisis inside China of the kind that unleashes China's ethnic minorities. Suddenly China would be more vulnerable to ethnic unrest on the Tibetan plateau, abutting the Indian Subcontinent. This would alleviate the Chinese threat on India's northern borderlands, even as it gives India greater diplomatic leverage in its bilateral relations with Nepal, Bangladesh, Sri Lanka, and Burma, all of which have been venues for India's quiet great game that it has been playing with China. Burma has historically been where Indian and Chinese cultural and political influence overlap. Though China has been the dominant outside economic influence in Burma in recent decades, prior to World War II Indian economic middlemen were a major force in the capital of Rangoon. Look for the Indian role in Burma to dramatically ramp up in the event of a partial Chinese political meltdown. Given Burma's massive stores of natural gas, coal, zinc, copper, precious stones, timber, and hydropower, this would not be an insignificant geopolitical development. It would ease India's naval entry into the South China Sea. The glory days of Vietnam's Indianized Champa civilization would find an echo in a twenty-first-century strategic reality.

This is all theoretically possible, were China to experience a form of economic meltdown. However, now I must return to the situation as it is at the time of my writing.

Thucydides writes that the "real cause" of the Peloponnesian War was the rise of Athenian sea power and "the alarm which this inspired in Sparta."[29] Indeed, wars often start over seemingly inconsequential matters—uninhabited islands, for instance—even as their underlying causes are anything but inconsequential. Thus, the rise of Chinese sea power should not be taken lightly. Athens may have been democratic, even as China may have no motives for conquest. Yet the very disturbance of the status quo caused by the ascendancy of a new power has throughout history raised the risk of hostilities. The fact that China's military rise is wholly legitimate (China is not a rogue state like clerical Iran) makes little difference, given that China's air and naval acquisitions are altering the regional balance of power, something which in and of itself is destabilizing. Of course, the status quo is not sacrosanct. History as we know is dynamic. And the status quo can be unfair and deserving of change. But it is a fact that war often breaks out when there has been a significant change in the status quo.

As China's naval position in the Western Pacific grows, increasingly altering the status quo, "a grand and protracted bargaining process" between the United States and China will go on for the geopolitical fate of the Western Pacific and the adjacent Indian Ocean, writes Swarthmore College political scientist James Kurth. "In the end, there might be constructed an explicit and effective system of mutual deterrence, based upon such concepts as red-lines, salient thresholds, and tit-for-tat actions and reactions."[30]

We can see the beginning of this process in recent years. In 2011, Secretary of State Hillary Clinton declared a "pivot" to Asia. At the same time, Secretary of Defense Leon Panetta declared that Pentagon budget cuts would not come at the expense of U.S. force posture in the Pacific. These were both strong messages indicating U.S. resolve to maintain and perhaps strengthen U.S. air and sea forces in the face of China's military rise. Meanwhile, President Obama's announcement, also in 2011, that the United States would begin rotating 2,500 marines through bases in northern and western Australia, near the confluence of the Western Pacific and Indian oceans—coupled with the stationing of new littoral combat ships in nearby Singapore—demonstrated an American desire to distribute forces across two oceans rather than across one: so that the maritime security systems of the Greater Middle East and East Asia would begin to merge into one grand geography uniting the southern Eurasian rimland. The more immediate result of this would be to bring South Asia into the same conflict system of which the South China Sea is the center. Remember, the advancing technology of war compresses distance. Henceforth, the term Indo-Pacific would be used more and more. The scholar Michael Auslin of the American Enterprise Institute writes, "Conceptually, this new strategic arrangement can be thought of as a set of 'concentric triangles,' based on rough geographic coverage. The outer triangle links Japan, South Korea, India, and Australia; the inner triangle connects Indonesia, Malaysia, Singapore, and Vietnam."[31] Meanwhile, an emerging Asian power web designed to balance against China links countries like India and Vietnam in a "robust strategic partnership."[32]

So now let us look at the larger map. In 2050, close to seven out of nine billion people in the world will live generally in East Asia, Southeast Asia, South Asia, the Middle East, and East Africa. The maritime organizing principle of this global demographic heartland is the Greater Indian Ocean, along with the Western Pacific. It is a map that unites Eurasia by sea, assuming that the northern Eurasia coastline, comprised mainly of Russia, remains ice-blocked or partially ice-blocked for significant portions of the year. From the Horn of Africa across the Indian Ocean, bending around archipelagic Indonesia, up to the Sea of Japan, constitutes one world in this vision. And whereas the Indian Subcontinent, Japan, and Australia are the outer points of this map, the countries of the South China Sea constitute the inner points, or strategic core of it. The South China Sea is the Mitteleuropa of the twenty-first century.

The South China Sea, whether in peace or in war, allows one to imagine the world as it is, and as it is to become. It is a nervous world, crowded with warships and oil tankers, one of incessant war games without necessarily leading to actual combat: a world in which actions taken by a country such as Vietnam, the political bellwether of the South China Sea region, can affect the highest decisions of state in Beijing and Washington. It is a world where sea denial is cheaper and easier to accomplish than sea control, so that lesser sea powers like China and India may be able to check the ambitions of a greater power like the United States, and submarines and mines and land-based missiles may combine to inhibit the use of aircraft carriers and other large surface warships.[33] It is a world in which it is just not good enough for American officials to plan for continued dominance in these waters. For they must be prepared to allow, in some measure, for a rising Chinese navy to assume its rightful position, as the representative of the region's largest indigenous power. True, America must safeguard a maritime system of international legal norms, buttressed by a favorable balance of power regimen. But the age of simple American dominance, as it existed through all of the Cold War decades and immediately beyond, will likely have to pass. A more anxious, complicated world awaits us.

EPILOGUE

The Slums of Borneo

Oily-green forests slashed by sludgy, curvilinear rivers; tree-lined ridges crouching under rain clouds; a moldy, bottle-green sea offering a confused reflection of the tormented sky above: an entire landscape that signaled confinement. The town of Kota Kinabalu near the northern tip of Borneo—the Jesselton of British colonial days—had, despite the ratty sprawl and overpasses, a carved-out-of-the-jungle feel. Weeds ate up many a sidewalk; stone walls were blackened from decades of rain; the rusted balconies were crammed with water tanks, machine-molded plastic chairs, and sagging clothes lines. After the glittering postmodernism of Kuala Lumpur in peninsular Malaysia, this capital of the Malaysian state of Sabah, with its tacky, concrete pink- and cream-colored facades, had, nevertheless, a faded black-and-white aura. Whereas on the Malay Peninsula, the state of Malaysia with its confection of ethnic groups appeared subtle and dynamic, here in far-off East Malaysia, separated from the peninsula by Indonesian territorial waters, the idea of *Malaysia* seemed tenuous; more desperate.

I came to the Malaysian state of Sabah to visit a naval base where two Scorpène-class diesel-electric submarines were berthed. The subs were there to announce Malaysia's intention of defending the southeastern corner of the South China Sea against Chinese, Vietnamese, and Philippine maritime incursions. I was denied permission to visit the base, however.

Instead, with the help of a Malaysian friend, I paid a young man with a small wooden boat and outboard motor the equivalent of forty-five dollars to take me across the bay from Kota Kinabalu to a *kampung air,* or water village, adjacent to the island of Gaya. The village was a vast slum city on stilts, stretching far out from the island into the rolling sea.

Warrens of shacks and alleyways, built of cheap wood and patches of corrugated iron, rested on twisted tree limbs sunk vertically in the water. Half-naked children were everywhere, as though each was about to fall off the edge of the narrow and corroded planks connecting the houses. A gold-painted mosque dome made of hammered sheet metal punctuated the marine encampment that held thousands. These people were, for the most part, illegal Muslim Filipino migrants from the Sulu archipelago: the southern extremity of the Philippines racked by Islamic insurgencies—insurgencies caused, ultimately, by the failure of a weak and corrupt Roman Catholic power structure in the capital of Manila to properly govern its own far-flung ethnic reaches.

These people made their living as fishermen, construction workers, and at a medley of other jobs that frankly no Malaysians wanted. Typhoons and fires had wiped out this and other, even larger seaborne encampments. But the migrants quickly rebuilt them, and more destitute Filipinos kept coming. Roughly a quarter of Sabah's population were illegals. Geography was an enabler. It was only seven minutes by motorboat—as a Malaysian coast guard admiral later told me—from the southernmost Philippine island to the northernmost Malaysian one.

The admiral then spoke to me of that other reality of the South China Sea, one in which the water village was a window onto a world of disease, piracy, and smuggling. While the region's navies were concerned with the twenty-first-century strategic chessboard of strong states and their overlapping blue-water territorial claims, the region's coast guards dealt with a *Back to the Future* nineteenth-century world before the modern state had existed—a world where the southern Philippines, Malaysia, and Indonesia were a unitary, archipelagic mass of Muslim peoples, Malays and Javanese both, to-ing and fro-ing between the former British and Dutch empires of the East Indies. (Because of its ethnic Malay insurgency, southern Thailand, too, is part of this Muslim world.)

Abetted by a convenient geography, global Islam—an undeniable form of globalization—was undoing the nation-state of Malaysia here in northern Borneo, just as peninsular Malaysia with its strong institutions (a product of Mahathir bin Mohamad's authoritarian rule) was building it up. Of course, Mahathir represented global Islam, too, in its political and ideological form. The question was how would Islam finally be deployed here: as a force for modern state building, or for transnational refugee movements that undermined the modern state?

Sabah was one place in the South China Sea region where no one talked about the Chinese naval threat—but instead about illegals. "They are the mother of all our problems," said one *bumiputra* (indigenous) Christian, whose ancestors were baptized by Roman Catholic missionaries, referring to the Muslim *kampung air* across the bay. This man, a prominent local politician, sat at a long wooden table with some of his colleagues, members of the Kadazan and Dusun tribes all, who, while native to Sabah, now accounted for less of the population than the illegals. Rather than a world of upscale malls and tinted glass, as in peninsular Malaysia and much of the rest of the South China Sea region, here beside me were homely statues of Jesus and the Virgin Mary and angry voices set amidst the encroaching jungle. They kept me at the table for hours with their intensity, their obsessive bitterness about the illegal Muslim Filipinos, and the peninsular colonizers who in their minds had merely taken over from the British and made a mess of it.

So it was with my other meetings in Kota Kinabalu. *Oh Jesselton,* they all seemed to cry out in almost fond memory of the British North Borneo Company, *where the Chinese dominated the cities, the Malays and* bumiputras *dominated the* kampungs, *and the Indians the plantations. Everyone got along because everyone knew his place under a European flag. And so peace reigned more or less.* But now, despite the impressive levels of intermarriage between *bumiputras,* Malays, Chinese, and Indians, as well as between Christians, Muslims, and animists—creating identities far more subtle than on the peninsula—the threat of political Islamization from peninsular Malaysia and demographic Islamization from the southern Philippines was inviting all sorts of zero-sum ethnic and religious tensions—and thinking.

It turns out that the challenges of the South China Sea are, at least in part, the challenges of postcolonialism, in which newly formed polities emerging out of world empires must now settle which group or faction controls what internally, and which state controls what externally in the waters beyond.

And it isn't only in the waters beyond, since, for example, the Philippines has a latent claim on Sabah itself, arising out of a dispute about whether the sultan of Sulu in the late nineteenth century had ceded or merely leased northern Borneo to the British. Thus, these sprawling *kampungs* pockmarking the Sabah coast represented a deeper puzzle than the specific social problems brought by the illegals themselves: they represented the problem—the fear—of Malaysia being not altogether legitimate but, rather, a legalistic contraption inherited from the British part of the Malay archipelago, theoretically always open to challenge. For had Singapore not been brought into the Federation of Malaysia in 1963, upsetting the ethnic balance to the benefit of the Chinese, then Kuala Lumpur would not have needed to include the Malays and other *bumiputras* of northern Borneo in the federation in the first place. The creation of Malaysia had all been so ad hoc: a product of the complex relationship between Tunku Abdul Rahman and Lee Kuan Yew as much as a product of geography and the territorial boundaries between Great Britain and the Netherlands on Borneo.

"We are still ethnic groups and races, we are not yet a state composed of citizens," the tribal politician told me, summing everything up. "Mahathir's Islamic state on the peninsula oppresses us. The Filipino illegals are convenient to the Muslim power structure in Kuala Lumpur because these illegals from Sulu are altering the demographic balance in the Muslims' favor. Sabah is responsible for 60 percent of the oil in Malaysia and gets only 5 percent of it back in revenue," he went on. "It won't happen in my lifetime, but eventually the Malaysian federation may break up."

He said this as though it were a hope. For he now spoke of Sabah in the same tone as he spoke about South Sudan or former East Pakistan. While the maritime disputes of newly hardened states in the region dominated the present, and therefore something I have been forced to write about, he seemed to suggest that globalization itself could encourage the emergence of distinct micro-regions in Asia just as it already had in Europe.

So while I had been concentrating on the rise of modern nationalism in the South China Sea, Sabah—like the ruins of Champa in central Vietnam—spoke of the possible reemergence of a medieval world in which nationalism had yet to be invented.

Borneo was indeed a throwback: a place that, like Champa in Vietnam, challenged my theories about the present—about how China was the principal reality; and about how it was all about warships, oil tankers, and modernizing autocrats. For next door in northern Borneo in the Malaysian state of Sarawak there was a chief minister, Abdul Taib Mahmud, a member of the minority Melanau tribe of *bumiputras,* who had been in power since 1981 and governed like a petty despot, in premodern paternalistic fashion, even as he was democratically elected. Here was a world of cronyism and kickbacks governing everything from logging contracts to the control of local newspapers. The chief minister's thirty-year reign lubricated the wheels of development, yet it also left the indigenous tribes in the interior in a state of poverty and prevented the emergence of real institutions. Sarawak's somnolent capital of Kuching was dominated by fantasy structures that were the trophies of his rule, such as a $300 million, umbrella-like state assembly building used only sixteen days a year when the legislators were in session.

Sarawak had actually been governed by a series of British "white rajahs" from the mid-nineteenth to the mid-twentieth century. The first was James Brooke, who, having grown up in British India and journeyed around Madras, Penang, Malacca, and Singapore—the whole region where the Indian Ocean meets the Pacific—bought a schooner with an inheritance and sailed up the Sarawak River, arriving in Kuching in 1839. Brooke proceeded to make himself the *Tuan Besar* (Great Lord) of the territory, engaging in local wars, suppressing piracy, playing one tribe against the other, even as he established a nascent administration and legal system, in a drama that Joseph Conrad might have written. Brooke was succeeded by his nephew, Charles Brooke, who in turn was succeeded by his own son, Charles Vyner Brooke, who ruled until World War II.[1] Chief Minister Taib's paternalistic style was similar enough to that of the Brookes that he was referred to as the "brown rajah." The worry in Kuching in 2013 was not about China but about the chaos that might follow the demise of the chief minister, leading, perhaps, to a strengthening of the peninsula's involvement in local affairs.

Borneo—even the relatively developed Malaysian states of Sabah and Sarawak in the island's north—was a window onto a poorer and more chaotic world signaled by the sprawling immensity of Indonesia just to the south.[2] The navies and air forces that figure prominently in the contest over the South China Sea and in this book are themselves manifestations of successful modern development and the strong in-

stitutions that go along with it. But this part of the South China Sea—
the archipelago stretching from the Philippines to Indonesia—echoes
a different reality entirely.

So here I am at the end of my journey with more questions. What
if, as I intimated in the previous chapter, China eventually has a messy
decentralization of sorts as a result of a truly profound economic and
political crisis yet to come? How would that affect its ability to continually enlarge its air and naval forces and to make war, and thus to
intimidate its neighbors? What if the future of the South China Sea is
not just about newly strong states asserting their territorial claims,
but also about a new medievalism born of weak central government
and global Islam? Of course we could have a combination of both: of
a comparatively weaker China that, coupled with a more decentral-
ized Malaysia, Philippines, and Indonesia, might reignite such problems as piracy and refugee flows, even as the U.S. Navy and Air Force
retain their relative regional dominance. Don't think of the region as
necessarily going in one direction, in other words.

Because different futures are possible, all that I have written is a
mere period piece: I have focused on the central drama of the beginning of the second decade of the twenty-first century, that of China's
military rise in the area where the Western Pacific and the Indian
Ocean intersect. But as much as I heard about submarines throughout my journeys, the image of the slum encampment on stilts in the
water lingers, too.

ACKNOWLEDGMENTS

Foreign Policy, The Atlantic, and *The National Interest* each published works-in-progress of this book, for which I thank the editors and fact-checkers at those publications. A one-thousand-word section on Philippine history is reprinted from my 2005 book, *Imperial Grunts,* as noted on the copyright page.

As in all my past books, I am in debt to Brandt and Hochman Literary Agents in Manhattan, especially the late Carl D. Brandt and Marianne Merola. Indeed, Carl Brandt, who tragically passed away as I completed this book, was my most necessary friend over the past quarter century. I must also thank Gail Hochman and Henry Thayer. At Random House, much thanks are due to my editor, Jonathan Jao, and his assistant, Molly Turpin.

My colleagues at Stratfor, too numerous to name, assisted me greatly in the content of this book, as well as giving me the freedom to complete it. Nevertheless, I want to especially mention two of

Stratfor's Asia analysts, Matt Gertken and John Minnich, and Stratfor's founder, George Friedman, for helping me with some of the details of the manuscript. My colleagues at the Center for a New American Security, again too numerous to name, provided me with the encouragement to start the project in the first place, and helped it in all its phases. Patrick Cronin, Richard Fontaine, and Robert Work stand out among those now at CNAS who over the years educated me about things Asian and things naval. The Smith Richardson Foundation once again proved generous in its willingness to support my work: for which I thank Nadia Schadlow, among others.

In Beijing, Paul Haenle and his colleagues at the Carnegie-Tsinghua Center for Global Policy hosted me splendidly in every detail. In Kuala Lumpur, Sean Foley and Tang Siew Mun initially introduced me to Malaysia, even as Shahriman Lockman provided me with contacts there, arranged logistics, and most of all provided the gift of his altogether delightful and brilliant friendship. In Singapore, Peter Beckman, Ian Storey, and the late Barry Wain were generous with their expertise. In the Philippines, Dante Francis Ang and his staff at *The Manila Times* very ably arranged my schedule. The Diplomatic Academy of Vietnam did likewise for me in Hanoi. The Taiwanese government funded a trip to Taipei and arranged the logistics of getting me to one of the disputed islands in the South China Sea. Elizabeth Lockyer, my assistant, arranged the maps (with Stratfor's assistance) and many other details of this project. My wife, Maria Cabral, once again made it all possible by tolerating my long absences.

NOTES

PROLOGUE: THE RUINS OF CHAMPA

1. Jean-François Hubert, *The Art of Champa,* Parkstone Press, Ho Chi Minh City, 2005, pp. 7–8, 17–18, 20, 22–23, 28–29, 31–32.
2. The full photographic archives of ancient Champa are housed at the Musée Guimet in Paris.

CHAPTER I: THE HUMANIST DILEMMA

1. John J. Mearsheimer, *The Tragedy of Great Power Politics,* W. W. Norton, New York, 2001, p. 114.
2. U.S. Energy Information Administration, "South China Sea: Oil and Natural Gas," March 2008; Robert D. Kaplan, "China's Caribbean," *Washington Post,* September 26, 2010.
3. Regional Program on Partnerships in Environmental Management for the Seas of East Asia, "Current Activities in GEF-UNDP-IMO PEMSEA Programme Relating to Maritime Safety and Security";

Center for a New American Security, "The South China Sea: The First Testing Ground of a Multipolar Age," Washington, D.C., September 2010.

4. U.S. Energy Information Agency and Scott Snyder, "The South China Sea Dispute: Prospects for Preventive Diplomacy," United States Institute for Peace, August 1996; Center for a New American Security, "The South China Sea: The First Testing Ground of a Multipolar Age." Oil deposits in the Spratlys may be overhyped, with natural gas the more abundant hydrocarbon resource. See Sam Bateman and Ralf Emmers, eds., *Security and International Politics in the South China Sea: Towards a Cooperative Management Regime,* Routledge, New York, 2009, p. 17; John C. Baker and David G. Wiencek, *Cooperative Monitoring in the South China Sea: Satellite Imagery, Confidence-Building Measures, and the Spratly Islands Disputes,* Praeger, Westport, Connecticut, 2002, p. 6.

5. Rear Admiral (ret.) Michael A. McDevitt in conversation at a conference at the Center for a New American Security, Washington, D.C., September 29, 2011.

6. BP Statistical Review of World Energy, London, 2011; Andrew Higgins, "In South China Sea, a Dispute over Energy," *Washington Post,* September 17, 2011.

7. Carl Ungerer, Ian Storey, and Sam Bateman, "Making Mischief: The Return of the South China Sea Dispute," Australian Strategic Policy Institute, Barton, Australia, December 2010.

8. Energy Information Administration, "South China Sea: Country Analysis Briefs."

9. Geoffrey Till and J. N. Mak, essays in Bateman and Emmers, eds., *Security and International Politics in the South China Sea,* pp. 38–39, 117–18; Robert D. Kaplan, *Monsoon: The Indian Ocean and the Future of American Power,* Random House, New York, 2010, p. 7.

10. Baker and Wiencek, *Cooperative Monitoring in the South China Sea,* p. 7.

11. Rommel C. Banlaoi, "Renewed Tensions and the Continuing Maritime Security Dilemma in the South China Sea," paper presented at the International Forum on Maritime Security, Keelung, Taiwan, April 2010.

12. Kaplan, "China's Caribbean."

13. Robert B. Strassler, ed., *The Landmark Thucydides: A Comprehensive Guide to the Peloponnesian War,* trans. Richard Crawley, Simon & Schuster, New York, 1998, p. 352. Actually, there is a similar Chengyu saying, "The weak are prey to the strong."

14. Andrew Marshall, "Military Maneuvers," *Time,* New York, September 27, 2010; "China's New Naval Base Triggers U.S. Concerns," SpaceWar.com, May 12, 2008.
15. "Map of Nineteenth Century China and Conflicts," www.fordham .edu/halsall, reprinted in *Reshaping Economic Geography,* World Bank, Washington, D.C., 2009, p. 195.
16. Jonathan D. Spence, *In Search of Modern China,* W. W. Norton, New York, 1990, pp. 300, 450–51.
17. Piers Brendon, "China Also Rises," *The National Interest,* Washington, November/December 2010.
18. Mearsheimer, *The Tragedy of Great Power Politics,* pp. 2, 168.
19. Mark J. Valencia, "The South China Sea: Back to the Future?," *Global Asia,* Seoul, December 2010.
20. Andrew F. Krepinevich, "China's 'Finlandization' Strategy in the Pacific," *Wall Street Journal,* New York, September 11, 2010.
21. Mark Helprin, "Farewell to America's China Station," *Wall Street Journal,* New York, May 17, 2010.
22. Abraham M. Denmark and Brian M. Burton, "The Future of U.S. Alliances in Asia," *Global Asia,* Seoul, December 2010.
23. Hugh White, "Power Shift: Australia's Future Between Washington and Beijing," *Quarterly Essay,* Collingwood, Australia, 2010, pp. 1, 2, 48.
24. Ibid., pp. 4–5.
25. Ibid., p. 12.
26. Ibid., p. 22–26.
27. Ibid., p. 65.

CHAPTER II: CHINA'S CARIBBEAN

1. Bill Emmott, *Rivals: How the Power Struggle Between China, India, and Japan Will Shape Our Next Decade,* Allen Lane, London, 2008, p. 16.
2. Desmond Ball, "Asia's Naval Arms Race: Myth or Reality?," Asia-Pacific Roundtable, Kuala Lumpur, May 30, 2011.
3. Leslie P. Norton, "Dragon Fire," *Barron's,* New York, June 27, 2011.
4. Amol Sharma, Jeremy Page, James Hookway, and Rachel Pannett, "Asia's New Arms Race," *Wall Street Journal,* New York, February 12–13, 2011.
5. Ball, "Asia's Naval Arms Race."
6. Ibid.; W. S. G. Bateman, *Strategic and Political Aspects of the Law of*

the Sea in East Asian Seas, Australian Defence Force Academy, Canberra, 2001, p. 85.

7. James C. Bussert and Bruce A. Elleman, *People's Liberation Army Navy: Combat Systems Technology, 1949–2010,* Naval Institute Press, Annapolis, Maryland, 2011, p. 183.

8. Sharma, Page, Hookway, and Pannett, "Asia's New Arms Race"; Carl Ungerer, Ian Storey, and Sam Bateman, "Making Mischief: The Return of the South China Sea Dispute," Australian Strategic Policy Institute, Barton, Australia, December 2010.

9. Jonathan Holslag, *Trapped Giant: China's Military Rise,* Routledge Journals, Oxfordshire, 2011, p. 103; Jonathan Holslag, "Seas of Troubles: China and the New Contest for the Western Pacific," Institute of Contemporary China Studies, Brussels, 2011.

10. David Axe, "Relax: China's First Aircraft Carrier Is a Piece of Junk," Wired.com, June 1, 2011.

11. Fumio Ota, "The Carrier of Asia-Pacific Troubles," *Wall Street Journal, Asia Edition,* Hong Kong, August 11, 2011.

12. "China Expanding Fleet of Warships at a Fast Clip: Stepped-Up Construction of Amphibious Vessels Part of Drive to Be Maritime Power," Reuters, February 16, 2012; David Lague, "Firepower Bristles in the South China Sea," Reuters, June 11, 2012.

13. Stephanie Kleine-Ahlbrandt, "A Dangerous Escalation in the East China Sea," *Wall Street Journal,* New York, January 5, 2013.

14. Hugh White, *The China Choice: Why America Should Share Power,* Black, Inc., Collingwood, Australia, 2012, p. 69.

15. Norton, "Dragon Fire."

16. Wayne A. Ulman, "China's Military Aviation Forces," in Andrew S. Erickson and Lyle J. Goldstein, eds., *Chinese Aerospace Power: Evolving Maritime Roles,* Naval Institute Press, Annapolis, Maryland, 2011, p. 45.

17. Office of the Secretary of Defense, August 16, 2010; Andrew S. Erickson, "Beijing's Aerospace Revolution: Short-Range Opportunities, Long-Range Challenges," in Erickson and Goldstein, eds., *Chinese Aerospace Power,* p. 7.

18. Paul Bracken, *The Second Nuclear Age: Strategy, Danger, and the New Power Politics,* Times Books, New York, 2012, pp. 207–9, 211.

19. Ball, "Asia's Naval Arms Race"; Richard A. Bitzinger and Paul T. Mitchell, "China's New Aircraft Carrier: Shape of Things to Come?," *RSIS Commentaries,* Singapore, May 6, 2011.

20. Aaron L. Friedberg, *A Contest for Supremacy: China, America, and*

the Struggle for Mastery in Asia, W. W. Norton, New York, 2011, p. 201.

21. Michael D. Swaine, *America's Challenge: Engaging a Rising China in the Twenty-First Century,* Carnegie Endowment for International Peace, Washington, D.C., 2011, p. 53.

22. Erickson, "Beijing's Aerospace Revolution," in Erickson and Goldstein, eds., *Chinese Aerospace Power,* p. 14.

23. Ding Ying, "FTA Driving ASEAN Growth," *Beijing Review,* January 22, 2011; cited in Swaine, *America's Challenge,* p. 4.

24. Mingjiang Li, "Reconciling Assertiveness and Cooperation? China's Changing Approach to the South China Sea Dispute," *Security Challenges,* Kingston, Australia, Winter 2010, pp. 51–52.

25. Friedberg, *A Contest for Supremacy,* p. 7.

26. James R. Holmes, "Maritime Outreach in the South China Sea," Center for a New American Security, Washington, D.C., 2011; John Pomfret, "U.S. Takes a Tougher Tone with China," *Washington Post,* June 30, 2010; June Teufel Dreyer, "The Growing Chinese Naval Capacity," *Topics,* American Chamber of Commerce, Taipei, August 1, 2011; George Will, "The 'Blue National Soil' of China's Navy," *Washington Post,* March 18, 2011.

27. Mingjiang Li, "Reconciling Assertiveness and Cooperation? China's Changing Approach to the South China Sea Dispute," p. 53.

28. Ibid., pp. 63–65.

29. Bussert and Elleman, *People's Liberation Army Navy,* p. 186; Bruce A. Elleman, "Maritime Territorial Disputes and Their Impact on Maritime Strategy: A Historical Perspective," in Sam Bateman and Ralf Emmers, eds., *Security and International Politics in the South China Sea: Towards a Cooperative Management Regime,* Routledge, New York, 2009, p. 51.

30. Elleman, "Maritime Territorial Disputes and Their Impact on Maritime Strategy," in Bateman and Emmers, eds., *Security and International Politics in the South China Sea,* p. 42.

31. Bussert and Elleman, *People's Liberation Army Navy,* pp. 141, 180.

32. Andrew S. Erickson and David D. Yang, "Chinese Analysts Assess the Potential for Antiship Ballistic Missiles," in Erickson and Goldstein, eds., *Chinese Aerospace Power,* p. 340.

33. Gabriel Collins, Michael McGauvran, and Timothy White, "Trends in Chinese Aerial Refueling Capacity for Maritime Purposes," in Erickson and Goldstein, eds., *Chinese Aerospace Power,* pp. 193, 196–97.

34. Felix K. Chang, "China's Naval Rise and the South China Sea: An Operational Assessment," *Orbis,* Philadelphia, Winter 2012.

35. John J. Mearsheimer, *The Tragedy of Great Power Politics,* W. W. Norton, New York, 2001, p. 401, and in conversation.

36. B. W. Higman, *A Concise History of the Caribbean,* Cambridge University Press, New York, 2011, pp. 98, 109, 189–90, 197–98.

37. James R. Holmes, "Monroe Doctrine in Asia?," *The Diplomat,* Tokyo, June 15, 2011.

38. David Healy, *Drive to Hegemony: The United States in the Caribbean, 1898–1917,* University of Wisconsin Press, Madison, 1988, pp. 3–4, 9.

39. Richard H. Collin, *Theodore Roosevelt's Caribbean: The Panama Canal, the Monroe Doctrine, and the Latin American Context,* Louisiana State University Press, Baton Rouge, 1990, p. x.

40. Ibid., pp. 56–57.

41. Ibid., p. 308.

42. Ibid., pp. 410, xiii.

43. Healy, *Drive to Hegemony,* p. 261.

44. Higman, *A Concise History of the Caribbean,* p. 230.

45. Collin, *Theodore Roosevelt's Caribbean,* p. 561.

CHAPTER III: THE FATE OF VIETNAM

1. Henry Kissinger, *On China,* Penguin, New York, 2011, pp. 342–43.

2. Clive Schofield and Ian Storey, "The South China Sea Dispute: Increasing Stakes and Rising Tensions," Jamestown Foundation, Washington, D.C., November 2009.

3. Lee Kuan Yew, *From Third World to First: Singapore and the Asian Economic Boom,* HarperCollins, New York, 2000, pp. 309–10, 314.

4. Carlyle A. Thayer, "Vietnam's Defensive Diplomacy," *Wall Street Journal, Asia Edition,* Hong Kong, August 19, 2010.

5. David Lamb, *Vietnam, Now: A Reporter Returns,* PublicAffairs, New York, 2002, p. 43.

6. M. C. Ricklefs, Bruce Lockhart, Albert Lau, Portia Reyes, and Maitrii Aung-Thwin, *A New History of Southeast Asia,* Palgrave Macmillan, New York, 2010, pp. 33–34.

7. Robert Templer, *Shadows and Wind: A View of Modern Vietnam,* Penguin, New York, 1998, p. 294.

8. David C. Kang, *East Asia Before the West: Five Centuries of Trade and Tribute,* Columbia University Press, New York, 2010, p. 166.

9. Neil L. Jamieson, *Understanding Vietnam,* University of California Press, Berkeley, 1993, pp. 8–10.

10. Keith Weller Taylor, *The Birth of Vietnam,* University of California Press, Berkeley, 1983, pp. 298, xix–xxi.

11. Ricklefs, Lockhart, Lau, Reyes, and Aung-Thwin, *A New History of Southeast Asia,* pp. 7, 34.

12. Templer, *Shadows and Wind,* p. 297.

13. Lee, *From Third World to First,* p. 314.

14. Thayer, "Vietnam's Defensive Diplomacy."

15. Jamieson, *Understanding Vietnam,* p. 235.

CHAPTER IV: CONCERT OF CIVILIZATIONS?

1. Thorstein Veblen, *The Theory of the Leisure Class,* Oxford University Press, New York, (1899) 2007, pp. xix–xx, 24, 59, 60–61, 75.

2. V. S. Naipaul, *Among the Believers: An Islamic Journey,* André Deutsch, London, 1981, pp. 270, 272.

3. V. S. Naipaul, *Beyond Belief: Islamic Excursions Among the Converted Peoples,* Random House, New York, 1998, p. 365.

4. Ernest Gellner, *Muslim Society,* Cambridge University Press, New York, 1981, pp. 1–2, 4.

5. Clifford Geertz, *The Interpretation of Cultures,* Basic Books, New York, 1973, p. 36.

6. Ibid., p. 283.

7. Samuel P. Huntington, *The Clash of Civilizations and the Remaking of World Order,* Simon & Schuster, New York, 1996.

8. Harold Crouch, *Government and Society in Malaysia,* Cornell University Press, Ithaca, New York, 1996, pp. 20–21, 23.

9. Virginia Matheson Hooker, *A Short History of Malaysia: Linking East and West,* Allen & Unwin, Crows Nest, Australia, 2003, pp. 27–28.

10. M. C. Ricklefs, Bruce Lockhart, Alber Lau, Portia Reyes, and Maitrii Aung-Thwin, *A New History of Southeast Asia,* Palgrave Macmillan, New York, 2010, p. 110.

11. Huntington, *The Clash of Civilizations and the Remaking of World Order,* p. 82.

12. Samuel P. Huntington, "The Clash of Civilizations?," *Foreign Affairs,* New York, July/August 1993.

13. Joel S. Kahn, *Other Malays: Nationalism and Cosmopolitanism in the Modern Malay World,* University of Hawai'i Press, Honolulu, 2006, p. 55.

14. Anthony Milner, *The Malays,* Wiley-Blackwell, Malden, Massachusetts, 2008, pp. 49, 238.

15. Malays and Indonesians essentially spoke the same language, even as the culture of Java was more richly endowed materially speaking.

16. Leonard Y. Andaya, *Leaves of the Same Tree: Trade and Ethnicity in the Straits of Melaka,* University of Hawai'i Press, Honolulu, 2008, pp. 18–19, 80–81.

17. Ibid., pp. 108, 124.

18. Joseph Chinyong Liow, *Piety and Politics: Islamism in Contemporary Malaysia,* Oxford University Press, New York, 2009, pp. xi, 192.

19. Milner, *The Malays,* pp. 14, 216, 219.

20. Banyan, "The Haze and the Malaise: Ethnic Politics Makes Malaysia's Transition to a Contested Democracy Fraught and Ugly," *The Economist,* London, September 10, 2011.

21. John Stuart Mill, *On Liberty,* Introduction by Gertrude Himmelfarb, Penguin, New York, (1859) 1974, p. 34; John Stuart Mill, *Considerations on Representative Government,* Digireads.com, Lawrence, Kansas, 1861, p. 162.

22. Barry Wain, *Malaysian Maverick: Mahathir Mohamad in Turbulent Times,* Palgrave Macmillan, New York, 2009, pp. 3–4, 8, 10–11, 25–26, 29; Crouch, *Government and Society in Malaysia,* pp. 156–57; Mahathir Mohamad, *The Malay Dilemma,* Marshall Cavendish, Tarrytown, New York, (1970) 2008.

23. Wain, *Malaysian Maverick,* pp. 86–87, 217, 219–20, 227, 236–37, 243.

24. Ibid., pp. 54, 85, 341; Hooker, *A Short History of Malaysia,* p. 272.

25. Crouch, *Government and Society in Malaysia,* pp. vii, 4–7, 56, 75, 150–51, 189, 192.

26. Ibid., p. 246.

27. The other rocks with a Malaysian military presence are Mariveles Reef, Ardasier Reef, Erica Reef, and Investigator Reef.

CHAPTER V: THE GOOD AUTOCRAT

1. The Singaporeans have since relieved their dependence on Malaysia for freshwater considerably by desalination projects, sewage recycling, and the tapping of rainwater.

2. Robert D. Kaplan, *Hog Pilots, Blue Water Grunts: The American Military in the Air, at Sea, and on the Ground,* Random House, New York, 2007, pp. 96, 98.

3. Owen Harries, "Harry Lee's Story," *The National Interest,* Washington, June 1999.

4. Lee Kuan Yew, *The Singapore Story,* Times Editions, Singapore, 1998, pp. 74, 77, 131.

5. Lee Kuan Yew, *From Third World to First: Singapore and the Asian Economic Boom,* HarperCollins, New York, 2000; Plutarch, *The Lives of the Noble Grecians and Romans,* trans. John Dryden (1683–86), rev. Arthur Hugh Clough (1864), Modern Library, New York, 1992.

6. Lee, *The Singapore Story,* p. 23.

7. Ibid., pp. 202–3; Harries, "Harry Lee's Story"; Kaplan, *Hog Pilots, Blue Water Grunts,* p. 97.

8. Lee, *The Singapore Story,* pp. 207, 211, 228, 322, 324, 427.

9. M. C. Ricklefs, Bruce Lockhart, Alber Lau, Portia Reyes, and Maitrii Aung-Thwin, *A New History of Southeast Asia,* Palgrave Macmillan, New York, 2010, p. 337.

10. Lee, *The Singapore Story,* p. 539.

11. Ibid., pp. 474, 558, 608, 610–11.

12. Ibid., p. 640.

13. Ibid., p. 649.

14. Lee, *From Third World to First,* p. 47.

15. Niccolò Machiavelli, *The Prince,* trans. Russell Price, Cambridge University Press, New York, (1513) 1988.

16. Lee, *From Third World to First,* pp. 53, 106.

17. Ibid., pp. 57–58, 159.

18. Ibid., pp. 166, 173–74, 182–83, 185, 213.

19. Ibid., p. 452.

20. Ibid., p. 467.

21. Hugh White, *The China Choice: Why America Should Share Power,* Black, Inc., Collingwood, Australia, 2012, p. 12.

22. John Stuart Mill, *On Liberty,* Penguin, New York, (1859) 1974, p. 68.

23. Ibid., pp. 86–87.

24. Ibid.

25. Ibid., p. 69.

26. John Stuart Mill, *Considerations on Representative Government,* Digireads.com, Lawrence, Kansas, 1861, p. 121.

27. Isaiah Berlin, *Four Essays on Liberty,* Oxford University Press, New York, 1969, p. xlii.

28. Isaiah Berlin, "Two Concepts of Liberty," 1958, in ibid., pp. 124, 129–30.

29. Mill, *Considerations on Representative Government,* pp. 116, 118.

30. Ibid., pp. 143, 161.
31. Aristotle, *The Politics,* translated and with an introduction, notes, and glossary by Carnes Lord, University of Chicago Press, Chicago, 1984, pp. 66, 120.
32. Mill, *Considerations on Representative Government,* p. 124.
33. Leo Strauss, *On Tyranny: Including the Strauss-Kojeve Correspondence,* University of Chicago Press, Chicago, 1961, pp. 45, 55, 57.

CHAPTER VI: AMERICA'S COLONIAL BURDEN

1. Jillian Keenan, "The Grim Reality Behind the Philippines' Economic Growth," www.TheAtlantic.com, Washington, D.C., May 7, 2013.
2. Ibid.
3. Stanley Karnow, *In Our Image: America's Empire in the Philippines,* Random House, New York, 1989, pp. 12, 119.
4. Robert D. Kaplan, *Imperial Grunts: On the Ground with the American Military, from Mongolia to the Philippines to Iraq and Beyond,* Random House, New York, 2005, pp. 136–37.
5. Max Boot, *The Savage Wars of Peace: Small Wars and the Rise of American Power,* Basic Books, New York, 2002, p. 125.
6. Karnow, *In Our Image,* p. 140.
7. Kaplan, *Imperial Grunts,* p. 139.
8. Karnow, *In Our Image,* p. 197.
9. Samuel K. Tan, *The Filipino-American War, 1899–1913,* University of the Philippines Press, Quezon City, 2002, p. 256.
10. Ibid.
11. Kaplan, *Imperial Grunts,* p. 140.
12. Ibid., pp. 140–41.
13. P. Kreuzer, "Philippine Governance: Merging Politics and Crime," Peace Research Institute, Frankfurt, 2009.
14. Karnow, *In Our Image,* p. 366.
15. John Minnich, "The Philippines' Imperatives in a Competitive Region," www.Stratfor.com, Austin, Texas, June 18, 2012.
16. Ibid.
17. Scarborough Shoal or Shoals, labeled as Scarborough Reef on some maps, is named after the British East India Company tea trade ship *Scarborough,* wrecked on one of its rocks on September 12, 1784, with everyone aboard perishing.
18. James Holmes and Toshi Yoshihara, "Small-Stick Diplomacy in the South China Sea," www.nationalinterest.org, Washington, D.C.,

April 23, 2012; Max Boot, "China Starts to Claim the Seas: The U.S. Sends a Signal of Weakness over the Scarborough Shoal," *Wall Street Journal,* New York, June 25, 2012.

19. Mischief Reef was discovered in 1791 by Henry Spratly and named by the German sailor Herbert Mischief, one of his crew. Henry Spratly is oddly no relation to Richard Spratly, the nineteenth-century British sailor for whom the islands west of the Philippines are named.

CHAPTER VII: ASIA'S BERLIN

1. Joseph Conrad, "Typhoon," *Typhoon and Other Stories,* G. P. Putnam's Sons, New York, 1902.

2. Taiwan not only makes all the territorial claims that mainland China does, but also claims Mongolia, with which the mainland has a peace treaty.

3. Kuan-Hsiung Wang, "The ROC's [Republic of China's] Maritime Claims and Practices with Special Reference to the South China Sea," *Ocean Development and International Law,* Routledge, London, 2010.

4. The Taiwanese have also exercised jurisdiction over nearby Sand Cay, also in the Spratlys.

5. James R. Holmes, associate professor of strategy, Naval War College, in conversation at the Center for a New American Security, Washington, D.C., 2011.

6. Jonathan Manthorpe, *Forbidden Nation: A History of Taiwan,* Palgrave Macmillan, New York, 2005, pp. xi, 21–22, 25.

7. Ibid., pp. 80, 83–96.

8. Ibid., pp. 111–12.

9. Ibid., p. 225.

10. Bill Emmott, *Rivals: How the Power Struggle Between China, India, and Japan Will Shape Our Next Decade,* Allen Lane, London, 2008, p. 236.

11. Aaron L. Friedberg, *A Contest for Supremacy: China, America, and the Struggle for Mastery in Asia,* W. W. Norton, New York, 2011, pp. 218–19.

12. John J. Mearsheimer, *The Tragedy of Great Power Politics,* W. W. Norton, New York, 2001.

13. Joseph S. Nye Jr., *Soft Power: The Means to Success in World Politics,* PublicAffairs, New York, 2004.

14. James R. Holmes, "Taiwan's Navy Gets Stealthy," *The Diplomat,* Tokyo, April 30, 2012.
15. Robin Kwong and David Pilling, "Taiwan's Trade Link with China Set to Grow," *Financial Times,* London, March 7, 2011.
16. Jay Taylor, *The Generalissimo: Chiang Kai-shek and the Struggle for Modern China,* Harvard University Press, Cambridge, Massachusetts, 2009, p. 399.
17. Jonathan Fenby, *Chiang Kai-shek: China's Generalissimo and the Nation He Lost,* Carroll & Graf, New York, 2003, pp. 12–13.
18. Theodore H. White, *In Search of History: A Personal Adventure,* Harper & Row, New York, 1978, pp. 116, 118, 150, 159, 176–77, 179, 182, 195–97; Taylor, *The Generalissimo,* p. 31.
19. Taylor, *The Generalissimo,* pp. 2, 12, 14.
20. Ibid., pp. 21–22, 51–52, 89–90.
21. Fenby, *Chiang Kai-shek,* pp. 501, 503; Taylor, *The Generalissimo,* p. 152.
22. Steven Pinker, *The Better Angels of Our Nature: Why Violence Has Declined,* Viking, New York, 2011, p. 195.
23. Taylor, *The Generalissimo,* pp. 7, 192, 213–14, 220, 297; Pinker, *The Better Angels of Our Nature,* p. 195; Fenby, *Chiang Kai-shek,* p. 253.
24. Barbara W. Tuchman, *Stilwell and the American Experience in China, 1911–1945,* Macmillan, New York, 1970, pp. 93, 322, 379, 412, 464.
25. Ibid., p. 531; Fenby, *Chiang Kai-shek,* p. 380; Taylor, *The Generalissimo,* p. 400.
26. Taylor, *The Generalissimo,* pp. 411–12, 414, 419, 485, 487–88, 589.

CHAPTER VIII: THE STATE OF NATURE

1. Lyle Goldstein, "Chinese Naval Strategy in the South China Sea: An Abundance of Noise and Smoke, but Little Fire," *Contemporary Southeast Asia,* Institute of Southeast Asian Studies, Singapore, 2011.
2. Jonathan Holslag, "Seas of Troubles: China and the New Contest for the Western Pacific," Institute of Contemporary China Studies, Brussels, 2011.
3. David C. Kang, *East Asia Before the West: Five Centuries of Trade and Tribute,* Columbia University Press, New York, 2010, pp. 2, 4, 8, 10, 11.
4. Gideon Rachman, "Political Crises or Civil War Will Not Stop China," *Financial Times,* London, March 20, 2012.

5. Mark C. Elliott, *Emperor Qianlong: Son of Heaven, Man of the World,* Longman, New York, 2009, p. 126.

6. Aristotle, *The Politics,* trans. Carnes Lord, University of Chicago Press, Chicago, 1984, p. 153.

7. Kenneth N. Waltz, *Realism and International Politics,* Routledge, New York, 2008, pp. 59, 152, 200.

8. Harvey Mansfield and Nathan Tarcov, Introduction to Machiavelli's *Discourses on Livy,* University of Chicago Press, Chicago, 1996.

9. Paul Kennedy, "The Pivot of History: The U.S. Needs to Blend Democratic Ideals with Geopolitical Wisdom," *The Guardian,* London, June 19, 2004.

10. "East Asia and Pacific Economic Update (2010)," World Bank, Washington, D.C.

11. Clive Schofield and Ian Storey, "The South China Sea Dispute: Increasing Stakes and Rising Tensions," Jamestown Foundation, Washington, D.C., November 2009.

12. John C. Baker and David G. Wiencek, "Cooperative Monitoring in the South China Sea: Satellite Imagery, Confidence-Building Measures, and the Spratly Islands Dispute," Praeger, Westport, Connecticut, 2002.

13. Nick A. Owen and Clive H. Schofield, "Disputed South China Sea Hydrocarbons in Perspective," *Marine Policy* 36 (3), May 2011.

14. Ian Storey, "China's Diplomatic Engagement in the South China Sea," Institute of Southeast Asia Studies, Singapore, 2011.

15. M. Taylor Fravel, "Maritime Security in the South China Sea and the Competition over Maritime Rights," Center for a New American Security, Washington, D.C., 2012.

16. Peter A. Dutton, "Cracks in the Global Foundation: International Law and Instability in the South China Sea," Center for a New American Security, Washington, D.C., 2012.

17. Hillary Clinton, "Asia's Pacific Century," *Foreign Policy,* Washington, D.C., September/October 2011.

18. Aristotle, *The Politics,* p. 114.

19. Stanley A. Weiss, "Imagining 'Eastphalia,'" *Strategic Review,* Jakarta, January/March 2012.

20. Holslag, "Seas of Troubles."

21. Jacques deLisle, "China's Claims and the South China Sea," *Orbis,* Philadelphia, Fall 2012.

22. Robert Kagan, *The World America Made,* Alfred A. Knopf, New York, 2012.

23. Jonathan Holslag, *Trapped Giant: China's Military Rise,* Routledge

Journals, Oxfordshire, 2011, pp. 31–35, 44–45, 48. Holslag's sources include the following: Park Sung-hyea and Peter Chu, "Thermal and Haline Fronts in the Yellow/East China Sea," *Journal of Oceanography* (62); and Andrew S. Erickson, Lyle J. Goldstein, and William S. Murray, "Chinese Mine Warfare," *China Maritime Study,* U.S. Naval War College, Newport, Rhode Island, June 2009.

24. "China Enhances Its Maritime Capabilities," www.Stratfor.com, Austin, Texas, May 12, 2012.

25. Holslag, *Trapped Giant,* p. 56.

26. Ibid., p. 64, map and commentary.

27. John J. Mearsheimer, *The Tragedy of Great Power Politics,* W. W. Norton, New York, 2001, p. 401.

28. M. Taylor Fravel, discussion on the South China Sea, Center for a New American Security, Washington, D.C., 2011.

29. Robert B. Strassler, *The Landmark Thucydides: A Comprehensive Guide to the Peloponnesian War,* Free Press, New York, 1996, p. 16.

30. James Kurth, "Confronting a Powerful China with Western Characteristics," *Orbis,* Philadelphia, Winter 2012.

31. Michael Auslin, "Security in the Indo-Pacific Commons: Towards a Regional Strategy," American Enterprise Institute for Public Policy Research, Washington, D.C., December 2010.

32. Sumit Ganguly and Manjeet S. Pardesi, "Can China and India Rise Peacefully?," *Orbis,* Philadelphia, Summer 2012.

33. Hugh White, *The China Choice: Why America Should Share Power,* Black, Inc., Collingwood, Australia, 2012, p. 71.

EPILOGUE: THE SLUMS OF BORNEO

1. Nigel Barley, *White Rajah: A Biography of Sir James Brooke,* Little, Brown, London, 2002; S. Baring-Gould and C. A. Bampflyde, *A History of Sarawak: Under Its Two White Rajahs, 1839–1908,* Synergy, Kuala Lumpur, (1909) 2007.

2. I write about Indonesia at length in *Monsoon: The Indian Ocean and the Future of American Power,* Random House, New York, 2010, Chapter 13.

INDEX

About the Author

ROBERT D. KAPLAN is chief geopolitical analyst for Stratfor, a private global intelligence firm. He is the author of fifteen books on foreign affairs and travel, including *The Revenge of Geography: What the Map Tells Us About Coming Conflicts and the Battle Against Fate, Monsoon: The Indian Ocean and the Future of American Power, Balkan Ghosts: A Journey Through History,* and *Warrior Politics: Why Leadership Demands a Pagan Ethos.* He has been a foreign correspondent for *The Atlantic* for nearly three decades. In 2011 and 2012 he was named by *Foreign Policy* magazine as one of the world's Top 100 Global Thinkers.

From 2009 to 2011 Kaplan served on the Pentagon's Defense Policy Board, appointed by Secretary of Defense Robert Gates. Since 2008 he has been a senior fellow at the Center for a New American Security in Washington. From 2006 to 2008 he was the Class of 1960 Distinguished Visiting Professor at the United States Naval Academy, Annapolis.

www.RobertDKaplan.com
www.Stratfor.com

About the Type

This book was set in Sabon, a typeface designed by the well-known German typographer Jan Tschichold (1902–74). Sabon's design is based upon the original letter forms of sixteenth-century French type designer Claude Garamond and was created specifically to be used for three sources: foundry type for hand composition, Linotype, and Monotype. Tschichold named his typeface for the famous Frankfurt typefounder Jacques Sabon (c. 1520–80).